26.82

D1035288

THE AMERICAN
COLLEGE NOVEL

GARLAND REFERENCE LIBRARY
OF THE HUMANITIES
(VOL. 253)

THE AMERICAN COLLEGE NOVEL
An Annotated Bibliography

John E. Kramer, Jr.

GARLAND PUBLISHING, INC. • NEW YORK & LONDON
1981

Library of Congress Cataloging in Publication Data

Kramer, John E., 1935–
  The American college novel.

  (Garland reference library of the humanities ; v. 253)
  Includes indexes.
  1. American fiction—Bibliography.   2. Universities
and colleges in literature—Bibliography.   3. American
fiction—Stories, plots, etc.   I. Title.   II. Series.
  Z1231.F4K7   [PS374.U52]   016.813'008'0379   80-8971
  ISBN 0-8240-9365-8   AACR2

Printed on acid-free, 250-year-life paper
Manufactured in the United States of America

CONTENTS

ACKNOWLEDGMENTS

At each stage in the creation of this book I was assisted by willing and helpful individuals. Gloria Condoluci, Colleen Donaldson, Joan Kramer, John Kramer, Sr., John Kramer III, Dorothy A. Mariner, Richard Newman, Brenda Peake, Richard A. Terry, and Ken Young all made important contributions. John O. Lyons offered sage advice, but his major input was through his monograph *The College Novel in America*, a work which not only served as my guide throughout the project but which also inspired my initial curiosity about college fiction. Many of the novels included in the bibliography were first discovered (and read) by me during the summer of 1978 when I attended a National Endowment for the Humanities seminar at the University of North Carolina. Robert N. Wilson, the seminar director, provided me with significant encouragement. Finally, and with a special note of gratitude, I must make note of the heroic labors of Robert Gilliam and Norma Lawrence. These two individuals, members of the inter-library loan staff of Drake Memorial Library at the State University of New York College at Brockport, kept me provisioned with fugitive college novels drawn from libraries across the full length and breadth of the United States.

INTRODUCTION

For purposes of this book, the term "college novel" refers to a full-length work of fiction which incorporates an institution of higher learning as a crucial part of its total setting and which includes, among its principal characters, graduate or undergraduate students, faculty members, administrators, and/or other academic personnel.[1] The annotated bibliography which forms the substance of this book lists and describes 425 "American" college novels. All of these novels employ American institutions of higher learning as critical components of their settings, and all of them have American college or university characters as protagonists or as major supporting players. The bibliography begins with the first American college novel, Nathaniel Hawthorne's *Fanshawe*, published in 1828, and it concludes with the fifteen American college novels published in 1979.

The bibliography is designed for two, perhaps overlapping, audiences. First, it is intended for individuals who simply enjoy reading college novels for pleasure. Second, it is aimed at scholars who might wish to utilize American college novels for research purposes. As long as the proper safeguards regarding the use of fiction as data are employed, the college novel would seem to offer a rich lode of information about higher education in America. However, this lode has seldom been mined.[2] Nor has the American college novel itself been the subject of an abundance of literary scrutiny.[3] An impediment to both research ventures has been the lack of an extensive annotated bibliography through which prospective students of the genre could easily obtain the titles of American college novels, and through which they could quickly ascertain the novels' dominant themes. It is my hope that the bibliography which follows will rectify this situation.

This book had its origin in my own professional and personal encounters with college fiction. Although my usual field of study is urban political sociology, I have twice dipped into college novels to write articles on academic imagery.[4] And, during my fifteen years as a college faculty member, I have taken a great deal of perverse delight in reading fictional accounts of people very much like my administrative overseers, my faculty colleagues, my students, and myself.

All bibliographies must have boundaries. In order to keep the bibliography in this book to manageable proportions, and in order to limit it to "hard-core" American college novels, I have excluded from the listing eight quantitatively vast but thematically marginal sub-species of college fiction. Not included in the bibliography are:

1. Anthologies of college short stories (except for those anthologies in which the stories are linked together by a common character or common set of characters).

2. Novels intended expressly for juvenile consumption.

3. Science-fiction novels.

4. Conventional mysteries and suspense stories.

5. Novels which deal exclusively with intercollegiate sports.

6. Novels set at West Point and Annapolis.

7. Novels in which faculty members and/or students are depicted largely or entirely at significant distance from their academic institutions. In particular, novels about faculty members vacationing and/or working in non-academic settings are not included in the bibliography.

8. Novels which have as their total rationale the commercial exploitation of sexual themes. Specifically excluded under this restriction are novels which describe the operations of fictional campus sex-research institutes.

In an effort to make the bibliography as exhaustive as possible—within the confines of my operational definition of the college novel; within the limits of my exclusionary strictures; and within the American context—I engaged in what can best be described as a long and tedious process of search, evaluate, discard, or include. As a first step I scoured the meager supply of literature about college fiction for the titles of potentially includable novels. From these sources I uncovered the titles of approximately 350 works of fiction which touch, in one way or another, upon American college or university life.[5] This list of possible inclusions was then augmented by systematic scrutiny of several general bibliographies of American fiction, and it was expanded even further by an item-by-item examination of book reviews in such past and present publications as *Literary World*, *Bookman*, *Library Journal*, and *Publishers Weekly*. A provisional roster of well over 500 likely novels was thereby generated. Each work on the provisional roster was then perused in hand, often after being obtained via inter-library loan. Through this screening procedure I admitted novels to or excluded novels from the final listing.[6]

The works in the bibliography display immense thematic and stylistic diversity. The 425 novels in the list include masterpieces of fiction as well as potboilers, and novels of manners, novels of morals, and novels of incident. Some of the books are serious in tone while others are satirical. The authors of the novels have set their stories in almost every conceivable type of American higher educational facility. And as focal characters they have employed students of all description, faculty members from the entire spectrum of academic disciplines, administrators of high rank and low, spouses and children of all of the above, and even campus security guards, cafeteria workers, and college photographers. For the most part, this diversity has gone unappreciated by the few literary experts who have offered analyses of the American college novel. The prevailing view among these scholars has been that the American college novel is internally derivative, a repository of literary underachievement, and heavily conventionalized. Through my search procedures I was able to uncover a great many American college novels which have heretofore eluded students of the genre. I would not claim that the existing literary assessments of the American college novel are incorrect. However, I would contend that this bibliography, by identifying a great many previously unexamined American college novels, suggests the need for a general reassessment of the genre.

As novels were admitted to the bibliography, all those which I had not read before beginning the project were read for the first time for purposes of annotation. Each annotation in the bibliography contains plot information, an identification of the book's college or university setting, and an identification of the academic discipline of the faculty protagonist (if any). In most cases the annotations also include author information, with emphasis placed upon the author's academic credentials and the locus of the book under consideration in the course of the author's career. Some of the authors of the works in the bibliography rank as giants of American literature, but the more usual American college novel has been the product of a nostalgic former student or a professor of English. A great many authors of American college novels do not appear in the standard biographic compendia; hence acquisition of author data required yet another long and often tedious set of research enterprises. Some information about authors was taken from dust jackets (when available), some from obituaries, some from college alumni records, and some from direct inquiries to publishers, to authors' agents, and to the authors themselves. In some cases, no information was available.

The annotations vary in both length and format. These variations are, in part, a result of the unevenness of available author data. They are also, in part, a consequence of the books' uneven merit both as works of literature and as fictive descriptions of college life. In general I have lingered longest over those novels which, in my view, are likely to be most useful and/or interesting to the prospective consumers of the bibliography. Although the annotations feature little of my own literary criticism, in some instances I have referred to or quoted from reviewers' assessments of the books in question. In all cases I have provided first-edition bibliographic citations.

In order to give the bibliography form, I have organized it chronologically, and within each major time period I have subdivided it into "student-centered" and "staff-centered" novels. Though this dichotomous arrangement is not an absolutely perfect classification device, most American college novels fit easily into one of the two categories. As the term implies, a student-centered novel focuses upon the behavior and concerns of students. Staff-centered novels, on the other hand, deal primarily with the milieux of faculty members, administrators, and the members of their families.[7]

Sixty of the 425 novels listed in the bibliography are marked with an asterisk, and the titles of these novels are listed in an appendix of "Major American College Novels" which follows immediately after the bibliography's final entry. In my opinion, the sixty novels in this appendix are the most heuristically important and/or entertaining works in the bibliography. The outstanding qualities of these novels are explained in their annotations. There is a danger, of course, in designating sixty out of 425 novels for special citation. My choice of "major" college novels necessarily reflects my own biases, and users of the bibliography are warned that their own particular research requirements, reading tastes, and/or emotional needs may better be satisfied by many of the works which I have not elevated to "major" status. The appendix of "Major American College Novels" is best seen, perhaps, as a starter syllabus for those individuals who have yet to discover the marvels of American college fiction. Certainly, exclusion from this list should not be interpreted as a sign that a particular novel is in any way an inferior or uninspired piece of literature. In the last analysis, all of the novels in the bibliography deserve respect and all of their authors warrant admiration. After all, as a perceptive acquaintance of mine once observed, even the most ill-composed college novel is a heroic attempt to fabricate reality out of an environment dominated by fictions.

NOTES

1. Some writers have employed the terms "academic novel" and "campus novel" to designate this same body of literature.

2. The most extensive use of American college novels in a work about American higher education is found in Earnest Penney Earnest's *Academic Procession: An Informal History of the American College* (Indianapolis and New York: Bobbs-Merrill, 1953). In the relatively few other works about American higher education which cite college novels, the authors generally limit themselves to brief discussions of one or two of the more prominent exemplars of college fiction.

3. By far the most exhaustive treatise on the American college

novel is John O. Lyons, *The College Novel in America* (Carbondale, Illinois: Southern Illinois University Press, 1962). Two doctoral dissertations also offer fairly wide-ranging assessments of the genre. These are Michael Victor Belok, "The College Professor in the Novel, 1940–1957" (1958, the University of Southern California) and Robert Charles Lee, "Portrayal of the College in Modern American Novels, 1932–1942" (1943, George Peabody College for Teachers). Novels set at Harvard are subjected to painstaking scrutiny in Hamilton Vaughan Bail, "Harvard Fiction: Some Critical and Bibliographical Notes," *The Proceedings of the American Antiquarian Society* (April 16, 1958–October 15, 1958, pp. 211–347). Harvard-centered fiction is also reviewed in Theodore Hall, "Harvard in Fiction: A Short Anthology," *The Harvard Graduates Magazine* (Vol. 40, 1931, pp. 30–54). Other attempts to come to grips with the literary merits and demerits of American college fiction include Richard C. Boys, "The American College in Fiction," *College English* (Vol. VII, 1946, pp. 379–387); Frederic I. Carpenter, "Fiction and the American College," *American Quarterly* (Vol. 12, 1960, pp. 443–456); Benjamin DeMott, "How to Write a College Novel," *Hudson Review* (Vol. 15, 1962, pp. 243–252); and William Randel, "Nostalgia for the Ivy," *Saturday Review of Literature* (November 29, 1947, pp. 9–11, 39).

4. These two articles are "Images of Sociology and Sociologists in Fiction," *Contemporary Sociology* (Vol. 8, 1979, pp. 356–376) and "College and University Presidents in Fiction," *The Journal of Higher Education* (Vol. 52, 1981, pp. 81–95).

5. Most of these titles came from Lyons' *The College Novel in America* and from a subsequent Lyons article entitled "The College Novel in America: 1962–1974," *Critique* (Vol. 16, 1974, pp. 121–128). In his book Lyons provides an unannotated bibliography of 214 works of American college fiction. In his article Lyons offers an unannotated list of 101 more fictive treatments of American academe, most of them published between 1962 and 1974.

6. All marginal or doubtful cases were admitted. Readers who compare my bibliography with Lyons' two bibliographies will find that I have omitted a few of the works in his listings. Several of the books in Lyons' bibliographies proved to be multi-focus anthologies of college short stories, and several more were banished from my bibliography because they strayed within one or more of my seven other grounds for exclusion.

7. While the American staff-centered college novel—especially the novel about professorial life—seems to have had its birth in melo-

dramatic American romances of the late nineteenth and early twentieth centuries, the genealogy of American student-centered novels can be traced to British college novels of the mid-Victorian period. The initial American student-centered novel was Nathaniel Hawthorne's *Fanshawe*. But *Fanshawe* did not provide the impetus for the first great wave of American student-centered works which broke upon the publishing scene in the 1880s and 1890s. These novels were modeled, instead, upon such best-selling British college epics as Edward Bradley's *The Adventures of Mr. Verdant Green* (London: Nathaniel Cooke, 1853) and Thomas Hughes' three-volume work *Tom Brown at Oxford* (London: Macmillan Co., 1861). The British novels had as their protagonists callow freshmen at Oxford or Cambridge who were quickly indoctrinated by upperclassmen into the joys of collegiate revelry and good fellowship. Many early-day American authors of student-centered fiction imported these British plots, set them in elite institutions of higher education in this country, and added appropriate local detail. For more information about British college fiction in the Victorian era see Mortimer Proctor, *The English University Novel* (Berkeley: University of California Press, 1957) and Carroll A. Wilson, "Verdant Green," *The American Oxonian* (January, 1933, pp. 27–33).

The American College Novel
1828–1899

*1. Hawthorne, Nathaniel. *Fanshawe*. Boston: Marsh and Capen, 1828.

Fanshawe is a melodrama set at "Harley College," a small institution in a remote part of New England. Edward Fanshawe is a student so serious about his work that he studies day and night. However, he leaves his books to rescue Ellen Langton from the clutches of an evil kidnapper. Ellen is the comely young ward of Dr. Melmoth, Harley's president. Just when it appears as though Edward and Ellen will wed, Edward dies of consumption brought on by an overdose of studying, and Ellen eventually marries another, less scholarly, Harley student. Harley College is modeled after Bowdoin, Nathaniel Hawthorne's alma mater. The book contains only modest detail about Harley, but as a college novel it is noteworthy for Hawthorne's sympathetic portrait of Dr. Melmoth. The school's president is described as kindly, well-meaning, and devoted both to his institution and his family. Few other American college novels treat presidents with such affection. The good Dr. Melmoth seems to have been entirely a product of Hawthorne's fertile imagination. Dr. William Allen, the real president of Bowdoin during Hawthorne's days as a student, was a stern and autocratic taskmaster whom Hawthorne detested.

Nathaniel Hawthorne was born in Salem, Massachusetts, in 1804. He graduated from Bowdoin in 1825, in a class which also included Henry Wadsworth Longfellow. *Fanshawe*, Hawthorne's first novel, was privately printed. Later in his life Hawthorne reevaluated the work, found it lacking in literary virtues, and attempted to purchase and destroy all copies.

2. Bailey, Charles, M.D. *The Reclaimed Student: A Tale of College Life*. Springfield, Massachusetts: Benjamin F. Brown, 1844.

Edmund Marvin and Charles Washburn are undergraduates at "B---- University," an institution of higher learning

in Massachusetts. The year is "18--." Edmund and Charles
are both devilishly handsome, though the former's natural
beauty "has been dimmed by indulging too freely in midnight
revel." The two students attempt to outdo one another in
scoundrelism. Edmund is the clear winner. He impregnates
Mary Wentworth, a local girl, and then deserts her after
arranging a bogus marriage ceremony. Charles is a model
of propriety by comparison. His vices are compulsive
gambling and an occasional act of campus arson, after which
he throws "dirty water" on the responding fire apparatus.
Charles is expelled from B---- and eventually drifts into
debtor's prison. Edmund is shot to death by police when
he flees arrest for walking out on Mary, who has come under
the protection of Davis, a compassionate member of the
B---- student body. Suddenly the book leaps ahead five
years. Charles, now miraculously "reclaimed," has become
a prominent attorney, and Mary, fully restored to respec-
tability, is Davis' wife. All of the above is augmented
by a series of sub-plots, most of which involve Edmund in
various exercises of perversity. Considering all of the
extracurricular action which is jammed into the mere sixty
pages of this melodrama, it is little wonder that the
students of B---- are seldom pictured in scholarly pursuits.
     Charles Bailey, M.D., has met that cruel fate known as
literary invisibility. Benjamin F. Brown, the publisher
of *The Reclaimed Student*, owned a combination bookstore
and book bindery in Springfield.

3. [Jones, Justin]. *The Belle of Boston: Or, The Rival
    Students of Cambridge*. By Harry Hazel (pseud.). Bos-
    ton: F. Gleason, 1844.

    The Belle of Boston is generally thought to be the first
fictionalized account of Harvard undergraduate life. The
protagonists are Philip Percy, an undergraduate of impec-
cable virtue, and his classmate George Thornton, a
wastrel, who lacks any redeeming qualities. The two students are rivals for the hand of the title character, a
fair Boston maiden. George uses underhanded tactics, including physical assault upon Percy, but Percy wins the
girl and the nefarious George is expelled from Harvard.
Only the first portion of the novel takes place at Harvard.
The later sections follow the continuing rivalry between
Percy and George after their college years.
     Little is known about Justin Jones except that he was
the author of numerous mid-nineteenth-century melodramas
and that he also was a book and job printer in Boston.
Indeed, even though *The Belle of Boston* was published

by the firm of F. Gleason, the book was printed in Jones'
shop.

4. Whippoorwill, Tim (pseud.). *Nelly Brown: Or, The Trials,*
   Temptations and Pleasures of College Life. Boston: "The
   Yankee Office," 1845.

   The protagonists of this slight, breezy tale are three
   Harvard students, two of whom spend most of their time in
   assorted dissipations and one of whom is a diligent scholar.
   The scholar, Stephen Brown, is poor while his two associates
   are wealthy. Nelly Brown, the title character, is Stephen's
   nubile sister and the novel begins a long tradition of in-
   corporating romances between male students and the sisters
   of their classmates.
   Nothing is known about the actual author of this epic,
   but the title page contains the statement that "He knows
   'tis true, for he's been thru' the Mill."

5. Vose, John Denison. *Yale College "Scrapes."* New York:
   Bunnell and Price, 1852.

   Twenty-six Yale students, one representing every state
   then in the Union, form a secret society. The organization,
   appropriately named "The Philistine Society," has as its
   aim the creation of mischief. It accomplishes such feats
   as placing a live rooster in the desk of a professor. But
   when the sobering prospect of graduation arises many of the
   lads assume a new seriousness about life. Some actually
   swear off liquor, and Joggles, the leader of the group,
   announces his intention to become a clergyman. The frontis-
   piece of the book offers excerpts from what apparently were
   pre-publication reviews. The reviewer for *The Critic*
   claimed that "nothing of the kind has ever appeared before."
   In the sense that this novel appears to be the first saga
   of Yale undergraduate life, the reviewer for *The Critic*
   may have been correct.
   John Denison Vose was the editor of the *New York Picayune*
   before becoming a highly successful author of popular morality tales.

*6. Washburn, William Tucker. *Fair Harvard: A Story of American*
    College Life. New York: G.P. Putnam's Sons, 1869.

   Fair Harvard centers largely upon undergraduate pranksterism. The protagonist is one Wentworth Saulsbury, who, along
   with his classmates, spends the greatest portion of his
   college career in such pursuits as stealing the clapper

from the bell atop Harvard Hall. In between pranks, Saulsbury and his clique go to parties, to the theater, and to
various sporting events. Occasionally they settle down,
not to study, but to concoct grandiose plans for self-
improvement. *Fair Harvard* obviously was inspired by the
British *Verdant Green* series. It received unfavorable reviews. *The Harvard Advocate*, in particular, criticized the
work as a caricature of the real Harvard milieu, and warned
that the book was likely to do serious harm to Harvard's
reputation. The book's negative notices only served to
stimulate sales, however, and the work became required extracurricular reading for Harvard undergraduates of the
period.

William Tucker Washburn graduated from Harvard in 1862,
sixth in his class and Phi Beta Kappa. He became a New
York City lawyer, but continued to write novels, some of
which were advertised as from the pen of the author of *Fair
Harvard*.

7. Loring, Frederick Wadsworth. *Two College Friends*. Boston:
    Loring Publisher, 1871.

Two College Friends is a brief (161-page) and tragic saga
about Ned and Tom, two Harvard chums, and their professor.
The professor's name is never given but "his reputation was
cosmopolitan, his head bald, and his life a matter of routine." Tom is the son of the professor's long-lost sweetheart, hence the professor readily takes the two boys under
his advisory wing. When the Civil War breaks out, halfway
through the book, the chums join the Union army. On a foray
behind Confederate lines they are captured by rebel troops
led by Stonewall Jackson. Tom becomes deathly ill with
fever and Jackson paroles Ned to care for his buddy. Ned
violates the parole by carrying Tom back to the Union trench-
es for medical care. Then, knowing full well that he will
be shot by firing squad for breaking the rules of war, Ned
recrosses the battlefield and, in the true Harvard spirit,
presents himself to Jackson for execution. Tom survives
the war, marries, and with the approval of the professor
names his first son Ned.

Frederick Wadsworth Loring graduated from Harvard in 1870.
Two College Friends was his only novel. In 1871 he joined
the staff of *Appleton's Journal* and was sent to report upon
a United States exploring expedition in the West. On November 5, 1871, Loring was killed by Apache Indians who attacked
the stagecoach in which he was a passenger.

8. Anonymous. *Lloyd Lee: A Story of Yale*. New Haven: Privately Printed, 1878.

   The author of this novel, who did not care to be identified, notes in a preface that the book was composed "in pencil between the duties and pleasures of seven weeks of college life." He dedicates the book "with all reverence and love to that manly independent little college world known as Dear Old Yale." The plot follows manly Lloyd Lee through four Yale undergraduate years. It includes a few student pranks and some hazing episodes but the main thrust of the story concerns Lloyd's tortured pursuit of Belle Gadsen, the sister of a classmate. Eventually Lloyd and Belle swear their eternal love, but not before a series of misunderstandings, one of which almost leads to a duel between Lloyd and Belle's brother.

9. Severance, Mark Sibley. *Hammersmith: His Harvard Days*. Boston: Houghton, Osgood and Co., 1878.

   This saga of Harvard undergraduate life is set in the days just preceding the Civil War. The protagonist is Tom Hammersmith who spends four years engaged in the usual fatuous pursuits of fictional nineteenth-century Harvard students. The book differs from other Harvard novels of the period principally in its attention to detail. When Hammersmith and his friends attend the class crew race, for example, the novel contains a full reproduction of the race card for "July 13, 185-."
   Mark Sibley Severance graduated from Harvard in 1869, after a brilliant student career capped by his election to the presidency of *The Harvard Advocate*. Following college he had a varied work history. Severance first went into academe and, indeed, *Hammersmith* was written while he was acting president of Santa Barbara (California) College in 1876. Tiring of the academic life, Severance went to work as a freight agent for the Southern Pacific Railroad. Then, after rising to an executive position with the railroad, he left Southern Pacific for the more profitable business of California fruit farming. His farming enterprises brought him immense wealth and, at the time of his death in 1931, he was a prominent member of southern California's economic and social elite. *Hammersmith* was his only novel.

10. Anonymous. *His Majesty, Myself*. Boston: Roberts Brothers Publishers, 1880.

    Two cousins, Steven Trent and Thirlmore McGregor, attend "Old Orange University," a private institution which gives every appearance of being Princeton. The time is the mid-nineteenth century. Steven is from the South. Thirlmore is from Vermont. The first person Steven meets on the Old Orange campus is Caesar Courteous, a "very fat, exceedingly black" Negro who is selling pies from a wheelbarrow. Caesar, it seems, is a runaway slave from Steven's family plantation. But in the liberal spirit of Old Orange Steven tells him that he will not reveal his identity. After that singular occurrence the two lads begin to immerse themselves in undergraduate life. Though they differ in their political views they become close friends. The book includes a number of portraits of professors, most of whom are described as tiresome pedants. Student high-jinks are kept to a minimum. The comic relief is provided principally by Caesar. While wheeling his pies through the Old Orange precincts Caesar strives in vain to imitate the cultured speech and manners of the school's president, Dr. McMasters, a man whom he admires. After graduation Steven goes on to medical school and Thirlmore enters the Old Orange Seminary. At the conclusion of the book Thirlmore gives up the ministry--after his church in New York City goes bankrupt--and he returns to Vermont to be a farmer.

His Majesty, Myself was published as part of a "No Name Series" of unsigned works marketed by Roberts Brothers in the 1870s and 1880s.

11. Hageman, Samuel Miller. *Once: A Novel*. New York: W.B. Smith and Co., 1881.

Once is a rambling epic which centers upon Claire Thornington, a Princeton undergraduate, and Amine, a poor but beautiful waif who lives in the town. The two innocent young people fall in love but Claire's mother, a society matron, orders Claire to give up the girl or leave college. Claire chooses to continue his education and Amine drifts away into a life of abject poverty. Years later, as Claire evicts a haggard and ragged woman from one of the family-owned tenements he realizes that the woman is Amine. But all does not end happily ever after. Upon discovering that the rent collector is Claire, Amine goes into a "prolonged swoon" and spends the rest of her life in a mental asylum. *Once* offers only limited views of Princeton as an academic institution, but those views which are provided are decidedly unfavorable. Thus, the Princeton student body is referred to as "the perfumed exquisite" and the university as "a sanitarium for the healthy."

Samuel Miller Hageman was born in 1848. He was raised in Princeton and educated at the Princeton Theological

Seminary, an institution founded by Samuel Miller, his grandfather. For a short time after his graduation Hageman was a Presbyterian clergyman but he broke with the Presbyterians over the issue of predestination and began his own church in Brooklyn. *Once* seems to have been Hageman's only novel, but he wrote many theological works and contributed poems and literary criticism to the periodicals of his day.

12. Brown, Helen Dawes. *Two College Girls*. Boston: Ticknor and Company, 1886.

Two College Girls deals with student life at an unnamed college for women. The protagonists are Edna Howe and Rosamund Mills. Edna is a poor girl who is a serious student. Rosamund is wealthy and giddy. The two are roommates for four years and, while they often disagree about the proper approach to higher education, they graduate fast and eternal friends. In many respects the book is a feminine version of the more popular male undergraduate novels of the era. And, like many of the male oriented novels, it ends with a moral lesson. Rosamund, who has devoted much of her time to meeting the "right" boys, is elected "class historian" at graduation. This is an honor reserved for the most popular girl in the class. Edna, on the other hand, wins a bigger prize. Although she has concerned herself very little with the social aspects of college, she receives a proposal of marriage from Jack, a handsome and wealthy Harvard senior.

Helen Dawes Brown received an A.B. from Vassar in 1878 and an M.A. from the same institution in 1880. *Two College Girls* was her first novel. She continued to write popular light fiction and, in 1907, returned to the academic scene for the plot of *Mr. Tuckerman's Nieces* (56).

13. Jones, L.L. *Oberlin and Eastern School Life*. Warren, Ohio: The Trumbull Publishing Co., 1889.

This wordy satire compares nineteenth-century student life at elite Eastern institutions with that at Oberlin. George Clark, a self-proclaimed sophisticate, enters "B---- College," an Eastern school. At B---- George finds that pranksterism is the order of the day and he joins in with enthusiasm. Among the more jolly student frolics at B---- is the pouring of sewage ("laden with disagreeable fumes") from dormitory windows onto unsuspecting passersby. George's disregard for his studies prompts the B---- faculty to ask him to leave, and he then enrolls in

Oberlin. Deep in Ohio George finds an entirely different
academic world. As the author points out, Oberlin's re-
moteness renders it "without parallel as a place to avoid
trouble." At first George attempts to fight the Oberlin
environment, and to behave as he did in the effete East.
But he soon sees the error of his ways and becomes a model
student.

Whoever L.L. Jones may have been, he or she clearly was
familiar with Oberlin. The campus is described in great
detail in this novel and, on occasion, Jones adds foot-
notes which tell about plans for new buildings.

14. Hancock, Anson Vriel. *John Auburntop, Novelist: His
     Development in the Atmosphere of a Fresh-Water College.*
     Chicago: Charles H. Kerr and Co., 1891.

Set at the University of Nebraska, this novel describes
the undergraduate experiences of John Auburntop, an aspiring novelist. John is one of the most erudite students
in American college fiction. Almost all of his conversations consist of analysis of such writers as Nathaniel
Hawthorne, Victor Hugo, and Ambrose Bierce. Moreover,
John's own manner of speech reflects his preoccupation
with literary style. For instance, when he is stopped by
some riotous fellow students one night in Lincoln John
asks: "Are you cognizant of the fact that it is now midnight, when all good people should be in bed? This city
of mud and darkness is now in stertorous bliss: only bat-
like souls are now abroad." Despite John's verbosity the
novel contains some interesting scenes of late nineteenth-
century life in a Western state university. Among the
more arresting incidents in the plot are a two-day zoology
class field trip made by horse and wagon and an abortive
student protest over compulsory military training.

15. Phelps, Elizabeth Stuart [Mrs. Elizabeth Ward]. *Donald
     Marcy.* Boston and New York: Houghton Mifflin Co., 1893.

Donald Marcy, the son of a wealthy New York financier,
enters "Harle University" as a spoiled, though charming
adolescent. For a time he is the leader of his class in
fun and games. But in his sophomore year one of his
pranks nearly ends the life of another student. Under
Donald's direction a group of sophomores forces a freshman
into a coffin and buries him alive in a local graveyard.
The freshman almost dies of "exposure and fright," and
Donald reforms. During the latter part of the novel Donald
demonstrates his new outlook on life by winning the college

debating contest and by capturing the heart of a clergyman's daughter. The name "Harle" is, of course, a blend
of Harvard and Yale but the university depicted in this
novel could be any upper status institution of the era.
Elizabeth Stuart Phelps was one of the most popular
novelists of the late nineteenth and early twentieth centuries. All of her novels contained moral lessons. She
also was an early day American feminist. Indeed, in
Donald Marcy it is Donald's beloved, a Smith College student, who discovers that Donald's opponent in the debating
match has plagiarized his speech from an obscure oration
by Rufus Choate. This fact, when made public, causes the
judges to award the prize to Donald. Of even more significance, the all-male Harle student body finds to its surprise that a female is capable of sophisticated investigatory scholarship. Another of Phelps' novels, *Walled
In* (58), is included in this bibliography.

*16. Wood, John Seymour. *College Days: Or Harry's Career at
     Yale*. New York: The Outing Club, Ltd., 1894.

In a preface, dated April 1894, John Seymour Wood notes
that the object of *College Days* is "to give a picture of
(Yale) student life as it was twenty years ago." And so,
through 429 pages, Wood takes his readers on an exhaustive
examination of Yale and its student rituals during the
1870s. The protagonist of the novel is Harry Chestleton,
a wealthy lad from the Midwest. Only a fair student, but
a brick of a Yalie, Harry spends four action-packed years
following every conceivable undergraduate pursuit. Something of a devotee of the dance, Harry even blacks his
face and attends a "cakewalk" held by a Negro church in
New Haven. There is a brief epilogue at the end of the
book. Harry and a classmate are back at Yale fifteen
years after their graduation. As they stand amidst the
familiar scenes of their college days Harry, now a wealthy
lighting company magnate in Cleveland, observes that "Yale
men out in the world get ahead by work and energy--that's
what Yale teaches."
John Wood graduated from Yale in 1874 and from Columbia
University Law School in 1876. Although he became a
prominent New York City attorney he found time to produce
a sizeable output of light fiction. *College Days* was his
first novel. Another of Wood's books, a collection of
short stories entitled *Yale Yarns* (New York: G.P. Putnam's
Sons, 1897) also deals with undergraduate life in New
Haven.

17. Garland, Hamlin. *Rose of Dutcher's Coolly*. New York:
     Harper and Brothers, 1895.

     Rose Dutcher, a bright Midwestern girl, aspires to a
     life beyond the family farm. Her father, a progressive
     thinker, sends her to the University of Wisconsin at Madi-
     son. After graduation Rose wends her way to Chicago where
     she marries a newspaper editor. Less than a quarter of
     the novel takes place at Madison, but this portion of the
     book is important because it is at Wisconsin that Rose
     begins to realize her intellectual potential. Much of the
     novel will delight feminist readers. In Madison, for
     instance, Rose meets a female lawyer who advises her to
     stay single until she is thirty. In Chicago Rose is taken
     under the wing of a female doctor who nurtures her ambi-
     tions as a poet and who makes certain that she is intro-
     duced into the city's literary circles. And, when the
     newspaper editor proposes, he agrees that in the interests
     of her creative work Rose will not necessarily have to
     bear children or follow his orders.
     Rose of Dutcher's Coolly was one of Hamlin Garland's
     early "realistic" novels. Some literary scholars argue
     that the characterization of Rose was Garland's fictive
     tribute to his younger sister, Jessica, who died while
     still in high school. Garland never attended college.
     Other than receiving a host of honorary degrees late in
     his life, his only connection with academe came in 1885
     when, badly in need of funds, he served as "Professor of
     English" during the summer term of the Boston School of
     Oratory.

18. Barnes, James. *A Princetonian: A Story of Undergraduate*
     Life at the College of New Jersey. New York: G.P.
     Putnam's Sons, 1896.

     Newton Wilberforce Hart, a strapping former sheriff,
     comes from Nebraska to enroll at Princeton. With his
     countrified ways he has some difficulty gaining accept-
     ance into the sophisticated Princeton milieu. But when
     he becomes the hero of the football team he finds that
     his fellow students are suddenly willing to overlook his
     less-than-elite background. Hart also finds that women
     are impressed by his football exploits. During the course
     of the novel he woos and wins a girl from the upper eche-
     lons of Eastern society.
     James Barnes graduated from Princeton in 1891. After
     college he entered the magazine business serving, at vari-
     ous points in his career, on the editorial staffs of

Scribner's and *Harper's Weekly*. Barnes was best known as
a writer of military histories and biographies about military figures.

19. Elliott, Sarah Barnwell. *The Durket Sperret*. New York:
    Henry Holt and Co., 1898.

    This romantic tragedy is set, in part, at Sewanee Uni-
    versity in Tennessee. Max Dudley, an undergraduate, be-
    comes enamored of Hannah Warren, a girl from the nearby
    Cumberland Mountains. Hannah, who peddles apples and
    potatoes on the campus, can barely read and she speaks in
    unadulterated hill country dialect. When Max proposes,
    at the end of the novel, Hannah replies "I'm obleeged."
    But she then goes on·to reject his marriage offer because
    she does not see herself fitting into his world. The
    crestfallen Max is left alone with his memories and with
    a sudden appreciation of the evils of the American class
    system. Although less than half of the story takes place
    at the university—much of the plot concerns Hannah's life
    in the mountains—interesting college-related passages
    are scattered throughout the text. In one episode, for
    example, Hannah's mountaineer grandfather is asked for
    his opinion of the strange university folk down in the
    town. "God made all the critters, book-larnin' critters,
    too," says the old man, "an' all has a right to live."
    Sarah Barnwell Elliott was the daughter of Steven
    Elliott, a Protestant clergyman who was the founder of
    Sewanee University. She never married and lived most of
    her life in the town of Sewanee. A popular author of
    moralistic novels, she is sometimes credited by literary
    scholars as being the pioneer of "realistic" fiction about
    poor Southern Whites. Her reputation in literary circles
    rests less on *The Durket Sperret*, however, than on *Jeremy*
    (New York: Henry Holt and Co., 1891), a study of family
    life in the Tennessee hills. Elliott was a fervent ex-
    ponent of women's rights and, at one point in her life,
    she served as president of the Tennessee State Equal
    Suffrage Association. She died in 1928.

20. Young, Eleanor Dey. *Two Princetonians and Other Jersey-
    ites*. Trenton, New Jersey: MacCrellish and Quigley,
    1898.

    This brief (154-page) and innocuous novel is about a
    Princeton undergraduate whose younger sister marries one
    of his classmates. The stolid protagonist, improbably
    named Alexander Hamilton, engages in no pranks or high-
    jinks. Nor, it must be observed, does he study to excess

since much of his time is taken up escorting his sister
on repeated tours of the Princeton campus. These excur-
sions allow the author to offer detailed views of the
Princeton scene. After graduation Alexander marries and
has a daughter. Ever loyal to his alma mater, he insists
that his daughter must always wear orange and black ribbons
in her hair.

Eleanor Dey Young was a well-respected author of historical fiction. This novel, however, is autobiographical
in nature. The book is introduced by a brief, if non-
specific, preface in which Young teases her readers by
informing them that the novel "is a concentrated collection of the pleasant happenings of my past life." "Almost
without exception," she adds, "the incidents related herein
are founded upon fact."

21.   Fuller, Caroline Macomber. *Across the Campus: A Story of
      College Life*. New York: Charles Scribner's Sons, 1899.

Across the Campus is a rather bland but detailed story
of undergraduate life at "Harland College," an exclusive
college for women in the Northeast. The protagonists are
Christine, Ruth, and Claire, three members of the class
of 1895. They and their classmates share a series of
tepid adventures over a four-year period. Christine, the
daughter of a Senator from Iowa, is the most intriguing
of the three central characters. One of her favorite
pastimes is to take long strolls in the forest where she
talks with the trees. Toward the end of the book Christine
acquires a new interest, a young zoology professor who,
as the author takes pains to point out, is independently
wealthy and not reliant upon his presumably meager salary.
When the professor asks Christine if he might visit her
in Washington after graduation the reader knows that
Christine is about to acquire more than a diploma from
her college experience.

Caroline Macomber Fuller received a B.Litt. from Smith
College in 1895. *Across the Campus* was her first novel.
In later life she was a regular contributor of romantic
stories and poems to popular magazines, and she produced
a number of commercially successful romantic novels.

*22. Williams, Jesse Lynch. *The Adventures of a Freshman*.
      New York: Charles Scribner's Sons, 1899.

The undergraduate hero of this story, one William
"Deacon" Young, arrives at Princeton from the rustic Midwest. In the course of the narrative Deacon overcomes his

ignorance of Eastern ways to become a leader of his class.
The book pays particular attention to the question of
freshman hazing. Early in the novel Deacon suffers grievously at the hands of Princeton's sophomores. Although
the author suggests that hazing can be carried to excess
he also notes, in several asides, that it can serve a
democratic purpose. Hazing, in the author's view, reduces
all freshmen, regardless of their social background, to
a common level of obsequiousness.

Jesse Lynch Williams came to Princeton from rural Illinois, graduated in 1892, and then went on to become a
successful author of light drama and fiction. He began
his rise to literary prominence with a book of college
vignettes entitled *Princeton Stories* (New York: Charles
Scribner's Sons, 1895). *The Adventures of a Freshman* was
his first novel. During the late 1890s Williams served on
the editorial staff of *Scribner's Magazine*. In 1900 he
founded the *Princeton Alumni Weekly* and acted as the publication's first editor until 1903. In 1917 Williams'
Broadway comedy, *Why Marry?*, won the first Pulitzer Prize
for drama. Princeton awarded him an honorary Doctor of
Letters in 1919. In 1921 Williams was named president of
the Author's League of America. He maintained a home in
Princeton during most of his adult life and when he died
in 1929, at the age of fifty-eight, he was buried in a
Princeton cemetery.

23. MacGregor, Annie Lyndsay. *The Professor's Wife: Or,*
    It Might Have Been. Philadelphia: J.B. Lippincott Co.,
    1870.

    The principal characters in this early-day academic
    family saga are John Ashton, a professor of Greek and
    Latin at New London (Connecticut) College, his wife, and
    their two daughters. Ashton is the archetypical absent-
    minded professor. "A man of wonderful acquirements" and
    "a great scholar," he is nonetheless "totally unfitted
    for the everyday business of life." In fact, halfway
    through the book Ashton's carelessness with mundane mat-
    ters brings about his death. Late for an examination
    which he is scheduled to proctor, he hurries without hat
    or coat through a rainstorm and contracts terminal chills.
    The final portion of the story is taken up with the strug-
    gles of the remaining Ashtons to adjust to the professor's
    demise.
    The identity of Annie Lyndsay MacGregor is a biblio-
    philic mystery. However, it is known that she published
    three melodramatic romances during the nineteenth century.
    Her first novel was *John Ward's Governess* (Philadelphia:
    J.B. Lippincott Co., 1868). *The Professor's Wife* was her
    second novel. After a twenty-two-year absence from the
    publishing scene she burst forth once again in 1892 with
    Bound, Not Blessed (New York: G.W. Dillingham), a non-
    college saga about a loveless marriage.

24. Quincy, Josiah Phillips. *The Peckster Professorship.*
    Boston and New York: Houghton-Mifflin Co., 1888.

    The "Peckster Professorship" is an endowed chair of
    osteology at a renowned but unnamed American college.
    Its occupant, Ernest Hargrave, is convinced that the
    human mind exists beyond the body and he launches a series
    of experiments into spiritualism. Hargrave's explorations
    into the occult anger his less imaginative faculty

colleagues and they vote to abolish his chair. But Hargrave has married a wealthy widow. Rather than fight the action of his colleagues, Hargrave leaves with his wife for Brazil, where he plans to continue his research. This novel defies easy classification. It is part romance, part melodrama, and part satire. When Professor Hargrave courts the widow, for example, the pair enjoy long discussions about the philosophies of Herbert Spencer. And when the college president calls on prospective donors he carries with him blank checks from all of the local banks.

Josiah Phillips Quincy graduated from Harvard in 1850. He then attended Harvard Law School but he practiced law only sporadically. During his adult life most of his energies were devoted to the writing of poetry, fiction, and New England local histories. He was the grandson of Josiah Quincy, president of Harvard from 1829 until 1845.

25. Hubbard, Elbert Green. *This is the Story of the Legacy*. East Aurora, New York: The Roycroft Printing Shop, 1896.

This is the Story of the Legacy is a long (448-page) and multi-barbed satire. Among the book's many targets are Harvard, its faculty, and academe in general. The plot centers on Chilo Wilson, a Harvard biology professor. Wilson is swindled out of nearly a quarter of the $20,000 left to him in the will of a former student. Distraught over the loss of his money, and harassed by a shrewish wife, he flees with what remains of the legacy and attempts to forge a new life in the wild West. Eventually Wilson is located by his wife, whom the author uncharitably describes as "an animated blank." But before Mrs. Wilson can nag her husband back to Cambridge the unhappy couple is killed by the professor's two pet bears. Only the first third of the novel takes place in Cambridge, but that portion is laden with sardonic observations about the Harvard environment. Charles W. Eliot, president of Harvard during the late nineteenth century, and Professors Alexander Agassiz and Charles T. Copeland make unflattering cameo appearances.

After a checkered career as a newspaperman, soap salesman, and advertising writer, Elbert Green Hubbard entered Harvard in 1893 at the age of thirty-six. He remained only for a year. A disciple of William Morris, whose Kelmscott Press he had visited in Great Britain, Hubbard then opened a combination pottery, jewelry, and printing shop in East Aurora, New York. *This is the Story of the Legacy* was printed in his East Aurora establishment. Hubbard was a prolific author. One of his earlier works,

Forbes of Harvard (Boston: Arena Publishing Co., 1894)
concerns a Harvard dropout who, like Professor Wilson,
seeks his fortune in the West. In his later years Hubbard
became a popular lecturer on art and literature. He and
his wife were drowned in 1915 in the sinking of the *Lusi-
tania*.

26. Pier, Arthur Stanwood. *The Pedagogues: A Story of the
     Harvard Summer School*. Boston: Small, Maynard and Co.,
     1899.

This romantic farce is set at Harvard during a summer
term. Miss Jessie Deagle, an impressionable schoolteacher
from Peru, Ohio, thinks that her young instructor of
English, the dashing Arthur Palatine, has singled her out
for amorous attention. But, to her sorrow, Jessie eventually finds that she has been mistaken and that Arthur
really loves another. There is some interesting material
in the novel about Harvard junior faculty in the 1890s.
Arthur, portrayed as an insensitive egotist, teaches summer
school not for the money but because he can think of nothing
else to do. An especially arresting segment of the book
comes toward the end when Arthur asks his students for
written evaluations of his course. George Gorch, Jessie's
regular beau, takes out his vengeance on Arthur with a
three-page excoriation. Among George's milder comments:
"Mr. Palatine is a shallow, prating, affected fop, preju-
diced in his likes and dislikes, unpatriotic and unAmerican
in his judgments, and unable to discern good work when he
sees it." Captivated by the eloquence of George's prose,
Arthur reads the critique aloud to the class.
     Arthur Stanwood Pier received an A.B. from Harvard in
1895. He then joined the editorial staff of *Youth's
Companion*, a magazine for boys. From 1916 until 1921 Pier
taught English composition at Harvard and Radcliffe, and
from 1918 until 1930 he was editor of *The Harvard Graduate's Magazine*. *The Pedagogues* was Pier's first novel.
Before his death in 1966 he produced thirty-one more books,
including sports stories for juveniles, histories, biographies, and additional novels for adults.

The American College Novel
1900–1919

27. Holbrook, Richard Thayer. *Boys and Men: A Story of Life
    at Yale*. New York: Charles Scribner's Sons, 1900.

    The aim of this novel, according to advertisements which
    appeared shortly after its publication, was to demonstrate
    how colleges turn boys into men. The plot focuses on John
    "Jack" Eldredge and Thomas "Tarb" Tarbell, two lads who
    enter Yale in 1891. Jack is a wealthy Easterner. Tarb is
    a poor son of the Arizona soil. The two excel in football
    and they become close friends. In their junior year they
    find that they both love the same girl, one Margaret Glenn,
    the inevitable sister of a classmate. When both of Jack's
    parents die unexpectedly Tarb steps aside, out of sympathy,
    so that Jack may have Margaret. Overwhelmed by this act
    of generosity, Jack in turn steps aside for Tarb. At the
    end of the novel we are led to presume that Tarb and the
    highly confused Margaret will wed. *Boys and Men* is lush
    with detail about late nineteenth-century Yale. In addi-
    tion to the usual college minutiae readers can find that
    dialect-spouting "darkies" cleaned the rooms of the "Yalen-
    sians," that "small Jews" sold newspapers on the campus,
    and that "dagos" operated many of the local New Haven
    markets.
    Richard Thayer Holbrook received an A.B. from Yale in
    1893 and a Ph.D. from Columbia in 1902. From 1896 until
    1901 Holbrook was an instructor of romance languages at
    Yale and it was during this period that *Boys and Men* was
    written. After leaving Yale Holbrook continued his aca-
    demic career at Bryn Mawr. Then, in 1919, he moved to the
    University of California where he was a professor of French
    until his death in 1934. *Boys and Men* was his only novel.
    As an academician he was best known for his writings on
    Dante and Balzac.

28. Stark, Harriet. *The Bacillus of Beauty*. New York: Fred-
    erick A. Stokes Co., 1900.

    Helen Winship, a plain girl with a bachelor's degree

from a Western state university, journeys to Barnard College for graduate work in biology. Her mentor, one Professor Darnstetter, is an elderly eccentric. After years of labor Darnstetter has created a bacillus which he hopes will produce beauty in living organisms. Helen volunteers to be his guinea pig. In the space of a few weeks Helen is transformed into a paragon of pulchritude. She becomes so beautiful, in fact, that she causes riots when she appears in public. For a time Helen revels in her new physical condition. Suitors beat a path to her door and, as the world's only gorgeous biologist, she finds that newspapers and magazines vie for exclusive rights to her pronouncements on scientific matters. But, sad to relate, it all begins to turn sour. Professor Darnstetter is so smitten by Helen's face and figure that one day he makes amorous advances right in the laboratory and suffers a fatal heart attack. Deprived of her teacher, beset by mounting debts caused by her need for exotic clothes to drape her spectacular physique, and repelled by most of the men who seek her attention, Helen commits suicide. The book includes a few descriptive passages about Barnard and, on occasion, the characters engage in discussions about the plight of female graduate students training for occupations dominated by men.

The Bacillus of Beauty is written with considerable polish, and without the verbose, flowery prose which characterizes most turn-of-the-century fiction. And yet, despite Harriet Stark's obvious talents for writing and invention, she seems to have faded into total literary obscurity.

*29.   Flandrau, Charles Macomb. *The Diary of a Freshman*. New
        York: Doubleday, Page and Co., 1901.

The diarist referred to in the title of this work is "Granny" Wood, a Harvard freshman. Along with Berri Berrisford, his roommate, Granny has most of the adventures and misadventures which were customary for fictive Harvard students of the era. Although the plot of the novel is not especially noteworthy, the book is heaped with descriptive detail and it offers a great deal of information for anyone interested in turn-of-the-century undergraduate life at Harvard.

The Diary of a Freshman first appeared in serial form in *The Saturday Evening Post*. The book was Charles Macomb Flandrau's second excursion into college fiction. In 1897 he published *Harvard Episodes* (Boston: Copeland and Day), a collection of seven stories about Harvard

undergraduates. *Harvard Episodes*, which focuses more on
student rowdyism than does *The Diary of a Freshman*, pro-
voked anguished cries of dismay from those reviewers who
were concerned with Harvard's image. After completing *The
Diary of a Freshman* Flandrau continued to write stories
about Granny and Berri for *The Saturday Evening Post*.
Shortly before his death in 1938 some of these stories--
about the chums' exploits in Europe during a college summer
vacation--were collected in book form and published as
Sophomores Abroad (New York: D. Appleton-Century Co.,
1935). *Sophomores Abroad* includes a thirty-nine-page
author's preface in which Flandrau gives his views on
Harvard fiction in general and tells how he came to make
his own contribution to the genre. Flandrau graduated
from Harvard in 1895 and spent most of his career writing
for and editing magazines and newspapers.

30. Kauffman, Reginald Wright. *Jarvis of Harvard*. Boston:
    L.C. Page and Co., 1901.

Richard Jarvis arrives for his freshman year at Harvard
having already surrendered his virginity to a worldly girl
in his hometown of Philadelphia. With little left to lose,
Richard then plays havoc with the fair young maidens of
Cambridge. And along with some of his more bumptious
classmates he becomes a master of pranksterism. During
one episode, for instance, Richard and his chums hijack
a Boston streetcar, and on another occasion Richard and
his pals bully a passing M.I.T. student into singing "Fair
Harvard." Eventually Richard meets the girl he wishes to
marry and he begins a long and difficult process of re-
pentance. The book offended many members of the Harvard
community and the reviewer for *The Harvard Advocate* (November 7, 1901) observed that *Jarvis of Harvard* "is so foul
as to be sickening."
Reginald Wright Kauffman entered Harvard in 1896 but
left after one year. During his adult life he combined
newspaper and magazine work with fiction writing. *Jarvis
of Harvard* was Kauffman's first novel. It was begun when
he was a preparatory student at St. Paul's School and it
was carried forward in creative writing classes during
his one year on the Harvard campus. In most of Kauffman's
subsequent novels, none of which have academic settings,
the protagonists are Harvard graduates or dropouts.

31.   Lichtenstein, Joy. *For the Blue and Gold: A Tale of Life
      at the University of California*. San Francisco: A.M.
      Robertson, 1901.

      Jim Rawson, a poor but ambitious lad of twenty-three,
      enters the University of California at Berkeley. Jim
      lacks a high school degree, but thanks to years of studying
      by himself he has no difficulty with California's entrance
      examinations. Once enrolled as a freshman Jim excels at
      both studies and football. The book concludes at the end
      of Jim's first college year, when he already has attained
      the status of big-man-on-campus. The plot of this book is
      relatively routine. In terms of descriptive particulars,
      however, the novel is virtually without parallel in college
      fiction. Turn-of-the-century Berkeley is portrayed in
      painstaking detail, and the text of the novel is augmented
      by twelve full-page photographs of Berkeley scenes.
      Joy Lichtenstein graduated from the University of Cali-
      fornia at Berkeley in 1901. After a brief career as a
      librarian in San Francisco he became an insurance agent.
      Lichtenstein prospered in the insurance trade, became a
      prominent member of the San Francisco business community,
      and served as a sometimes professor of insurance at Stan-
      ford. *For the Blue and Gold* was his only novel.

32.   Johnson, Shirley Everton. *The Cult of the Purple Rose*.
      Boston: Richard G. Badger, 1902.

      This brief (170-page) novel about Harvard undergraduate
      life differs significantly from most other turn-of-the-
      century Harvard sagas. The protagonist is Lucian Denholm,
      the fabulously wealthy son of a Buffalo bank president.
      Unlike his counterparts in other early Harvard epics,
      Lucian does not waste his time with drink and pranks.
      Instead, he dedicates himself to literature and art. Mid-
      way through the novel he founds the "Cult of the Purple
      Rose," a society which publishes magazines and books con-
      taining the creative prose of Harvard students. The ef-
      forts of the Cult reach their zenith when the society
      publishes "The Pink Mule," described on its title page as
      "an artistic book of inordinate cleverness containing
      unique poems and stories." The final sixty-seven pages
      of *The Cult of the Purple Rose* reproduce "The Pink Mule"
      in its entirety. Perhaps because Shirley Johnson wrote
      the book within the book, as well as the main body of the
      novel, "The Pink Mule" seems no more inordinately clever
      than *The Cult of the Purple Rose* itself.

Shirley Everton Johnson graduated from Harvard in 1895 and then went into the banking business in Kentucky. *The Cult of the Purple Rose*, published by an early-day "vanity press," was his only novel.

33. Barbour, Ralph Henry. *The Land of Joy*. New York: Doubleday, Page and Co., 1903.

This Harvard novel stresses the romantic aspects of student life while downplaying pranksterism and idle dissipation. The plot centers on John North and Philip Ryerson, two undergraduates who, during most of the book, find their attentions monopolized by ardor for the sisters of fellow students. There are some modestly picturesque descriptions of the Harvard environs in the story, but the central characters lack the good-natured, dilettantish qualities of the protagonists in many other turn-of-the-century student epics. The reviewer for *Literary World* (July, 1903), conditioned perhaps by his or her reading of other student-centered novels of the period, commented that the heroes of *The Land of Joy* "bear little resemblance to the real Harvard articles."

Ralph Henry Barbour was born in Cambridge, Massachusetts, in 1870. His birthplace was only a four-minute walk from the Harvard Yard, but he did not attend college. After graduating from Highland Military Academy in Worcester, Massachusetts, Barbour went into the newspaper business, serving as a reporter and editor on papers in Boston, Denver, Chicago, and Philadelphia. He also wrote sports stories for older boys and became so successful at the craft that by early middle-age he was able to desert journalism and devote his full attentions to writing. Before his death in 1944 he wrote more than 100 books. *The Land of Joy* was one of his few attempts to write fiction for adults.

*34. Wister, Owen. *Philosophy 4: A Story of Harvard University*. New York: Macmillan Co., 1903.

This short (95-page) novella often is considered the classic story of early-day student life at Harvard. Bertie Rogers and Billy Schuyler hire a tutor to help them study for a philosophy examination. The tutor, a hard working student named Oscar Maironi, tries his best but Bertie and Billy go larking through the countryside on the day before the exam and then they stay up all night drinking champagne in the Bird-in-Hand Tavern. The examination goes famously, however, and Bertie and Billy overwhelm

their philosophy professor with their wit and orginality.
Indeed, they receive higher grades than does Maironi, whose
answers are correct but mere regurgitations of the professor's lectures. Wister intended the story as satire,
but some readers interpreted it as a fictive tribute to
free academic spirit. Hamilton Bail (see footnote 3,
Introduction) reports that Theodore Roosevelt, for instance,
wrote a praiseful letter to Wister extolling the "deep and
subtle moral" of the novel.

Owen Wister graduated from Harvard in 1882. *Philosophy
4* appeared first in *Lippincott's Magazine* of August 1901.
The story was written at the height of Wister's writing
career. His most famous novel, *The Virginian* (New York:
Macmillan Co.), was published in 1902.

35.   Holland, Rupert Sargent. *The Count at Harvard*. Boston:
      L.C. Page and Co., 1906.

"The Count" in the title of this book is an undergraduate
prankster who charms his way through Harvard. The novel
contains more than the usual complement of high-jinks and
partying but it is spiced with some sardonic attention to
the academic side of college life as well. Thus, The
Count and his cronies find that Harvard's courses all look
good in the catalog but "sink rapidly in charm with every
lecture." And, in order to pass essay examinations, The
Count perfects what he describes as "the gentle art of
drool."

The Count at Harvard was a popular, best-selling novel.
It was modeled, in part, after a British college novel,
E.F. Benson's *The Babe, B.A.* (New York: G.P. Putnam's Sons,
1896), the story of a charming, unscholarly undergraduate
at Cambridge. *The Count at Harvard* also was drawn from
Rupert Holland's own experiences. Holland graduated from
Harvard in 1900. After Harvard he attended law school at
the University of Pennsylvania, but he practiced law only
for a short time before turning to writing on a full-time
basis. Holland was the author of more than fifty books
including detective stories, adventure books for boys,
and biographies.

36.   Young, Rida Johnson, and Gilbert Payson Coleman. *Brown
      of Harvard*. New York: G.P. Putnam's Sons, 1907.

This novel of Harvard undergraduate life was adapted from
a play of the same name which ran on Broadway in 1906.
The plot involves a lad named Tom Brown in a variety of
escapades with fellow students, with sisters of classmates,

and even with a professional gambler. The play received
reasonably favorable notices even though some reviewers
thought it too reminiscent of George Ade's *The College
Widow*, a very popular satirical drama of the period. But,
according to Hamilton Bail (see footnote 3, Introduction),
when the touring version of the show opened in Boston on
April 8, 1907, Harvard students found the play so distaste-
ful they pelted the actors with lemons and eggs.

Rida Johnson Young attended Wilson College for the 1890-
91 academic year and then became a professional playwright.
During her career she wrote a number of successful shows.
Gilbert P. Coleman, who apparently had no hand in writing
the stage version of *Brown of Harvard*, but who collaborated
with Young on the novel, graduated from Trinity College in
Connecticut in 1890. During a multifaceted career he was
a lawyer, a newspaperman, and a member of the English de-
partments at Lehigh and the United States Naval Academy.

*37. Fitch, George Helgeson. *At Good Old Siwash*. Boston:
      Little, Brown and Co., 1911.

At Good Old Siwash is one of the classic satires on
college life, and a classic satire on college fiction as
well. The book is narrated by a recent Siwash graduate
who recounts a series of his undergraduate exploits.
Siwash is a private institution deep in the Midwest. Its
cultural life revolves around fraternities and football.
Among the more endearing characters in the story is Ole
Skjarsen, a giant Norwegian-American fullback who is so
dense he must be led around the campus at the end of a
rope. The faculty at Siwash are described as spoilsports,
nasty little men who serve only "to mar the joy of college
days and nights and early mornings."

George Helgeson Fitch was born in Galva, Illinois, in
1877. He graduated from Knox College. In an author's
preface he argues that Siwash is not modeled after Knox,
but his disclaimer is not very convincing. Fitch also
published two small books of stories about Siwash. *The
Big Strike at Siwash* (New York: Doubleday, Page and Co.,
1909) deals, in part, with Ole Skjarsen's refusal to play
in the big game because he is denied membership in a
fraternity. And *Petey Simmons at Siwash* (Boston: Little,
Brown and Co., 1916) is a set of stories in which Petey,
a cunning Siwash undergraduate, outwits various faculty,
administrators, and fellow students. *Petey Simmons at
Siwash* was published posthumously. Fitch died in 1915.

*38.   Johnson, Owen MacMahon. *Stover at Yale*. New York:
       Frederick A. Stokes Co., 1912.

       This classic novel of turn-of-the-century undergraduate
       life at Yale begins as a conventional college story. Ar-
       riving at Yale from Lawrenceville Prep, Dink Stover joins
       with a retinue of fictively orthodox classmates to experi-
       ence most of the usual joys and traumas of collegiate
       life. Although he begins his college career as something
       of an outsider (Yale is unaccustomed to Lawrenceville
       graduates, since most of the school's products go to
       Princeton), Dink quickly becomes the star of the football
       team and acquires exalted social status. Halfway through
       the book, however, the mood of the narrative changes.
       Dink begins to consort with students who are disenchanted
       both with Yale's social snobbishness and with its restric-
       tive classical curriculum. Through long discussions with
       these early-day student dissidents Dink finds his own
       attitudes changing. He becomes an outspoken critic of
       Yale's academic and social programs. And, in a dramatic
       scene, he resigns from his sophomore society by tearing
       his sacred pin from his shirt, throwing it to the floor,
       and stamping upon it. And yet, despite Dink's noncon-
       formity, he wins Yale's ultimate undergraduate honor. At
       the end of the book he is tapped for Skull and Bones.
          Owen MacMahon Johnson graduated from Lawrenceville Prep
       and then attended Yale. He graduated from Yale in 1900.
       During most of his life he combined writing with a career
       in the publishing industry. Much of his fiction was in-
       tended for older boys and many of his stories were set at
       Lawrenceville. None of his books ever matched *Stover at
       Yale* in sales. Indeed, in reissued editions the novel
       remains a steady best-seller at the Yale Co-Op.

39.   Webster, Jean [Mrs. Glenn Ford McKinney]. *Daddy-Long-Legs*.
       New York: The Century Co., 1912.

       Strictly speaking, *Daddy-Long-Legs* does not belong in
       this bibliography because Jean Webster, the author, in-
       tended the book primarily for a juvenile audience. How-
       ever, the novel became immensely popular with both children
       and adults and, through its many stage and film versions,
       the story has entertained international audiences of all
       ages. The novel consists of letters from Jerusha "Judy"
       Abbott, an orphan, to "Daddy-Long-Legs," a mysterious
       benefactor who is financing her through an unnamed college
       for women in the East. One of the people Judy meets at
       college is Jervis Pendleton, the wealthy uncle of a

classmate. Despite the fourteen-year difference in their
ages, Judy and Jervis fall in love. At the end of the
novel Judy finds to her surprise that Jervis has been her
benefactor. The various stage and screen versions of the
book emphasized the romantic aspects of the plot, but the
novel itself contains many interesting sequences about
student life.

Jean Webster graduated from Vassar in 1901 and immediately began writing fiction for children. *When Patty Went
to College* (New York: The Century Co., 1903), her first
novel, was a best-seller in its day and is now a classic
work of college fiction for juveniles. The first stage
adaptation of *Daddy-Long-Legs* opened on Broadway in 1914.
Webster died two years later, in childbirth, at the age of
thirty-nine. The first film version of the book was made
in 1919 and starred Mary Pickford. A second screen version
was made in 1931, with Janet Gaynor, and a film musical
based on the story--with Leslie Caron and Fred Astaire--
was released in 1955. Since its original publication in
1912 *Daddy-Long-Legs* has been reissued in innumerable
editions and it has never gone out of print.

40.   [Porter, Harold Everett]. *Henry of Navarre, Ohio.* By
       Holworthy Hall (pseud.). New York: The Century Co.,
       1914.

This brief (192-page) and lighthearted Harvard story
features Henry Chalmers--a lad from Navarre, Ohio--in its
title role. As Henry leaves homes for his freshman year
his solicitous sister presents him with a dictionary, a
history of Harvard, the latest *Who's Who in America*, and
a copy of *How to Grow Strong in Your Own Room*. On the
trip to Boston Henry throws all these tomes out of the
window of the train, but he keeps an issue of *The Football
Guide* with which he has taken care to provision himself.
During the course of his Harvard career Henry becomes an
all-American tackle and a star of the Crimson baseball
team. He also becomes a paragon of good undergraduate
fellowship and engages in far more than his fair share of
collegiate revelry. The Century Co. advertised the book
as "Henry's gay adventures" and "Just the thing for light
summer reading." Theodore Hall (see footnote 3, Introduction) also recommends the book for leisure-time relax-
ation. "Try it on a warm day," suggests Hall, "in a
window-seat looking out over the (Harvard) Yard if possible."

Harold Porter graduated cum laude from Harvard in 1909.
As an undergraduate he was on the board of *The Harvard*

Advocate and president of the *Lampoon.* He also was a
member of Phi Beta Kappa. Porter spent most of his post-
Harvard life as a professional writer. Among his many
books was *Pepper* (43), another breezy tale of Harvard student life which appears in this bibliography.

41. Canfield, Dorothy [Mrs. Dorothea Frances Canfield Fisher].
     The Bent Twig. New York: Henry Holt and Co., 1915.

This long (480-page) novel centers on Sylvia Marshall,
the daughter of an individualistic professor of political
economy at a Midwestern state university. Although Sylvia's girlhood is happy, she vaguely realizes that her
family does not quite "fit in." Their home is on the
wrong side of town and, what's more, Professor Marshall
has liberal political ideas which set him apart from most
of the other members of the university faculty. When
Sylvia enrolls at the university she discovers just how
far from local society her family has strayed. Sylvia is
not asked to join any of the higher-status undergraduate
social organizations. Nonetheless, through her own charm
and beauty, she gradually surmounts most of the social
obstacles placed in her path. Toward the end of the book
Sylvia goes on a European trip with her aunt, and it
appears that she might leave the family fold. But hearing
of the death of her mother, Sylvia rushes home to be of
assistance to her grieving father. Reviewing the book for
Publishers Weekly (October 15, 1916) Doris Webb found
that the book embodied a "rich, sweet philosophy." Viewed
as a college novel, the work is a detailed, if sentimental-
ized, study of a faculty family in the early part of this
century.
     Dorothy Canfield was born in 1879 in Lawrence, Kansas,
where her father was a member of the faculty at the University of Kansas. Her own childhood was spent on various
university campuses, as her father became chancellor of
the University of Nebraska, president of Ohio State, and
librarian at Columbia. She received a Ph.B. from Ohio
State in 1899 and a Ph.D. in French from Columbia in 1904.
From 1902 until 1906 she served as secretary of the Horace
Mann School in New York City. Married in 1907, she moved
with her husband to Arlington, Vermont, where she produced
a massive list of fictive and non-fictive works. *The Bent
Twig* was her third novel. Another Canfield novel, *Rough-
Hewn* (68) appears in this bibliography. One of the more
celebrated women writers of the early twentieth century,
Dorothy Canfield received honorary degrees from Middlebury,
Dartmouth, Columbia, Northwestern, Swarthmore, Ohio State,
Williams, and the University of Nebraska. She died in 1958.

42. Gilman, Dorothy Foster. *The Bloom of Youth*. Boston:
    Small, Maynard and Co., 1915.

    The Bloom of Youth is a first novel about a Boston so-
    ciety girl named Leslie Wyman who attends Radcliffe much
    against her parents' wishes. The elder Wymans would prefer
    that their daughter "come out" and find a socially promi-
    nent husband. Moreover, they fear for Leslie's virtue at
    Radcliffe, an institution viewed with deep suspicion by
    the turn-of-the-century Boston upper crust. And, indeed,
    Leslie does meet a number of threatening characters during
    her college days. One of them, a radical socialist stu-
    dent from Harvard, tries to capture her mind along with
    her body, but Leslie remains pure. At the end of her
    senior year she announces plans to marry a young man who
    meets with her parents' full approval. *The Bloom of Youth*
    includes considerable detail about Radcliffe and Harvard.
    The basic message of the novel is that aristocratic young
    ladies can survive, and even profit from, the Radcliffe
    experience.

43. [Porter, Harold Everett]. *Pepper*. By Holworthy Hall
    (pseud.). New York: The Century Co., 1915.

    Like *Henry of Navarre, Ohio* (40), an earlier Harold
    Porter work in this bibliography, *Pepper* is a light and
    amusing story of undergraduate life at Harvard. The title
    character and protagonist of the book is James "Pepper"
    McHenry, a diminutive young rogue who constantly schemes
    to achieve success. As a substitute quarterback on the
    sophomore football team, for instance, he protects a slim
    last-quarter lead over the dreaded seniors by arguing
    obscure rules with the referee while the timekeeper ticks
    off the final minutes of the game. Much of the text of
    Pepper first appeared as twelve stories in *Popular Magazine*
    during 1914.
        Harold Porter dedicated *Pepper* to three of his 1909
    Harvard classmates. In the preface to the work he notes:
    "Each one of us was partly Pepper." Holworthy Hall, the
    pseudonym which Porter adopted for both *Pepper* and *Henry
    of Navarre, Ohio*, was the name of the dormitory in which
    Porter and his three Harvard compatriots lived as upper-
    classmen.

44. Williams, Wayland Wells. *The Whirligig of Time*. New
    York: Frederick A. Stokes Co., 1916.

    This book is a light entertainment about two brothers,
    James and Harry Wimbourne, who are separated in early

childhood but who are reunited as students at Yale. James
is a graduate of an American prep school. Harry, who was
taken to live in Great Britain by his uncle, is a product
of Harrow. Although the two brothers get into many of the
usual undergraduate scrapes, the most interesting aspect
of the novel is the anglicized Harry's adjustment to American college life. Initially he finds Yale devoid of ci-
vility and lacking in intellectual rigor, but he is not
long in New Haven before he begins to grow accustomed to
the American ways of higher learning.

Wayland Wells Williams was born in New Haven, Connecticut, in 1888 and received a B.A. from Yale in 1910. He
entered newspaper work after graduation. A sometimes
painter as well as a sometimes novelist, Williams served
as a member of the New Haven Municipal Art Commission from
1935 until 1941. *The Whirligig of Time* was the first of
four novels which Williams wrote before his death in 1945.

45. [Morrow, Honore McCue Willsie]. *Lydia of the Pines.* By
     Honore Willsie. New York: Frederick A. Stokes Co., 1917.

Lydia Dudley grows up in "Lake City," the capital of a
state in the upper Midwest. Her father, a widower, is a
minor governmental official and Lydia develops both an
independent spirit and a deep concern for social justice.
Her particular cause is the plight of the state's Indians.
Midway through the story Lydia enters the state university,
which is conveniently located in her hometown. At the
university she continues to support Indian causes but she
also meets Professor Willis, a bachelor member of the
English department who has come west from Harvard to en-
lighten the locals. Willis takes a dim view of coeducation
but he takes a shine to Lydia. He pays court by giving
her individualized reading assignments, most of them poems
by eighteenth- and nineteenth-century British romantic
poets. Though Lydia is tempted by Willis' matrimonial
overtures, down deep she yearns for a life on the soil.
The only female in the university's dairy science program,
she rejects the disappointed Willis and marries Billy
Norton, a lad who plans to be a farmer.

Honore McCue Willsie Morrow was born in 1880 in Ottumwa,
Iowa. She received a B.Litt. from the University of Wisconsin in 1902. In 1904 she married Henry Willsie, a
construction engineer from New York City, and moved to
New York where she combined work in the magazine business
with creative writing. Divorced from Willsie in 1922,
she married William Morrow, a book publisher, in 1923.
Although she wrote many novels and nonfiction books before

her death in 1940, she was best known for her historical
novels about Abraham Lincoln and his family. *Lydia of
the Pines*, written before she began her work on Lincoln,
was her third novel.

46. Train, Arthur Cheney. *The World and Thomas Kelly*. New
    York: Charles Scribner's Sons, 1917.

The World and Thomas Kelly is a novel about social snob-
bery and its consequences at Harvard. Thomas Kelly, a
poor-but-proud student, is excluded from all of Harvard's
high-status clubs and organizations. But when he becomes
the star of the tennis team during his junior year his
social circumstances take a decided turn for the better.
Thomas is elected to a prestigious club and he finds himself a highly sought-after companion for all-night drinking and poker parties. Unfortunately, young Thomas loses
all sense of proportion and his senior year is passed in
a protracted alcoholic stupor. He barely graduates. Only
the death of his mother, which occurs after college while
he is attempting to make inroads into the sinful upper-
class life of Newport, brings Thomas back to his senses.
    Arthur Cheney Train graduated from Harvard College in
1896 and from Harvard Law School in 1899. In addition to
practicing law he turned out a steady stream of fiction.
Most of his novels and short stories were about the legal
profession.

47. Norris, Charles Gilman. *Salt: Or, The Education of Grif-
    fith Adams*. New York: E.P. Dutton and Co., 1918.

Salt is an admonitory novel about a young man who is
temporarily rendered unfit for polite society by higher
education. Griffith Adams, the son of a well-to-do Boston
family, is sent to the "University of St. Cloud," a state
institution in the Midwest. There he is indoctrinated
into fraternity life, cheating, and debauchery in general.
Griffith leaves the university before graduating. He
then makes a total mess of a marriage and is a failure in
business as well. Only when he considers the future of
his infant son does he realize the errors of his ways.
At the end of the story Griffith is well along the path to
becoming a success in the wool trade. E.P. Dutton and Co.
advertised the book as "graphic realism" and as a book
which "will make every father and mother stop and think,"
presumably about whether or not to send their children off
to college.
    Charles Gilman Norris graduated from the University of

California in 1903. He was the younger brother of novelist
Frank Norris and the husband of novelist Kathleen Norris.
Most of his life was spent in magazine work but he turned
out a number of "realistic" social novels about such issues
as marriage, birth control, and the plight of artists in
American society. *Salt*, his second novel, was published
when Norris was a Captain in the A.E.F. during World War I.

48.   Tarkington, Booth. *Ramsey Milholland*. New York: Double-
      day, Page and Co., 1919.

Booth Tarkington won two Pulitzer Prizes: for *The Mag-
nificent Ambersons* (New York: Doubleday, Page and Co.,
1918), and for *Alice Adams* (New York: Doubleday, Page,
and Co., 1921). *Ramsey Milholland* was written in between
these two prize-winning social novels, and represented a
brief return to Tarkington's earlier career as a writer of
stories about small-town boys in the Midwest. *Ramsey Milholland* was consciously intended as a tribute to America's
World War I servicemen. The title character is followed
through a rustic secondary school education and then on
to the "State University at Greenfield," which he enters
in 1914. When World War I begins Ramsey is torn between
his desire to serve his country and the pacifistic plead-
ings of his college sweetheart. At the end of the book
he leaves the university to join the army. Modern college
administrators will appreciate an impassioned speech by
the university president who, fearing that mass enlist-
ments will drastically reduce the size of his student
body, tries to dampen the patriotic zeal of his male undergraduates.
Booth Tarkington entered Purdue in 1890, but transferred to Princeton in 1891. Because he could not master
classical languages he never received a degree. Nonetheless, Tarkington considered Princeton his alma mater
and upon his death his papers were given to Princeton by
his wife.

49. [Wilson, Richard Henry]. *Mazel*. By Richard Fisquill
    (pseud.). Chicago: Herbert S. Stone, Co., 1902.

   Mazel is a satirical romantic farce set at the University
of Virginia. Robert E. Lee Jones, a fabulously wealthy
young man about Charlottesville, falls in love with Mazel
Hurepoix, a beauteous Frenchwoman who is serving as a
governess for a faculty family. Unfortunately, Jones and
Mazel cannot converse with each other since Jones' only
language is English and Mazel speaks only French. Therefore, Jones enlists Professor Auban to make his proposal
of marriage. Auban is a rotund, forty-nine-year-old
bachelor member of the university's romance languages department. The plot thickens when Auban falls in love with
Mazel. For a time the reader is led to believe that Auban
may actually score a triumph for the portly professors of
the world by stealing Mazel from his glamorous rival. But
Mazel proves to be as flighty as she is beautiful. She
chooses youth and money and Professor Auban retires from
the contest a sadder but wiser man. The book contains
many descriptive passages about the University of Virginia
and a sizeable number of Virginia faculty—identified only
as "the professor of biology," etc.—make appearances in
the story. Professor Auban is portrayed as having a crusty
(and round) exterior but a romantic inner core.
   Richard Henry Wilson received a B.A. from South Kentucky
College in 1889 and a Ph.D. from Johns Hopkins in 1898.
At the time *Mazel* was published he was a member of the
department of romance languages at the University of Virginia.

*50. Hopkins, Herbert Muller. *The Torch*. Indianapolis: Bobbs-
    Merrill Co., 1903.

   When Henry Babington, a distinguished historian, arrives
at the "State University" to take up its presidency the
future looks bright for all concerned. But Babington

proves to have "much of the bully" in his personality as
well as an unfortunate tendency toward tactless behavior.
Among his administrative strategies is the lowering of
admission standards in order to increase the university's
enrollment. And, even worse, when asked to raise faculty
salaries President Babington refuses, noting that the
funds are needed to refurbish his presidential mansion.
Professor Plow, a political economist, challenges Babington's policies and the president summarily fires him.
Plow then runs for governor, wins, and immediately fires
Babington. Babington is not especially inconvenienced,
however. He has just been personally enriched by a multi-
million dollar bequest from a recently deceased heiress
who had generally been expected to leave her estate to the
university. Despite the turn-of-the-century setting of
this novel, today's faculty--especially those at state
supported institutions--are likely to find the book fascinating.

Herbert Muller Hopkins received an A.B. from Columbia
in 1893 and a Ph.D. from Harvard in 1898. From 1898 until
1901 he was an instructor of Latin at the University of
California, and from 1901 until 1905 he was a professor
of Latin at Trinity College in Hartford, Connecticut.
Hopkins then switched careers. From 1906 until his death
in 1910 he was Rector of the Holy Nativity Church in the
Bronx.

51. Linn, James Weber. *The Chameleon*. New York: McClure,
     Phillips and Co., 1903.

The Chameleon is a college novel with a different plot
and an unusual cast of characters. Frank Bradford is a
young graduate of "Carfax College," a small, private institution in the West. He returns to the town of Carfax
to practice law. Frank marries Amy, the niece of John
Murdock. John is also a Carfax graduate and now a rich
pickle processor. John Murdock wants to give Carfax
$10,000,000. In return he plans to ask the college trus-
tees to dismiss Dr. Craven, the school's aged president.
Murdock hopes that his gift, along with new administrative
leadership, will make Carfax the equal of Harvard and
Yale. Amy, who doesn't want Dr. Craven hurt, persuades
her rich uncle to wait a year before announcing his dona-
tion. But Frank, the "chameleon" in the story, leaks
Murdock's intentions to members of the Carfax community.
Murdock's plan becomes known to Dr. Craven who immediately
resigns his post and, shortly thereafter, dies of a broken
heart. Amy stops speaking to Frank. The two resume a

normal marital relationship only after the sudden death
of their infant son. Although few faculty or students
appear in this novel, the book pays a great deal of attention to the fiscal problems and the academic qualities of
struggling, turn-of-the-century Western colleges.
James Weber Linn received a B.A. from the University of
Chicago in 1897. He began teaching at Chicago, as an instructor of English composition, while still a senior.
He remained at Chicago until his death in 1939. Two other
Linn novels, *This Was Life* (121) and *Winds Over the Campus*
(148), also appear in this bibliography.

*52. Sholl, Anna McClure. *The Law of Life*. New York: D.
      Appleton and Co., 1903.

      The Law of Life is a romantic tragedy richly textured
with the issues and trappings of academic life. The protagonist is Barbara Penfield, the young wife of Professor
Amos Penfield, a noted mathematician at "Hallworth University." Hallworth is one of America's stellar institutions of higher learning. Barbara falls in love with
Richard Waring, an assistant professor who is also her
husband's research collaborator. The romance goes on
without Professor Penfield's knowledge. He is too engrossed in scholarship to notice. In the end, Waring
leaves the university and Barbara resumes her role as
dutiful wife. Although the basic plot of *The Law of Life*
is hackneyed, even by turn-of-the-century standards, the
author injects a series of sub-plots which revolve around
such matters as academic freedom, job-hopping by faculty,
and the relationships between faculty and administrators.
Scholars concerned with the history of American higher
education will find much of interest.
      Anna McClure Sholl was both a novelist and a painter.
Some of her novels were published under the pseudonym of
Geoffrey Corson.

53. King, Basil. *The Steps of Honor*. New York: Harper and
     Brothers, 1904.

      The Steps of Honor is a novel about faculty life at
Harvard. Anthony Muir, a young and ambitious member of
the English department achieves national visibility with
a best selling book entitled, somewhat ironically, "Society and Conscience." Unfortunately, the book turns out
to be plagiarized from an obscure study published seventy
years earlier. Muir is forced to resign his Harvard appointment and he temporarily loses the affections of his

fiancée. But everything turns out for the best. Muir
reforms, goes into the business of private tutoring, and
eventually wins back the girl whom he loves. The novel
contains one memorable quote, from a senior professor:
"Good manners and bad morals, I always say, go together.
Thank the Lord, we don't have either of them at Harvard."
  Born in Canada in 1859, Basil King was educated for the
Episcopal ministry at Kings College in Windsor. He spent
much of his adult life offering religious guidance to the
denizens of Harvard from the pulpit of Christ Church in
Cambridge. He also wrote moralistic novels, some of which
became near best-sellers. *The Steps of Honor*, his third
novel, was the only one to deal expressly with academe.
In his later years King went blind, became a devotee of
spiritualism, and was associated with the spiritualist
movement led by Sir Arthur Conan Doyle.

54. Anonymous. *In the House of Her Friends*. New York: Robert
    Grier Cooke, Inc., 1906.

  This academic soap opera centers on Katherine Lawrence,
a middle-aged widow who lives with her teenage daughter
in "Littelton," the site of "Littel College." Littel is
a private institution, small in its physical size but,
as Katherine notes, "the men who have served it have been
great and have had great aims." Katherine keeps house for
her elderly father-in-law, the good and wise college dean.
She has a platonic affair with a married professor of en-
gineering--who dies of alcoholism midway through the book--
and her daughter falls in and out of love with a wastrel
student. Meanwhile, evil college trustees try to force
the dean to resign; age and worry bring about his death;
and the college is plunged into incipient bankruptcy.
Then, to make matters even worse, a local busybody finds
the love letters which Katherine wrote to the dipsomaniacal
professor and circulates them in the college community.
By the end of the book neither the college nor Katherine
have solved all of their problems. Yet, miraculously,
Katherine's travails have made her a better person.

55. Wright, Mary Tappan [Mrs. John Henry Wright]. *The Tower*.
    New York: Charles Scribner's Sons, 1906.

  Sylvia Langdon, the fortyish, unmarried daughter of the
president of "Great Dulwich College" keeps house for her
widower father and cherishes the memory of Robinson, a
former student with whom she once had a romance. Robinson,
who has been traveling in Europe for eighteen years, returns

to Great Dulwich as an instructor of Greek. Sylvia watches
and waits as Robinson pays court to a number of local
belles. Only after Sylvia becomes deathly ill with a mysterious fever does Robinson begin to renew his old attentions. When Sylvia recovers she and Robinson are wed,
and Robinson accepts an associate professorship. Robinson,
whose brooding personality leads him to long, introspective
debates with himself, is portrayed as a super-serious teacher. He hides away in his solitary room for weeks on end
preparing lectures. Great Dulwich College is distinguished
by having in its community a vast number of unwed faculty
daughters and nieces, as well as a sizeable coterie of
faculty widows. Most of the unattached ladies find the
enigmatic Robinson attractive. The book contains a series
of academically relevant sub-plots. These center on Robinson's efforts to write a biography of a deceased professor,
his aversion to teaching off-campus classes administered
by the college, and his rejection of a full professorship
offered him by "Coldston College," Great Dulwich's arch
rival. Modern-day faculty may especially appreciate the
interest in scholarship at Great Dulwich. When a book by
one of the school's professors is published, vendors roam
the campus hawking the tome to eager purchasers.

Mary Tappan Wright was born in Steubenville, Ohio, in
1851. She was the daughter of Eli Todd Tappen, president
of Kenyon College from 1868 until 1874. She married John
Henry Wright, a Harvard professor, in 1879 and spent most
of her adult life in Cambridge, Massachusetts. *The Tower*
was the third of four novels produced by Mrs. Wright before her death in 1916.

56.   Brown, Helen Dawes. *Mr. Tuckerman's Nieces.* Boston and
      New York: Houghton-Mifflin Co., 1907.

Ellery Tuckerman is a bachelor "lecturer" in history at
a small, unnamed university in New England. Books are
Ellery's passion. He reads and writes, but has few human
associates. His solitude is invaded by three young girls,
his nieces, who come from Chicago to live with him after
the death of their parents. The girls see Ellery as a
stuffy old man ("He must be forty!"). Gradually they make
him more sociable by such cute tricks as locking him out
of his home library and throwing away the key. As the
years go by the two older girls marry and Ellery, now a
de facto family man, can't stand the solitude. As the
story concludes he surprises the university community by
deserting bachelorhood and marrying a local lady. At the
start of Chapter 23 the author offers the following

admonition: "Nothing could be duller than this chapter,
the reader has fair warning." One might well ask why she
did not give this notice appropriate rephrasing and place
it at the beginning of the book.
Helen Dawes Brown was a popular turn-of-the-century
novelist. An earlier Brown novel, *Two College Girls* (12),
is included in this bibliography.

57. Keays, Hersila A. Mitchell [Mrs. Charles Henry Keays].
    The Road to Damascus. Boston: Small, Maynard and Co.,
    1907.

    Richarda Homfrey, the young wife of an attorney named
    Tim, is visited by a woman who claims that Tim has fathered
    her illegitimate infant son. The angelic Richarda takes
    the boy into her home, names him Jack, and tells the un-
    suspecting Tim that the child was abandoned on the door-
    step. Jack is raised by the Homfreys and eventually is
    sent to "Waverly University." At this point in the narra-
    tive, which occurs halfway through the book, Jack becomes
    the protagonist of the story. Jack proves to be a bril-
    liant student. He becomes the protégé of Professor Max-
    well, a philosopher. As Jack is about to graduate, Maxwell
    arranges for him to go to Berlin on a fellowship. But
    Jack has impregnated Betty, a Waverly co-ed who is now
    married to Bill Hutchinson, an instructor at the univer-
    sity. Hutchinson thinks that the yet-to-be-born child is
    his. Jack turns down the fellowship and plans to confess
    all to Hutchinson. Then Jack is suddenly afflicted with
    a mysterious disease, goes into delirium, and confesses
    his sin to Richarda instead. This event sets off a series
    of denouements. Richarda tells Jack that Tim is his fa-
    ther, and she tells Tim that Jack is his son. Jack re-
    covers and informs Hutchinson of the genealogy of Betty's
    child. Everyone forgives everyone else and Jack goes off
    to Berlin, presumably on the road to a brilliant academic
    career. Most of the scenes at Waverly focus upon Jack's
    relationship with Professor Maxwell. The latter is por-
    trayed as a dedicated misogynist but a sentimentalist at
    heart. For his part, Jack is not only precocious sexually
    but he is intellectually advanced as well. He and Maxwell
    have long discussions about religion, the nature of man,
    and the meaning of love.
    Hersila A. Mitchell Keays was born in Woodstock, Ontario,
    in 1861. She lived most of her adult life in Hamilton,
    Ontario. She began writing after the death of her husband
    in 1897. *The Road to Damascus* was the fourth of six novels
    Mrs. Keays published before her death in 1910. All of her

novels contained strong moral messages. Mrs. Keays' last novel, *The Marriage Portion* (61), also is included in this bibliography.

58. Phelps, Elizabeth Stuart [Mrs. Elizabeth Ward]. *Walled In*. New York: Harper and Brothers, 1907.

This romantic novel features a protagonist who finds an unusual, although not entirely desirable, way of becoming a college president. The setting is "Routledge College," a high-status private institution in New England. Myrton Ferris, a forty-three-year-old professor of rhetoric, is crippled in an automobile accident. Unable to walk, and confined to his home, he feels "walled in." Ferris' mental state is not improved by his wife, Tessa, who begins to spend her days with a handsome young instructor. Nor is it helped by his own growing attachment to Honoria, Tessa's attractive half-sister, who comes to nurse him back to health. Ever the loyal husband, Ferris represses his romantic feelings for Honoria. When Hubert Hildreth, the bachelor president of Routledge, begins to court Honoria poor Professor Ferris almost dies of frustration. But Tessa and her swain are drowned when their canoe capsizes, and Dr. Hildreth is suddenly appointed Ambassador to Austria. These matters taken care of, Ferris reveals his love for Honoria and they are married. Then the trustees of Routledge offer him the vacant presidency. At first the wheelchair-bound Ferris refuses, asking: "Who will make the collecting trips?" Assured that he will have an assistant to handle out-of-town fund raising, and told that his experiences with personal suffering will make him an ideal president, Ferris accepts the post.
Elizabeth Stuart Phelps was one of the most popular and best-selling novelists of her day. She was the daughter of Auston Phelps, a professor at Andover Theological Seminary. She began writing novels shortly after the death of her fiancé in the Civil War, and all of her stories contained uplifting moral messages. *Walled In* was one of her last novels. She died in 1911. One of her earlier sagas, *Donald Marcy* (15), also is included in this bibliography.

59. Ray, Anna Chapin. *Ackroyd of the Faculty*. Boston: Little, Brown and Co., 1908.

Andrew Ackroyd, an instructor of comparative philosophy, falls in love with Connie Everitt, the daughter of his wealthy department chairman. Unhappily, Andrew is not only very poor but, as the product of lower-middle-class

background, he also is lacking in polite social graces.
Connie considers him a bore. One day Andrew heroically
attempts to rescue Connie's brother from a burning train.
The effort is unsuccessful but, along with hapless brother
Fritz, romance begins to simmer. At the end of the book
it is evident that Andrew and Connie will wed. The setting
for the story is an unnamed, elite university in the East.
Most of the plot unfolds in Andrew's humble home, which
he shares with his overprotective, good-hearted mother,
and in the far more opulent abode of Professor Everitt.
The book is noteworthy because it probes in relentless
detail the social gulf between well-born and not-so-well-
born faculty in early-day American universities.

Anna Chapin Ray received a B.A. from Smith in 1885 and
an M.A. from the same institution in 1888. She lived most
of her adult life in New Haven, Connecticut. A well-known
and well-respected author of her era, she wrote more than
forty books. Many of her works were stories for children.
Some of her output was published under the pseudonym Sid-
ney Howard.

60. Glaspell, Susan. *The Glory of the Unconquered*. New York:
     A.L. Burt, 1909.

     Tragedy and ultimate triumph at the University of Chi-
cago! Karl Hubers, a brilliant thirty-nine-year-old cancer researcher, is recruited to the Chicago faculty. But
shortly after he arrives on campus he loses his sight in
a laboratory accident. His young wife, Ernestine, a
promising artist, retrains herself as a scientist in order
to be her husband's eyes. Just as Ernestine's retraining
is complete, however, Karl suddenly dies of appendicitis.
The grief stricken Ernestine returns to art and, three
years later, produces a masterpiece--an intensely sensitive portrait of her late husband.

     Susan Glaspell attended Drake University. After a brief
career in newspaper work she concentrated on writing novels
and plays. Her drama, *Alison's House*, won the 1931 Pulitzer Prize. *The Glory of the Unconquered* was her first
novel. For many years before her death in 1948 she was a
prominent member of the literary set in Provincetown,
Massachusetts.

61. Keays, Hersila A. Mitchell [Mrs. Charles Henry Keays].
     The Marriage Portion. Boston: Small, Maynard and Co.,
     1911.

     Set at "New Town College," one of America's "foremost"
institutions of higher learning, this involved romantic

novel has as its protagonist Adele Cleave, the twenty-eight-year-old widow of a former instructor. Adele also is the daughter of a New Town professor, with whom she lives after her husband's death. During most of the narrative Adele is pursued by two men of contrasting character. The first, Angus Kilborn, is a serious-minded, middle-aged archeologist, a specialist in deciphering the writings on Egyptian mummies. Angus is married to a young, former student who is bored with academic life. Since Angus limits himself primarily to writing love letters to Adele, he is no match for Julian Ware, a man of action. Julian is a sometime poet and sometime dilettante who is the wealthy son of the president of "Great Lakes University." Julian almost sweeps Adele off her feet, but he eventually finds Mary Skene, the wife of a low-level New Town administrator, more to his tastes. Julian jilts Adele, who then turns to David Windsor, a stolid, bachelor instructor of English. At the end of the book Adele and David are to be wed, but most of the other principals in the story seemed doomed to suffer the consequences of eternally tangled love lives. The reviewer for the *New York Times* (February 11, 1912) called the book "curiously unsavory and at the same time uninteresting." Although one would find it difficult to quarrel with this assessment, the work does contain several detailed portraits of New Town faculty members and their spouses.

The Marriage Portion was published posthumously. Hersila A. Mitchell Keays died in 1910. One of her earlier novels, *The Road to Damascus* (57), is also included in this bibliography.

62. Johnson, Alvin Saunders. *The Professor and the Petticoat.* New York: Dodd, Mead and Co., 1914.

The Professor and the Petticoat is a satire about a young Harvard Ph.D. (in philosophy) who takes a teaching position at "Asuncion University" in Texas. The novel includes a farcical romance between the professor and a headstrong Southern girl and some barbed observations about Southern coeducation of the period. The major thrust of the satire, however, is directed at Northern-Southern relations in general, and at the mistrusts still remaining from the Civil War. The book is told in the first person, and the professor-narrator takes relish in pointing out what he sees as ridiculous Southern customs and ludicrous Southern modes of speech.

Alvin Saunders Johnson received an A.B. from the University of Nebraska in 1897 and a Ph.D. from Columbia in

1902. During the years before World War I he served on
the faculties of Nebraska, the University of Texas, Stanford, and Cornell. In 1917 he became editor of the *New
Republic* and in 1919 he was one of the founders of the
New School for Social Research. Johnson wrote many scholarly monographs, textbooks, and articles for professional
journals. *The Professor and the Petticoat* was his only
novel.

63.   Fuller, Henry Blake. *Bertram Cope's Year.* Chicago:
      Ralph Fletcher Seymour/The Alderbrink Press, 1919.

This subdued novel of manners details a rather uneventful
year in the life of a twenty-four-year-old graduate stu-
dent/instructor of English at "Churchton University."
Churchton is a large coeducational institution in the Midwest. Bertram Cope, the book's title character, is portrayed as charming but too ambitious to develop meaningful
relationships with those around him. His goal is to obtain a teaching post at one of the prestigious universities
in the East. Though he is befriended by many Churchtonians,
Bertram is never willing to offer serious friendship in
return. Much of the plot is laid in the drawing room of
Medora Phillips, a wealthy widow who acts as Churchton's
unofficial social director and matchmaker. Medora introduces Bertram to Amy Leffingwell, another instructor at
the university, but Bertram makes no matrimonial advances
and Amy eventually marries one of the institution's petty
administrators. At the end of the book Bertram receives
the Eastern appointment he has coveted and he sends polite
but clipped farewell notes to his Churchton acquaintances.
After reading her abbreviated message from Bertram, Medora
concludes—perhaps along with most modern-day readers of
the novel—that Bertram was "scarcely worth the to-do we
made over him."
Henry Blake Fuller was born in 1857 in Chicago, where
his father was a banker. Fuller did not attend college.
A prolific writer, he is best remembered for his realistic
novels which focus upon turn-of-the-century social conditions in Chicago. In many of his later novels Fuller
turned to the exploration of the subtleties of human nature, and it was in this phase of his work that *Bertram
Cope's Year* was published. Various major American writers,
including H.L. Mencken and Theodore Dreiser, acknowledged
Fuller's influence upon their own writing careers. Fuller
died in 1929.

The American College Novel
1920–1939

*64. Fitzgerald, Francis Scott Key. *This Side of Paradise.*
      By F. Scott Fitzgerald. New York: Charles Scribner's
      Sons, 1920.

The protagonist of *This Side of Paradise* is Amory Blaine,
a wealthy and extraordinarily handsome young man from the
Midwest who attends Princeton. Only an indifferent student, Amory spends most of his time at Princeton immersed
in the school's extracurricular activities and in sampling
the pleasures of upper-class society life in New York
City. He has a number of abortive romances, drinks to
excess, and develops an amoral set of self-indulgent
personal values. Despite his crowded social calendar,
Amory also finds time to engage in romantic reflections
about Princeton and to discuss, sometimes with his classmates and sometimes with himself, his impressions of American society, his notions of success, and his assessments
of his own flamboyant personality. Now regarded as a
classic story about America's "flaming youth" of the World
War I period, the novel offers an intriguing portrait of
elite undergraduate life during the early part of this
century.
    F. Scott Fitzgerald entered Princeton in 1913 but left
in his junior year because of illness and poor grades.
After recuperating at his St. Paul, Minnesota, home he
re-entered Princeton in 1916 but left again in October of
1917, during his senior year, to enter officer's training
for the United States Army. He did not return to Princeton after World War I. *This Side of Paradise* was Fitzgerald's first novel. It was begun while he was still a
Princeton student. Even though Fitzgerald did not graduate from Princeton he remained loyal to that institution
throughout his brief and tragic life. In Alexander
Leitch's *A Princeton Companion* (Princeton, New Jersey:
Princeton University Press, 1978), Carlos Baker reports
that Fitzgerald was reading a copy of *The Princeton Alumni
Weekly* at the very moment of his fatal heart attack in

1940. In 1946 Fitzgerald's daughter gave her father's
papers to the Princeton University Library.

65. Nathan, Robert Gruntal. *Peter Kindred*. New York: Duffield
     and Co., 1920.

     The title character of this novel is a well-to-do lad
who is sent first to Phillips Exeter Academy and then to
Harvard. The plot concentrates upon Peter's intellectual
development. At Harvard Peter falls under the spell of
Professor Thomas Carver, a radical economist, and he renounces many of the values which he brought with him to
college. He also meets and marries a Radcliffe student
and after graduation they settle in New York City. *Peter
Kindred* includes a great amount of detail about Harvard
student life of the pre-World War I period. In fact, some
reviewers found the welter of Harvard minutiae overwhelming.
H.W. Boynton, evaluating the novel for *The Review* (April
17, 1920), commented: "Mr. Nathan has forgotten nothing;
it is all here; and it is vastly unimportant."
     Robert Gruntal Nathan entered Harvard in 1912 but left
after three years. *Peter Kindred* was his first novel.
It was written in the winter of 1917 when Nathan was a
neophyte advertising executive in New York. Nathan, of
course, eventually went on to become one of America's
premier novelists. His *Mr. Whittle and the Morning Star*
(221) is one of the classic novels about faculty life.

66. Benet, Stephen Vincent. *The Beginning of Wisdom*. New
     York: Henry Holt and Co., 1921.

     Stephen Vincent Benet, the celebrated American poet and
novelist, received an A.B. from Yale in 1919 and an M.A.
from Yale in 1920. *The Beginning of Wisdom* was his first
novel.
     The protagonist of *The Beginning of Wisdom* is Philip
Sellaby, a young man who enters Yale in 1912. Philip is
depicted as a budding intellectual. He reads voraciously
and writes for the literary magazine. Philip also meets
and marries a local New Haven girl, the daughter of a
"painless dentist." Philip's wife dies of pneumonia
shortly after the wedding and, unable to concentrate on
his final examinations, Philip fails to graduate. He
then drifts to California where he becomes a movie star
and, later, a successful writer. The novel is especially
well written and many reviewers praised it for its "poetic"
prose. One incident in the Hollywood portion of the narrative deserves special mention. When Philip auditions

for his first movie role the director asks if any of the
aspirants went to college. A number of hands go up and
the fledgling actors then take great pride in announcing
to the director the names of the mediocre institutions
they attended. Not wanting to look out of place by ad-
mitting he went to Yale, Philip tells the director he
attended Princeton.

67. Minnigerode, Meade. *The Big Year: A College Story.* New
     York: G.P. Putnam's Sons, 1921.

   The Big Year is a collection of vignettes masquerading
as a novel. The setting is Yale. The central character
is "Jimmy," a newsboy. Jimmy is a New Haven urchin who
sells papers on the campus. He befriends and is befriended
by a variety of undergraduates and, in large part, the
book recounts the students' adventures as seen through
Jimmy's eyes. The students are involved in the normal
fictive pursuits of undergraduates: football, secret
societies, the big prom, and the like. However, the students in this novel fail to display the wit or ingenuity
of their counterparts in other undergraduate epics of the
period. Indeed, the reviewer for the *New York Times*
(April 24, 1921) noted that the "average mentality (of
the students in *The Big Year*) seems to be about that of a
child of twelve."
   Meade Minnigerode was born in London of American parents.
He prepared for college at Harrow and was then sent to
Yale, from which he graduated in 1910. Along with George
S. Pomeroy, Minnigerode wrote--in 1909--the words to "The
Whiffenpoof Song." After graduation he worked for a time
in the publishing business and then became a full-time
writer. He died in 1967. His oeuvre consists of general
fiction, historical novels, biographies, social histories,
and literary criticisms.

68. Canfield, Dorothy [Mrs. Dorothea Francis Canfield Fisher].
     Rough-Hewn. New York: Harcourt, Brace and Co., 1922.

   The protagonists of this long (504-page) novel are
Marise Allen and Neal Crittenden. Marise is an American
girl raised in Europe. Neale, whose upbringing takes
place in New Jersey, is an undergraduate at Columbia during
much of the story. The book recounts the separate adventures of Marise and Neale up until their first meeting,
and then it follows them through courtship and into the
early days of their marriage. As a Columbia student Neale
discovers girls--including Marise--and plays halfback on

the Columbia football team. Neale also finds that he
dislikes big city living. When he and Marise are wed they
desert the urban scene for a more rustic existence in a
small town in Vermont.

Rough-Hewn was Dorothy Canfield's eleventh novel. An
earlier Dorothy Canfield novel, *The Bent Twig* (41), is
included in this bibliography.

69. Dell, Floyd. *Janet Marsh*. New York: Alfred A. Knopf,
     1923.

The title character of this epic is a bright, attractive
Midwestern girl who goes to the "State University." There
she has a series of romances, gets pregnant, undergoes an
abortion, and leaves school to seek her fortune in New
York City. She obtains a job as a clerk in a bookstore
owned by Roger Leyland, an old family friend. Once again
Janet gets pregnant, this time by Roger, and the couple
marries. Presumably, they live happily ever after in the
literary subculture of Gotham. Janet is portrayed as
introspective yet headstrong, anxious to avoid conventional
married life. Indeed, even by current standards Janet
would be thought of as "liberated."

Floyd Dell did not attend college. He began his working
life as a newspaper reporter in Chicago and by the age of
twenty-four he was an editor of the *Chicago Evening Post*.
In 1914, at the age of twenty-seven, Dell left Chicago
for New York, where he wrote novels and plays and became
a well-known figure in the Greenwich Village literary
scene. A socialist, he also was active in politics.
Janet Marsh was his third novel.

70. Husband, Joseph Biegler. *High Hurdles*. Boston and New
     York: Houghton Mifflin Co., 1923.

Harry Gray is a wealthy undergraduate at Harvard. The
"high hurdles" he must overcome are his own arrogance and
laziness. At the end of his sophomore year Harry fails
his examinations and is expelled from the university. He
then gets a job as a loader in an Illinois coal mine.
Manual labor works wonders. Following his stint in the
pits Harry enters the world of business in Chicago determined to be a success. By the end of the book, when Harry
revisits Harvard and surveys the scenes of his past fol-
lies, it is clear that he has been fully rehabilitated.

Joseph Biegler Husband graduated from Harvard in 1908.
His adult life was spent as an advertising and public relations executive. One of his first corporate posts was
with an Illinois coal mining company.

71. McNally, William James. *The Barb*. New York: G.P. Putnam's
    Sons, 1923.

    The Barb is a stridulous anti-fraternity novel. Bob
Whitney, a strong and self-assured young man, enters the
"State University" where he refuses to take part in fraternity pledging. As a "barb" (a non-fraternity man) he
is a social outcast. Bob also is an embarrassment to
Connie, his sister, who fears that her own social standing
as a coed will be jeopardized by her brother's independence.
Yet all turns out for the best. Bob becomes an honor student. He meets a beautiful girl who has refused to join
a sorority. And toward the end of the novel he inherits
a vast fortune from his aunt. The novel contains many unflattering depictions of fraternity men and fraternity
activities. It also includes some negative passages about
state universities. At one point Bob and his girlfriend
discuss higher education in America. Bob tells his sweetheart that state universities turn out far more graduates
than do elite private colleges. "No wonder, then, we're
a boob nation," says the girl.
    William James McNally received an A.B. in 1911 from the
University of Minnesota and an A.M. in 1913 from Harvard.
After service as an infantry officer in World War I he
entered the newspaper business in Minneapolis. Eventually
he became president of the Minnesota Tribune Company. *The
Barb* was the first of three novels which McNally published
during his lifetime. He died in 1967. McNally also wrote
a number of dramas. One of these, *Prelude to Exile*, was
produced on Broadway in 1936 by The Theater Guild.

72. Montross, Lynn, and Lois Seyster Montross. *Town and Gown*.
    New York: George H. Doran Co., 1923.

    Town and Gown is a set of thirteen humorous sketches and
vignettes held together by the presence throughout the
book of a series of common characters. The setting is
a Midwestern state university. The students in the episodes are for the most part representative of those devil-
may-care, "roaring twenties" adolescents who populated
American fiction in the decade after World War I. And
the school's faculty and administrators, when viewed in
the context of humorous college fiction, are typically
perverse, addled, and authoritarian.
    Eight of the episodes in *Town and Gown* were written by
Lynn Montross. The remaining five were written by his wife,
Lois. Lynn Montross was born in 1895. He attended the
University of Nebraska from 1914 until 1917. In later

years he became a well-known American military historian.
Lois Seyster Montross was born in 1897. She graduated
from the University of Illinois in 1919. Lynn and Lois
Montross were married in 1921 and *Town and Gown* was their
first collaborative book-length publication. Another Lynn
and Lois Montross collection of college sketches, *Fraternity Row* (85), appears in the bibliography. *Fraternity
Row* contains many of the same characters found in *Town and
Gown*. Lynn and Lois Montross were divorced in 1933. In
1934 Lois Montross published a student-centered college
novel, *The Perfect Pair* (115), and that book also appears
in this bibliography.

73. Clark, Ellery Harding. *Daughters of Eve*. Philadelphia:
    Dorrance and Co., 1924.

    The protagonist of this curiously moralistic Harvard
story is Dick Meredith, a star fullback on the Crimson
football team. Dick impregnates Dorothy Morrison, his
fiancée, but since Harvard does not allow its varsity athletes to be married Dick and Dorothy postpone their wedding until the conclusion of the gridiron season. The
birth of their child appears imminent on the day of the
final game, against Yale. In hopes of making the infant
"legitimate," Dick has a taxi waiting outside the stadium
to whisk a preacher, a marriage license, and himself to
Dorothy's bedside directly after the contest. Dick's
scheme goes awry, however, when he is knocked into prolonged unconsciousness while scoring the winning touchdown. He awakes a few days later to find that the child
was born dead. Dorothy, by contrast, is alive, well, and
loving, and the happy couple schedule a traditional marriage ceremony.
    Ellery Harding Clerk was an outstanding turn-of-the-
century Harvard athlete. A member of the class of 1896,
he led the Harvard track and football teams to innumerable
victories before winning gold medals for both the high
jump and the broad jump in the 1896 Olympic Games. After
the Olympics Clark attended Harvard Law School, from which
he graduated in 1899. During his adult life Clark practiced law in Boston and wrote many collegiate sports
stories for older boys. *Daughters of Eve* was one of his
few attempts to write fiction for adults.

74. Fitch, Albert Parker. *None So Blind*. New York: Mac-
    millan Co., 1924.

    The bulk of this novel is set at turn-of-the-century
Harvard. The protagonist of the story is Dick Blaisdell,

a Harvard undergraduate. At the beginning of the novel
Dick is more interested in drink and wild times than he is
in his studies. He is barely able to stay in college.
Toward the close of his college experience, however, Dick
undergoes a religious awakening and reforms. Meantime,
the girl whom Dick loves, one Felicia Moreland, decides
to marry Percy Barrett, a young man who has spent seven
years as a Harvard instructor. Felicia and Percy are wed
and the couple repairs to a new university far into the
Midwest, where Percy hopes for somewhat more rapid professional advancement. The last scenes of the novel take
place a decade later, in the Barrett homestead. Percy has
become a stodgy professor and Felicia is tired of life on
the prairie. Felicia's morale is not improved when she
learns that Dick, whose proposal she once rejected, is
now a prominent East Coast surgeon married to the glamorous
daughter of a former Canadian Prime Minister.

Albert Parker Fitch graduated from Harvard in 1920 and
immediately went on to Union Theological Seminary, from
which he graduated in 1923. He then began a varied career
which saw him move back and forth between the academic
world and the ministry. At the time *None So Blind* was
published Fitch was a professor of religious history at
Carleton College.

*75. Marks, Percy. *The Plastic Age*. New York: The Century Co.,
 1924.

The son of an immigrant from Poland, Percy Marks graduated from the University of California in 1912 and received an M.A. from Harvard in 1914. During the next ten
years he taught English at the Massachusetts Institute of
Technology, Dartmouth, and Brown. *The Plastic Age*, his
first novel, was written while he was at Dartmouth and it
was intended, in part, as a literary antidote to F. Scott
Fitzgerald's *This Side of Paradise* (64). It was Marks'
belief that Amory Blaine, the amoral Princeton protagonist
of Fitzgerald's novel, was not representative of American
college students. And so Marks, in *The Plastic Age*, set
out to offer a realistic portrait of an undergraduate.

The central character of *The Plastic Age*, one Hugh Carver,
is an upstanding and often moralistic youth who attends
"Sanford College." Sanford, a composite of various Ivy
League schools, possesses a pseudo-sophisticated student
body with a penchant for idle dissipation. Moreover, the
institution's faculty members, with only a few exceptions,
are either incapable of or disinterested in effective
teaching. Hugh begins his Sanford years full of enthusiasm.

But after partaking in a wide range of campus activities
he concludes, just before graduating, that the Sanford
experience is "pure bunk." Sanford, in Hugh's opinion,
provides little by way of intellectual stimulation and,
in terms of its undergraduate social life, it turns "nice
kid(s)" into "coarse snobs."

The Plastic Age received widespread critical attention.
Some reviewers praised it for its negative portrayal of
the American college system, but others thought that it
overlooked many of the positive aspects of American higher
education. In any event, the book sold extremely well
and, in 1927, it was adapted as a motion picture. Partly
on the strength of the novel's sales, Marks was able to
give up college teaching to devote his full energies to
writing. In 1927 he followed Hugh Carver into his post-
college career in *Lord of Himself* (New York: The Century
Co.). In 1929 he turned his attention once again to the
American college scene with *The Unwilling God* (94). And
in 1938, in *What's a Heaven For?* (New York: Frederick A.
Stokes Co.), Marks had his protagonist, Nathaniel Wayne,
attend the University of California. Since *What's a
Heaven For?* is primarily the story of Nathaniel's career
in the banking industry, it is not accorded a separate
entry in this bibliography.

76.   Wiley, John. *The Education of Peter: A Novel of the
      Younger Generation*. New York: Frederick A. Stokes Co.,
      1924.

Peter Carey, a bright lad from a wealthy family, attends
Yale. Peter's older brother Hugh, now a Yale alumnus,
offers him sage advice about how to meet the right people.
But Peter ignores his brother's injunctions and chooses to
spend most of his spare time working on the literary magazine. Peter also takes long, solitary walks through New
Haven, befriends a variety of socially unacceptable intellectual students, and meets a local girl whom he plans
to marry. During his senior year he pens a play for the
drama society and it is evident that after graduation he
will try his hand at professional writing. Unlike many
student-centered novels of the period, *The Education of
Peter* avoids the indolent side of collegiate life.

Born in 1899, John Wiley received a B.A. from Yale.
The Education of Peter was his first novel. Wiley later
became a prominent radio actor in New York City.

77. Crane, Clarkson. *The Western Shore*. New York: Harcourt, Brace and Co., 1925.

   The Western Shore consists of a series of vignettes linked together by a retinue of common characters. The setting is the University of California at Berkeley and the time is 1919. The character who appears most frequently is George Towne, a student from Wyoming. Poor and plodding, George is depicted as harboring ambitions as an intellectual. But he finds that Berkeley is sadly lacking in cerebral stimuli. Only Professor Burton, a displaced Easterner who lives in a world of books, seems capable of dispensing real wisdom. Burton is an oddball, however, and most Berkeley students suspect him of being a homosexual. Although George at one point moves into Burton's bachelor digs, his relationship with the professor never becomes especially close. Most of the other characters in the book are George's fellow students and, like George, they are depicted as both heterosexual and mentally drab.
   Clarkson Crane was born in Chicago in 1894. He graduated from the University of California at Berkeley in 1916. *The Western Shore*, Crane's first novel, was written during an extended stay in Paris after service as an ambulance driver during World War I. Crane returned to the United States in the late 1920s and thereafter combined writing, lecturing, and work as a librarian.

78. Dunton, James Gerald. *Wild Asses*. Boston: Small, Maynard and Co., 1925.

   The "wild asses" of this novel are five students who enter Harvard in the fall of 1919. Three of the students are worldly-wise veterans of World War I and the other two follow along as the veterans major in drinking and extracurricular sex.
   Like the central characters in his novel, James Gerald Dunton entered Harvard in 1919. During World War I he had driven an ambulance in France. Dunton graduated in 1923 and then stayed in Cambridge to take a master's degree in education. *Wild Asses* was written while he was doing his graduate work. It sold approximately 10,000 copies and film rights were purchased by a major Hollywood studio. Although no movie was made because the prospective producers feared that the plot would cause the film to run afoul of local "decency" regulations, the success of the

book encouraged Dunton to launch what proved to be a
commercially successful writing career. One of Dunton's
later novels, *A Maid and a Million Men* (New York: J.H.
Sears, 1928), sold over 1,000,000 copies.

79.   Gilman, Mildred Evans. *Fig Leaves*. New York: Siebel
        Publishing Co., 1925.

Lydia Carter, a pensive girl from Grand Rapids, Michigan,
attends the University of Wisconsin. She enters the university in 1915. During her four years at Madison she
grows to be an independent young woman. As a senior she
renounces her sorority membership, an act which makes her
an outcast among her former friends. She even spends a
night in a hotel room with David, her boyfriend. But both
David and Lydia are engulfed in remorse after this folly
of the flesh, and David joins the army in hopes of being
killed in World War I. Meanwhile, Lydia graduates from
the university. David survives the war and at the conclusion of the novel the two young people are about to be
married. The college scenes in *Fig Leaves* are reasonably
detailed, although the emphasis is upon the out-of-class
aspects of college life. Devotees of college fiction will
be gratified to learn that one of Lydia's favorite books
during her high school days was *When Patty Went to College*
by Jean Webster (39).
Mildred Evans Gilman was born in Chicago in 1898 but
spent most of her childhood in Grand Rapids, Michigan.
She received a B.A. from the University of Wisconsin.
Fig Leaves was her first novel.

80.   Holman, Russell. *The Freshman*. New York: Grosset and
        Dunlap, 1925.

This novel was adapted from the classic 1925 motion
picture comedy of the same title. The silent film was
scripted by Harold Lloyd and starred Lloyd in the title
role. The protagonist of the story is Harold "Speedy"
Lamb, a naive but determined lad from "Sanford," Ohio.
Harold attends "Tate University." Tate is described as
"a large football stadium with a college attached." The
bumbling Harold is kept on the football squad as a combination waterboy and mascot. During the final game of
the season, against arch rival Union State, injuries force
the Tate coach to send Harold into the fray as quarterback, and Harold scores the winning touchdown. Although
modern-day readers are not likely to learn a great deal
about actual college life in the 1920s from *The Freshman*,

the work is significant because it (and the movie upon
which it was based) provided millions of people around
the world with a "rah-rah" image of the undergraduate
collegiate experience.

81. Lehman, Benjamin Harrison. *Wild Marriage*. New York:
    Harper and Brothers, 1925.

    Wild Marriage is a novel of sexual intrigue at Harvard.
    The central character is Elam Dunster, the son of a Har-
    vard professor of geology. Elam is a Harvard undergradu-
    ate but his attentions stray from his studies to Medeline
    Colguhom, the young wife of a faculty member. Medeline's
    husband is conveniently away on a research trip to South
    America. Eventually Elam is forced to leave Cambridge
    and Medeline, after he is arrested in a police raid on a
    speakeasy. The novel has a number of sub-plots, including
    one which involves the desertion of Professor Dunster by
    Elam's mother. Reviewers generally found the book to be
    a mature treatment of sexual entanglements and a promising
    first novel. But the literary critic for *The Nation*
    (May 6, 1925) commented that "the undergraduate soil--
    none too fertile to begin with--shows signs of exhaustion."
        Benjamin Harrison Lehman graduated summa cum laude from
    Harvard in 1911. He received a Ph.D. from Harvard in
    1920. Lehman was a member of the English department at
    the University of California when *Wild Marriage* was
    published.

82. Lewis, Sinclair. *Arrowsmith*. New York: Harcourt, Brace
    and Co., 1925.

    Sinclair Lewis graduated from Yale in 1907. *Arrowsmith*,
    published when he was forty years old, was written at the
    height of his creative life. Many literary scholars con-
    sider it his best work. The book won the 1926 Pulitzer
    Prize for fiction but Lewis rejected the award. Lewis'
    biographers disagree about whether he refused the honor
    to gain publicity or whether, as Lewis himself claimed,
    he was acting from the conviction that no committee should
    have the effrontery to designate a "best novel."
        Arrowsmith follows its title character, Martin Arrow-
    smith, through medical school and then into a distinguished
    career as a physician, researcher, and director of a medi-
    cal institute. Martin's experiences at the "University
    of Winnemac Medical School," from 1906 until 1910, occupy
    the first quarter of the 448-page story. A somewhat in-
    different student, Martin is uncertain about what direction

his medical studies should take and, at times, he con-
templates leaving medical school altogether. At one point,
after incurring the displeasure of Dr. Gottlieb, a brilliant but eccentric instructor of bacteriology, Martin is
put on temporary probation. But his often tumultuous
association with Dr. Gottlieb, a pupil-mentor relationship
which Lewis describes in detail, ultimately provides
Martin with the inspiration he needs to become a dedicated man of science.

83. Brush, Katherine Ingham. *Glitter.* New York: A.L. Burt
     Co., 1926.

     Jock Hamill is a handsome undergraduate. He attends an
     unnamed, elite university a few hours' drive from New York
     City. A dedicated fraternity man, Jock has romances with
     one girl after another, performs student pranks, and gener-
     ally leads a profligate existence. However, his outlook
     on life begins to change when he learns that his widowed
     mother--whom he thought had been left filthy rich by his
     late father's will--really supports his college dissipa-
     tions by running a gambling den in her home. His attitudes
     change, too, when one of his lady friends, a seductive
     nightclub singer, jilts him. Finally, toward the end of
     the novel, Jock leaves the university before graduating.
     When last seen he is preparing to marry Cecily Graves, a
     serious-minded young woman who undoubtedly will give him
     the direction he needs to live a successful life. The
     book offers many extensive descriptions of out-of-class
     campus activities, but the academic aspects of Jock's
     college career are ignored.
       Born in 1900, Kathleen Ingham Brush attended Centenary
     Collegiate Institute (later Centenary Junior College) from
     1913 until 1917. After completing her formal education
     she entered newspaper work in Boston. *Glitter* was her
     first novel. Before her death in 1952 Brush produced a
     large roster of short stories, motion picture scripts,
     and light novels.

84. Hormel, Olive Deane. *Co-Ed.* New York: Charles Scribner's
     Sons, 1926.

     Co-Ed is a novel which parades the virtues of state
     universities. Lucia Leigh has her heart set on attending
     Vassar but at the last moment she is persuaded to attend
     her parents' publicly financed alma mater in the Midwest.
     Lucia has the usual undergraduate adventures and escapades,
     but by graduation she is a serious young lady ready to

make her way in the world. Midway through the book one
of Lucia's classmates develops a crush on her anthropology
professor, one Dr. Lovelace. The girl is saved from her
folly by Miss Carr, the dean of women, who offers her sage
motherly advice. Presumably, administrators at state universities in the 1920s really cared about their students.
Co-Ed is written in a plain, matter-of-fact style and, as
the reviewer for the *New York Times* (June 13, 1926) put
it: "[The novel is] without trace of a sense of humor."

Olive Deane Hormel received a bachelor's degree from
Lindenwood College in St. Charles, Missouri, and an M.A.
in English from the University of Illinois. After graduating from Illinois she worked for the University of Michigan Extension Service, lecturing on contemporary literature
and drama to groups throughout the upper Midwest. *Co-Ed*
was her first novel.

85. Montross, Lynn, and Lois Seyster Montross. *Fraternity
     Row*. New York: George H. Doran Co., 1926.

Fraternity Row is set at the same Midwestern state university as the Montross' earlier collaborative work, *Town
and Gown* (72). And, like *Town and Gown*, the book consists
of humorous sketches and vignettes which involve a common
set of characters. The protagonist of many of the *Fraternity Row* stories is Andy Protheroe, an undergraduate whom
the authors describe in a preface as embodying "the spirit
of young absurdity." Andy, who is also a prominent member
of the cast of *Town and Gown*, is a bright and charming
rogue, in many respects a throwback to the central characters of turn-of-the-century student-centered novels of
life at Harvard and Yale. Because Andy is thoroughly en-
joying himself at the university he has no wish to graduate. In one of the book's sixteen episodes he hands in a
blank blue book for his final examination in Professor Rutenber's economics class. But, as Andy finds to his dismay,
Rutenber has a habit of grading examinations without looking at them. The professor gives Andy a passing grade.
At this point it takes all of the ingenuity Andy can muster
to fail the course.

The Perfect Pair (115), a student-centered novel written
by Lois Seyster Montross without the collaboration of Lynn
Montross, also appears in this bibliography.

86. Hill, Carol Denny [Mrs. Carl Brant]. *Wild*. New York:
     John Day Co., 1927.

Wild is a roaring twenties novel about a Barnard College
student who finds the fleshpots of New York City considerably

more appealing than class work. The protagonist is Helen
Atchinson, an attractive girl from Ohio. Not lacking for
escorts, Helen spends most of her time being wined and
dined in New York's poshest restaurants, going to the
theater, and experiencing the cultural delights of speak-
easies. Helen also is something of a tease. Although she
is not averse to heavy petting she prides herself on re-
taining her virginity. There are a few classroom and
dormitory scenes in the novel but most of the real action
takes place off campus.

Carol Denny Hill graduated from Barnard in the early
1920s. She wrote *Wild*, her first novel, on an after-
graduation sojourn in France. During the 1930s Hill became a prominent literary agent. Among her clients were
Raymond Moley, Vincent Sheean, and Sigrid Undset.

87. Winslow, Horatio Gates. *Spring's Banjo: A Portmanteau
     Historical Novel and Hymn to Youth with a Musical Accom-
     paniment and Fashion Notes of the Period*. New York:
     Frank-Maurice Inc., 1927.

Spring's Banjo is a curious period piece about turn-of-
the-century student life at the University of Wisconsin.
The protagonist is a co-ed named Caria. An attractive and
charming young lady from "West Waunette," Caria is the
queen of the Wisconsin social scene. Maneuvering her way
through a series of fraternity and sorority parties, she
has romances with "Hungry" Hooper, the school's leading
undergraduate poet, and with Willett Gamm, the most snap-
pily dressed male student on the Wisconsin campus. Studies
prove to be Carla's undoing. After accumulating a debilitating array of failing grades she is asked to leave college. At the end of the book we see Carla wandering
through Chicago's Lincoln Park seven years after her en-
forced exit from Wisconsin. She is now a $23-per-week
clerk in an agency which places orphans in foster homes.
In the park she chances upon Willett Gamm, whose own
meager income as a drug salesman is barely enough for
basic food, clothing, and shelter. The two discuss their
separate post-college failures and agree to marry. The
text of the story is broken at many points by poetry (much
of it ostensibly written by Hungry Hooper) and it is inter-
rupted further by the author's suggestions about the appropriate popular songs which the reader might hum as he
or she reads each chapter.

Horatio Winston Gates was born in Racine, Wisconsin,
in 1882. He received a B.A. from the University of Wisconsin in 1904. A professional writer and editor, Winslow

produced many novels and short stories. During the years
which immediately preceded World War I he was editor of
The Masses.

88. Wolf, Robert Leopold. *Springboard*. New York: Albert and
      Charles Boni, 1927.

This novel follows Brian Hart from his birth through
his undergraduate days at Harvard. Brian is the son of
a Midwestern railroad owner. The early part of the book
details his unhappy life as a bullied Cleveland schoolboy.
At Harvard Brian blossoms into a man. He woos and wins
a Boston society girl and, in addition to his other student activities, he becomes president of the Harvard Equal
Suffrage League. *Springboard* won general critical praise
as a sensitive novel about adolescent awakening.
     Robert Leopold Wolf graduated from Harvard in 1915.
Springboard was his only novel. Wolf was one of the Harvard students whom Robert Nathan took as a model for the
title character in *Peter Kindred* (65).

89. [Adams, Samuel Hopkins]. *Unforbidden Fruit*. By Warner
      Fabian (pseud.). New York: Boni and Liveright, 1928.

Samuel Hopkins Adams was born in Dunkirk, New York, in
1871. After graduating from Hamilton College he embarked
upon a celebrated writing career that was to include novels,
mysteries, biographies, and muckraking exposes of various
American institutions. Warner Fabian was a pseudonym
which Adams reserved for his racier novels.
     Unforbidden Fruit is a fictional probe of undergraduate
life at exclusive women's colleges. The book is set at
"Sperry College," an institution populated largely by
foul-mouthed, intellectually disinterested, and sex-
crazed young ladies. The girls of Sperry, most of whom
eventually suffer grievously for their sins, jump out of
dormitory windows to meet their boyfriends and otherwise
behave in energetic, if unseemly, fashion. Adams claimed
that *Unforbidden Fruit* was written as a public service,
to alert parents to the dangers their daughters would face
in college. Many reviewers saw the book, instead, as a
crass attempt to exploit public concern over evils of
wanton "flapperism."

90. Suckow, Ruth. *The Bonney Family*. New York: Alfred A.
      Knopf, 1928.

This book chronicles twenty years in the life of a Midwestern academic family. Mr. Bonney, a sometimes Protestant

clergyman, is a minor administrator at "Vincent College," a small and struggling church institution. Two of his three children attend the school, and many of the scenes which take place on the Vincent campus focus upon their experiences as students. Son Warren is a shy, awkward redhead who attempts to find social salvation by becoming a violin virtuoso. Elder daughter Sarah, a lumpish young lady who is shunned by the college's eligible males, eventually leaves Vincent to become the family's mother-surrogate when Mrs. Bonney dies near the end of the story. The novel offers numerous insights into the life style of genteel, if penurious, academic families during the early part of this century.

Ruth Suckow was born in 1892 in Hawarden, Iowa. Her father was a Congregationalist minister. She attended Grinnell College for three years but left before graduating. She was a popular novelist and writer of short stories for mass circulation magazines. Many of the reviewers of *The Bonney Family*, her third novel, noted that the work was a fictionalized autobiography.

91. Wertenbaker, Charles Christian. *Boojum*. New York: Boni and Liveright, 1928.

Boojum is a novel about undergraduate disillusionment. But, unlike most epics about student disenchantment, it is spiced with comic incidents and the dialogue often crackles with wit. The protagonist is Stuart Lee Breckinridge and the setting is "Southern University." Stuart is an aspiring writer who rejects the "rah-rah" activities of his fellow students. Toward the end of the book, when the environment at Southern becomes too oppressive, Stuart hops a freight and embarks on a long odyssey across America. Some reviewers considered the book a satire, but the author's intent was to create a lively-but-serious study of a budding intellectual.

Charles Christian Wertenbaker attended the University of Virginia. Most of his adult life was spent with *Time Magazine* as a reporter and editor. At the time of his death in 1955 he was one of America's most respected journalists. *Boojum* was his first novel. Wertenbaker is now best remembered, perhaps, not for his own writing but as the central character in *Death of a Man* (New York: Random House, 1957). This book, written by his wife, Lael Tucker Wertenbaker, details Charles' death from cancer. *Death of a Man* was later adapted for the stage. The play, written by Garson Kanin, was entitled *A Gift of Time*. Produced on Broadway in 1962, it starred Henry Fonda as Charles.

92. Carter, Burnham. *Mortal Men*. New York: Albert and Charles Boni, 1929.

   The protagonist of this poetic novel is Allan Levering, a young aristocrat. The story follows Allan through prep school, into Princeton, and then to New York City where he becomes a junior executive with a copper conglomerate. The Princeton scenes occupy the middle third of the book. As a Princetonian Allan shuns student organizations and prefers to cultivate his aesthetic senses by reading *Tristram Shandy* and by taking solitary moonlight walks across the campus. He also courts an upper-class young lady from Trenton. At the end of his junior year Allan fails three examinations and leaves school. However, his exit from Princeton is not especially traumatic because Allan knows that his future does not depend upon a college degree. A few years later, when his father dies, Allan inherits stately "Levering Manor" as well as much of the vast family fortune. As the novel concludes, Allan is planning to retire from business--at the age of twenty-seven--to raise jumping horses on his estate. The author, whose identity has eluded the compilers of biographical reference works, does not indicate how the non-degreed but immensely wealthy Allan plans to deal with the constant dunning that he is certain to receive from the Princeton Alumni Fund.

93. Cary, Lucian. *The Duke Steps Out*. Garden City, New York: Doubleday, Doran and Co., 1929.

   Duke Wellington, lightweight boxing champion of the world, enrolls in the "University of Minnewaska," a large, state-supported bastion of academic absurdity north of Chicago. Duke's goal is to meet, woo, and wed Susan Corbin, a stunning co-ed whom he has secretly observed in the Windy City. Duke tells no one at Minnewaska his real identity. Nonetheless, because he arrives on campus in a chauffeur-driven Bentley, everyone at the university suspects that he is not an average student. Susan, who thinks Duke is a gangster, plays hard-to-get. Duke takes time off from his studies to successfully defend his title. Susan discovers his real vocation, agrees to marry him, and Duke retires undefeated from the ring. The novel includes a great amount of bald-faced satire. Duke proves to be Minnewaska's outstanding freshman--he reads voraciously-- and he clearly outdistances most of the university's faculty in knowledge about life beyond the campus. At one point Duke attends a dinner party in the home of a boorish sociology professor, and he must suffer in silence as his host--who does not know Duke's connection with pugilism--expounds at length on the innate stupidity of prizefighters.

Lucian Cary was born in Hamlin, Kansas, in 1886. Between 1902 and 1908 he attended the University of Wisconsin, Beloit College, and the University of Chicago. From 1908 until 1910 he was an instructor of English at Wabash College in Indiana. After leaving Wabash he became a reporter for the *Chicago Tribune* and eventually served as an editor for a variety of newspapers and magazines. *The Duke Steps Out* was his first novel. Two later Cary novels, *One Lovely Moron* (139) and *Second Meeting* (153), also appear in this bibliography. These novels, like *The Duke Steps Out*, are set at the University of Minnewaska. Toward the end of his career Cary became a noted authority on the history of firearms and published many books and articles on the subject. He died in 1971.

94.   Marks, Percy. *The Unwilling God*. New York: Harper and Brothers, 1929.

Percy Marks wrote *The Unwilling God* in what proved to be an unsuccessful attempt to repeat the sales success he had enjoyed with *The Plastic Age* (75). One reason for the relatively poor commercial showing of *The Unwilling God* may have been Marks' reversal of the theme of his earlier novel. Hugh Carver, the protagonist of *The Plastic Age*, enters college as an enthusiastic freshman and graduates four years later filled with disillusionment. Bill Boyer, the protagonist of *The Unwilling God*, enters "Raleigh College" at the ripe old age of twenty-four and has no time for the customary indolences of undergraduate life. In fact, Bill goes out of his way to avoid fraternities, societies, and other "rah-rah" activities. His only extracurricular enterprise is football, which he plays with great technical skill but with little fire. Bill pays the price for his aloofness. A social isolate, he is turned down for a scholarship because he does not embody the Raleigh ideal, and the girl whom he covets refuses to see him. Not until the late Fall of his senior year does Bill exhibit enthusiasm. Playing in the last football game of his career--against Raleigh's arch rival-- Bill makes a heroic effort in a losing cause, and he wins cheers from the crowd. He finally realizes the value of school spirit and, though he does not suddenly become Joe College, he becomes more tolerant of the adolescent collegiate environment which surrounds him. And, of course,

the girl who once shunned him now assents to his attentions.

Many of the same reviewers who had praised *The Plastic
Age* as a realistic expose of the evils of college life
dismissed *The Unwilling God* as mere sermonizing. Nonetheless, most critics agreed that *The Unwilling God*, like
its predecessor, contained an abundance of collegiate
atmosphere and many insightful characterizations of students, faculty, and administrators.

95. Millay, Kathleen [Mrs. Howard Irving Young]. *Against the
Wall*. New York: Macauley and Co., 1929.

Against the Wall is a bitter novel about snobbishness,
pretentiousness, and downright ignorance at "Matthew
College," a well-known institution for women in the East.
The protagonist is Rebecca Brewster, a girl from a small
town in Maine. Rebecca wants college to provide her with
mental stimulation. But, alas, at Matthew she finds that
the system works only to dull the students' intellects.
The book differs from most other novels about student
disillusionment in that Rebecca finds less fault with her
classmates than with Matthew's torpid faculty and with
the college's bureaucratic administrators. Unwilling to
subject herself to a full four years of Matthew's idea of
higher learning, Rebecca eventually leaves the institution
to seek a meaningful education in the school of life.

Kathleen Millay was the younger sister of Edna St. Vincent
Millay. She attended Vassar from 1917 to 1920 but left in
her junior year. Although Kathleen Millay did not attain
the literary eminence of her sister, she published extensively. *Against the Wall* was her second novel.

*96. Wolfe, Thomas Clayton. *Look Homeward, Angel: A Story of
the Buried Life*. New York: Charles Scribner's Sons,
1929.

Look Homeward, Angel is the first of three Thomas Wolfe
novels to deal, at least in part, with college life. The
other two are *Of Time and the River* (146) and *The Web and
the Rock* (129). As every student of American literature
knows, all three of these novels are heavily autobiographical. *Look Homeward, Angel* follows Eugene Gant, a gang-
ling North Carolina youth, through his childhood in the
town of Altamount and on to the "State University" at
Pulpit Hill. The son of a domineering mother and a father
who is dying of cancer, Eugene at first sees college
largely as an escape from his home life. During his four

years at Pulpit Hill, however, he investigates all of the
intellectual opportunities the university has to offer and
he decides upon a career as a writer. At the end of the
novel he is preparing to undertake graduate work at Harvard.

Thomas Wolfe was born and raised in Asheville, North
Carolina, and graduated from the University of North Carolina at Chapel Hill in 1920. After receiving his undergraduate degree Wolfe, like Eugene Gant, enrolled for
graduate work at Harvard. Wolfe's initial ambition was
to be a playwright and it was not until he wrote several
unproduced dramas that he turned to novels as an outlet
for his talents. *Look Homeward, Angel* was his first novel.
It was begun in the summer of 1926 and finished in March
of 1928. Much of the writing was done in time which Wolfe
snatched from his duties as an instructor of English at
New York University. The book was rejected by a number of
publishers before being accepted by Scribner's. It was
edited for publication by Maxwell Perkins and thus began
one of the most celebrated author-editor relationships in
American literary history.

97. Latimer, Margery Bodine. *This Is My Body*. New York:
     Jonathan Cape and Harrison Smith, 1930.

Megan Foster enters a Midwestern state university determined to become a great writer. Unfortunately, all those
required science and language courses get in the way of
her ambitions. So, too, do those intellectual dwarfs who
masquerade as university faculty members. And her fellow
students, who are interested only in frivolities, also
impede her quest for literary immortality. In her sophomore year Megan is expelled for cohabitating with the
male editor of the literary magazine. She drifts to New
York City's Greenwich Village, becomes pregnant, has an
abortion, and then caps her young life by having a nervous
breakdown. Megan is portrayed as an outspoken, aggressive
young woman against whom the world continually conspires.
Since she is often given to reviling men for their shabby
treatment of women, modern-day feminists may find her a
sympathetic character. In terms of its execution the book
is noteworthy for the author's attempts to intermix the
writing styles of James Joyce and Henry James. Most reviewers found the novel to be an ambitious literary under-
taking, flawed principally by its unremitting unpleasant-
ness.

Margery Bodine Latimer was born in Portage, Wisconsin,
in 1899. She attended Wooster College in Ohio, the University of Wisconsin, and Columbia University. *This Is
My Body* was her third novel.

98. Stein, Aaron Marc. *Spirals*. New York: Covici, Friede
     Publishers, 1930.

     Narrated by Tony Todd, an introspective Princeton under-
     graduate from the Boston area, this novel is more note-
     worthy for its execution than for its story line. The
     latter is a conventional tale of student social and in-
     tellectual awakening. In particular, Tony begins to real-
     ize some of the disquieting complexities of life when
     Sandy Price, one of his freshman classmates, is killed in
     a skiing accident. But if the plot of the book is routine,
     the author's writing style is unique in American college
     fiction. In 298 pages of undiluted stream-of-consciousness
     Tony offers the reader, often through sentence fragments,
     a constant outpouring of adolescent reaction to the hap-
     penings across four Princeton years. Tony quotes himself
     at great length, but since the other characters in the
     story have no dialogue they are realized only as shadows
     on the Princeton scene.
     Aaron Marc Stein was born in New York City in 1906. He
     received an A.B. from Princeton in 1927. *Spirals* was his
     first novel. In later years Stein became one of America's
     most prolific mystery writers, sometimes using the pseudo-
     nyms George Bagby and Hampton Stone.

99. [Stockwell, William Hume]. *Rudderless: A University*
     Chronicle. By W. Stock Hume (pseud.). Norwood, Massa-
     chusetts: The Norwood Press, 1930.

     Rudderless is a wordy recapitulation of the college
     career of Tom Benham, an undergraduate at "Harcourt Uni-
     versity." Located in the Midwestern city of "Belham,"
     Harcourt gives every appearance of being the University
     of Michigan. Tom joins a fraternity and, for two years,
     he leads a fairly routine collegiate existence. Then, in
     his junior year, he begins to question the value of a Har-
     court education. The institution, as Tom comes to see it,
     is "rudderless," a giant multidecked cruise ship floating
     without course or direction, and its students are as aim-
     less as the school itself. Over the objections of his
     father Tom leaves Harcourt, marries, and takes a job on
     a Detroit newspaper. Shortly thereafter Tom's father
     becomes gravely ill and in order to make his father's
     last days happier Tom returns to Harcourt after a year's
     absence. At the end of the book our dutiful hero receives
     his diploma, but even with his sheepskin in hand he has
     strong doubts about the usefulness of his Harcourt experi-
     ence. The novel provides painstaking detail about both
     the social and academic sides of the Harcourt milieu. A

great many faculty members appear in the story, most of
them reading stale lectures from yellowed note paper.
Only Mr. Pepys, a teacher of rhetoric, emerges as a dedicated educator, and it is through out-of-class meetings
with Pepys--whose own dislike of Harcourt is intense--that
Tom begins to see the lack of purpose which characterizes
the university.

William Hume Stockwell received a B.A. from the University of Michigan in 1928 and graduated from the University
of Michigan Law School in 1930. After a brief career as
a newspaperman he entered the advertising business and
spend the balance of his post-Michigan career as the co-
owner of an advertising agency in Detroit. *Rudderless*,
written while Stockwell was an undergraduate, was his only
novel.

100.   White, Betty. *I Lived This Story*. Garden City, New York:
       Doubleday, Doran and Co., 1930.

       I Lived This Story is a dour novel about co-ed life in
       the 1920s. Dorinda Clark enters a large university near
       Chicago expecting intellectual stimlulation and rewarding
       social experiences. Instead, she finds snobbishness,
       anti-intellectualism, and sexual exploitation. She is
       able to survive only by airing her grievances to a few
       sympathetic professors and by marrying, in her senior year,
       a young man who shares her disenchantments. The novel
       contains especially vivid portraits of Dorinda's empty-
       headed sorority sisters.

       Betty White attended Northwestern University. Doubleday,
       Doran published *I Lived This Story* after the manuscript
       won a competition, sponsored by the firm, for the best
       college novel submitted by an undergraduate or by a gradu-
       ate of less than a year.

101.   Aldrich, Bess Streeter [Mrs. Charles Sweetzer Aldrich].
       A White Bird Flying. New York: D. Appleton and Co.,
       1931.

       Laura Deal, the daughter of a small-town Nebraska law-
       yer, dreams of a career, preferably as a writer. She
       attends the University of Nebraska but, in the end, she
       marries a college-educated farmer and settles down as a
       happy rural housewife and mother. Laura's experiences
       at Nebraska occupy the middle third of the book. She
       finds the university a large, threatening place and much
       of her time is taken up with sorority activities. Laura's
       Aunt Grace is a spinster teacher at the university.

Grace warns Laura not to marry but, as the author makes clear, Laura's womanly yearnings for a home and family cause her to ignore her aunt's advice.

Bess Streeter Aldrich graduated from the Iowa State Teacher's College in 1901. She then taught for five years in public schools in Iowa and Utah before returning to her alma mater, for one year, as an assistant supervisor of primary training. Married to an attorney, Mrs. Aldrich raised four children. According to the dust jacket for *A White Bird Flying*, Mrs. Aldrich wrote her first published story in 1911, "while the baby was taking a nap." From that point Mrs. Aldrich turned out nearly 200 more stories for popular magazines and more than a dozen novels. *A White Bird Flying* was her fifth novel. A later Aldrich novel, *Miss Bishop* (142), also appears in this bibliography.

102. Clarke, Donald Henderson. *Young and Healthy*. New York: Vanguard Press, 1931.

The protagonist of this lusty period piece is Dick Raynor, a lad who enters Harvard in 1906 from a small town in northern New England. Taking full advantage of his social opportunities in turn-of-the-century Cambridge, Dick plays endless rounds of cards, consorts with women of both no and low repute, and exists largely on a liquid diet of beer, champagne, and "absinthe frappes." Dick finances some of his activities by writing term papers for his fellow students, but he can never take his own class work seriously. For example, when asked by his philosophy professor to write for an hour on his idea of the universe, Dick submits a paper which reads: "If I had any idea of the universe that was worth describing, I wouldn't be taking this course." The professor is not amused. Nor is the dean of students, who orders Dick to leave the Harvard scene during his sophomore year because of repeated drunken binges and failing grades. From Harvard Dick migrates to New York City where, during the last third of the book, he becomes an up-and-coming reporter on "The New York Planet."

Donald Henderson Clarke entered Harvard in 1904, left in 1906, was readmitted in 1909, and left again in 1911 without a degree. Following his on-again, off-again student career, Clarke became a well-known newspaperman in New York City. He also wrote many popular novels. *Young and Healthy* was one of Clarke's most commercially successful works. The book went through many printings and sold more than half a million copies.

103.   [Guest, Mary Lapsley Caughey]. *The Parable of the Vir-*
          gins. By Mary Lapsley. New York: Richard R. Smith,
          1931.

          The Parable of the Virgins is a critical look at under-
       graduate life at "Walton College," an exclusive Eastern
       institution for women. The principal character is Crosby
       O'Conner, a rebellious student poet whose major occupa-
       tion is testing the elasticity of Walton's rules. Crosby
       also is portrayed as a fledgling lesbian, as are many of
       her classmates. Indeed, although some of the Walton girls
       in the story become pregnant by male consorts, the theme
       of student homosexuality pervades the book. Among Wal-
       ton's faculty and administrators only Professor Clive
       Austin, a historian, seems able to face up to the Walton
       facts of life. She suggests to the president of the col-
       lege that Walton hire a live-in psychiatrist, but the
       president feels that a psychiatrist would only give his
       girls evil ideas.
          Reviewers generally saw *The Parable of the Virgins* as
       more reasoned and reasonable than Kathleen Millay's
       Against the Wall (95) and Samuel Hopkins Adams' *Unfor-*
       bidden Fruit (89), two other exposes of women's colleges
       of the period. Many reviewers interpreted "Walton College"
       as a fictive version of Vassar. John Lyons, in *The College*
       Novel in America (see footnote 3, Introduction) observes
       that part of the character of Crosby O'Connor may have
       been modeled on Edna St. Vincent Millay. Millay gradu-
       ated from Vassar in 1917, but only after President Harry
       Noble MacCracken overruled his faculty who tried to deny
       her a diploma on the grounds of flagrant rule-breaking.

104.   Uhler, John Earle. *Cane Juice: A Story of Southern*
          Louisiana. New York: The Century Co., 1931.

          Although *Cane Juice* is by any literary standards a
       rather conventional student-centered college novel, it
       generated a sharp backlash against its author. The book
       is set at Louisiana State University and its protagonist
       is Bernard Couvillon, a young man who comes to Baton
       Rouge to study the growing of sugar cane. As a freshman
       poor Bernard is hazed unmercifully, and when he seeks
       escape by joining the football team his studies suffer
       until he almost flunks out of the university. Many of
       the school's students are portrayed as drunken louts and
       its faculty members, with one notable exception, are
       depicted as intellectual pedestrians. Only after Bernard
       closets himself with the one outstanding teacher at LSU,

a Professor Gatz, does his collegiate career begin to
have real meaning. With Gatz' encouragement Bernard
develops a new strain of sugar cane which, we are led to
believe, will revolutionize the state's sugar industry.

John Earle Uhler was born in 1891 in Media, Pennsylvania.
He received an A.M. from Johns Hopkins in 1924 and a Ph.D.
from that institution in 1926. After teaching at Ogden
College in Kentucky and at Johns Hopkins, Uhler accepted
a professorship of English at LSU in 1928. When *Cane
Juice* appeared, in 1931, he was discharged by the LSU
administration for "misrepresenting the University."
After serving as a visiting professor at Stanford, Uhler
returned to LSU in 1936 where, among other pursuits, he
became an active member of the American Association of
University Professors.

105. Fales, Dean. *Bachelor of Arts*. New York: Dial Press,
1932.

Bachelor of Arts is a mild satire on undergraduate life.
The setting is the "University of Cornucopia." The central character is Barney Shirrel. Barney is followed
from his entrance as a freshman until his graduation.
Only semi-literate, Barney is a mainstay of his fraternity
and a star of the university football team. His younger
and considerably more cerebral sister, Barbara, also attends Cornucopia. During her junior year she marries Mr.
Danvers, a long-suffering instructor of English. Barbara
writes her own college novel, entitled "Clever Co-Ed."
The stuffy president of Cornucopia makes several appearances. In one moment of extreme frustration he utters
that time-honored line: "This university is not run for
the students." Connoisseurs of college novels will find
that *Bachelor of Arts* incorporates, under one cover, all
the stereotypic campus characters of inter-war college
fiction. It even includes one George Vesuvious Washington, an obsequious Black servant at Barney's fraternity
house. George rolls his eyes and speaks in dialect. Although George is the butt of the brothers' pranks, he
remains loyal to his "young gemmen of high-tone class."

106. [Wylie, Edmund Kiskaddon]. *Altogether Now!* By Kiskaddon
Wylie. New York: Farrar and Rinehart, 1932.

Altogether Now! is a strident critique of student life
at "a famous Eastern college." At the center of the
story is Slade Thompson, a sometimes well-meaning undergraduate who finds that drinking, dice playing, and girl

chasing--cultural staples at the college in question--
prevent him from acquiring an education. The cast of the
story includes a number of intellectually sterile professors, a clutch of Slade's hedonistic fraternity brothers, and a full roster of barely awake football players
with whom Slade cavorts, though not with much enthusiasm,
on the gridiron. Reviewers generally felt that *Altogether
Now!* was an immature work by a very young writer with
promise.

Edmund Kiskaddon Wylie was born in Delaware, Ohio, in
1913. He attended Amherst during the 1930-1931 and 1932-
1933 academic years. *Altogether Now!* was written when
Wylie was only eighteen years old and immediately after
his first stint on the Amherst campus. After leaving
Amherst for the second time Wylie became an associate
editor at Farrar and Rinehart, his publishers. He died
in 1936, at the age of twenty-three.

107. [Coffey, Edward Hope]. *She Loves Me Not*. By Edward Hope.
      Indianapolis: Bobbs-Merrill Co., 1933.

She Loves Me Not is a light college comedy which went
on to earn heavyweight royalties for its author. Curly
Flagg, a curvaceous dancer in a Philadelphia speakeasy,
becomes a witness to a gangland killing. In fear for her
life Curly flees the City of Brotherly Love and, when her
money runs out, she finds herself in Princeton, New Jersey. There she is befriended by Paul Lawton, an altru-
istic Princeton senior who hides her in his dormitory
room. Curly puts on Paul's clothes in an attempt to be
inconspicuous but her disguise proves ineffective. Various gangsters, policemen, and newspaper reporters discover she is in Princeton and all of them comb the campus
in search of her precise whereabouts. Then the Princeton
administration becomes concerned, and Paul is eventually
threatened with expulsion from the university, not only
for keeping a female in his room but for harboring a
fugitive from the law as well. It all ends happily.
Curly eludes her various pursuers. And Paul meets his
life's companion in Midge Mercer, the daughter of the
Princeton dean who is in charge of keeping speakeasy
dancers out of students' rooms.

Edward Hope Coffey was born in 1896. He received an
A.B. from Princeton in 1920. Sometimes called "the American Wodehouse," Coffey gained considerable prominence
during the early part of this century for his frothy
comic novels. Although *She Loves Me Not* was only a modest
commercial success as a novel, the book was adapted by

Harold Lindsay for a Broadway musical comedy of the same
title. The show, starring Burgess Meredith, Polly Waters,
and John Beal, opened in New York on November 30, 1933,
to rave reviews. In 1934 Paramount Pictures produced a
film version of the Broadway musical, starring Bing Crosby
and Miriam Hopkins. In 1955 yet another film musical
based on the novel was produced, though this version
differed significantly from both the book and the Harold
Lindsay show. The 1955 motion picture, entitled "How to
Be Very Very Popular," was to have starred Marilyn Monroe
as Curly Flagg. Ms. Monroe was replaced by Sheree North,
however, after she squabbled with the producers over pre-
filming costume fittings. The other stars of "How to
Be Very Very Popular" were Betty Grable, Charles Coburn,
Robert Cummings, and Orson Bean.

*108.   Erskine, John. *Bachelor--of Arts*. Indianapolis: Bobbs-
        Merrill Co., 1933.

   Bachelor--of Arts is a novel about undergraduate life
at Columbia during the Depression. The protagonist is
Philip ("Alec") Hamilton, and the story describes his
growing awareness, not only of his intellectual capaci-
ties but of the value of money as well. Alec's family
in New Jersey suffers Depression-connected fiscal reverses
and Alec goes into debt when his allowance is stopped.
His Barnard girlfriend meets an even worse fate. Her
father in St. Louis is wiped out and she must leave college to work in a drugstore. But just when Alec begins
to think that money is the most important of the world's
commodities he meets Professor Barth, a historian. Barth
is so wrapped up in his scholarship that he fails to
notice his own poverty. Alec works for Barth as a research assistant, is impressed by his mentor's dedication,
and finds that money is not the only item in life that
matters. Lively, and spiced with humor, *Bachelor--of
Arts* is one of the more readable stories of student
awakening in American college fiction.
   John Erskine received an A.B. from Columbia in 1900 and
a Ph.D. from the same institution in 1903. He taught at
Amherst before returning to his alma mater in 1909. From
that point until his retirement in 1937 Erskine was a
prominent member of Columbia's department of English.
His enormous oeuvre includes plays, novels, books of
poetry, and modern versions of ancient myths and legendary
romances.

*109.   Goodrich, John Thomas. *Cotton Cavalier*. New York:
        Farrar and Rinehart, 1933.

    This intriguing first novel takes place at "Blakely
College," a small Presbyterian institution in the South.
The protagonist is Peter Kimbrough, a bright but impulsive
undergraduate. At one point in the story Peter and three
of his classmates kill a local Black who is falsely accused of impregnating a White girl. When one of the
school's co-eds lies at an inquest, and claims that Peter
was with her at the moment of the homicide, Peter liter-
ally gets away with murder. In spite of Peter's unrecon-
structed attitudes on racial matters, he chafes under the
intellectual restrictions of Blakely. He is incensed,
for example, when one of his instructors, Professor Mac-
Elroy, is dismissed for teaching evolution. Interestingly
enough, though MacElroy is an outspoken exponent of truth
in the classroom he helps engineer the strategy through
which Peter escapes legal retribution for his crime. Another study in contradictions in this novel is Dr. Quimby,
the president of Blakely. A strident martinet when dealing with faculty and students, Quimby slavishly follows
the dictates of Richard Wyatt, the school's most powerful
trustee. Quimby's overriding motivation is to retain his
post, because he fears that if fired from Blakely he might
never obtain another college presidency.
    Cotton Cavalier was published after the manuscript won
a competition, sponsored by Farrar and Rinehart, for the
"best campus novel" submitted during 1932.

110.   [Lincoln, Joseph Freeman]. *Nod*. By Freeman Lincoln.
        New York: Coward-McCann, 1933.

    This light but involved novel has as its protagonist
John E.E. ("Nod") Grace, captain of the Harvard football
team and general big-man-on-campus. Orphaned at the age
of two, and brought up by his uncle, Nod falls in love
with Lee Forest, a wealthy society girl. Immediately
after his graduation from Harvard Nod invests what remains
of his small legacy in a private airport. Then, after
breaking his engagement to Lorna Clark, his childhood
sweetheart, he marries the super-rich Lee. But his airport investment quickly turns sour, and Lorna is killed
when a plane she is piloting crashes on Nod's landing
field at the very moment he and Lee are being wed. In a
daze brought on both by guilt and personal bankruptcy,
Nod deserts Lee and takes a back-breaking job as a day
laborer on a road-building crew. Only when Lorna's kindly

father visits Nod and convinces him that Lorna's death
was not a suicide does our hero return to his spouse,
her money, and a style of life which befits a Harvard man.
The Harvard scenes, all of which come in the first half
of the book, are written with care for Cambridge detail.
However, some readers--especially those who have always
wondered what one does with a bachelor's degree from Har-
vard--may find the graphic depictions of Nod's exhausting
work on the road gang more interesting.

Joseph Freeman Lincoln received an A.B. from Harvard in
1923. The son of Joseph Coffey Lincoln, a well-known
American novelist during the early part of this century,
he co-authored two novels with his father and wrote two
others, including *Nod*, without his father's collaboration.
During World War II Joseph Freeman Lincoln served as a
lieutenant colonel with the Office of Strategic Services.
After the war he became an editor with *Fortune Magazine*.
He died in 1962.

111. Stone, Irving. *Pageant of Youth*. New York: Alfred H.
      King, 1933.

Set at "Shockley University," a state institution near
San Francisco, this novel has sex and violence as its
principal ingredients. The protagonist of the story is
Ray Sharpe, an undergraduate. Ray is an economics major
who pays some of his college bills by playing saxophone in
a dance band. Although Ray shows signs of intellectual
inquisitiveness he finds the busy Shockley environment
full of distractions. He encounters a great many co-eds,
one of whom keeps a diary listing the 107 men with whom
she has had sexual relations. Moreover, Ray joins Psi
Beta, and life in the frat house is not conducive to
studying. Nonetheless, Ray manages to acquire a degree.
He then enters graduate school at Shockley and marries a
young lady named Paula. But Paula proves unfaithful.
After Ray applies a quick, punitive fist to Paula's face
he signs on as a merchant seaman and leaves for ports
unknown.

Irving Stone received a B.A. from the University of
California at Berkeley in 1923. While an undergraduate
Stone majored in economics and played saxophone in a
dance band. After obtaining his B.A. Stone entered graduate school at Berkeley and was awarded an M.A. in 1924.
Pageant of Youth was his first novel. In later years,
of course, Stone acquired literary prominence for his
many biographical novels of famous historical figures.
Included in his list of publications are *Lust for Life*

(New York: Longmans, Green and Co., 1934), *The Agony and the Ecstasy* (Garden City, New York: Doubleday and Co., 1961), and *The Origin* (Garden City, New York: Doubleday and Co., 1980).

*112.   Weller, George Anthony. *Not to Eat, Not for Love*. New York: Harrison Smith and Robert Haas, 1933.

Not to Eat, Not for Love is an exceptionally well-written novel about Harvard in the 1920s. The protagonist is Epes Todd, an introspective art history major and sometimes football player. The central thrust of the plot has Epes searching for the meaning of life and, in this sense, the book is like many other student-centered college sagas. But the novel rises well above the usual run of college fiction thanks to the richness of its detail and because of the kaleidoscopic view it presents of the Harvard scene. The book is decidedly reminiscent of the early prose of John Dos Passos, and it is the fast Dos Passos-like pacing of the novel, coupled with a long parade of characters, which allows Weller to present a multi-layered portrait of Harvard. The novel deals with the academic side of Harvard life, as well as the social, and it includes some arresting depictions of faculty members and administrators. *Not to Eat, Not for Love* was favorably reviewed when it appeared, and it is now generally regarded as the best of all Harvard novels.

George Anthony Weller graduated from Harvard in 1930 and then began a long and distinguished career as a journalist. During World War II he covered the fall of Singapore and later won a Pulitzer Prize for a story about an emergency appendectomy performed aboard a submarine.

113.   Coulter, John Gaylord. *In Freshman Year*. New York: William H. Wise and Co., 1934.

This pleasant but sometimes languid story is set at Wabash College in Indiana. The protagonist of the piece is Bill Hackson, a freshman from Syracuse, New York. Bill, who originally hoped to attend Yale, is persuaded by his father to try "a small college." Ultimately, after sampling Wabash's fraternities, girls, and football, Bill discovers that his father's advice was sound. The plot of the book is sometimes lost in the abundance of Wabash marginalia provided by the author. In a dust jacket commentary, William Mather Lewis, then the president of Lafayette College, praised the work as offering an accurate depiction of those small colleges "where the individual has room to develop."

John Gaylord Coulter was born in 1876 in Hanover, Indiana. He received a B.A. from Lake Forest College and a Ph.D. from the University of Chicago. Early in his career he taught biology at Syracuse, Emory, and Illinois State Universities. In 1929 Coulter became vice president of Wabash College and it was while serving in this post that he wrote *In Freshman Year*. Coulter's oeuvre includes a number of biology textbooks and historical studies. *In Freshman Year* was his only work of fiction.

114.   Fisher, Vardis. *Passions Spin the Plot*. Garden City, New York: Doubleday, Doran and Co., 1934.

The protagonist of this angry, sprawling novel is Vridar Hunter, a young man from rural Idaho. During much of the book Vridar attends "Wasatch College," a state-supported institution in Salt Lake City. Vridar is poor, introspective, and in search of his identity. An idealist, he constantly tests reality against his own standards. Although Wasatch falls considerably short of Vridar's notion of what a college should be, it does provide him with various intellectual stimuli and he decides to become a writer.

Vardis Fisher was born in Annis, Idaho, and graduated in 1920 from the University of Utah. Although many of the incidents in this novel are taken from Fisher's own experiences, Fisher's writing style is clearly derivative of that of Thomas Wolfe. During the late 1920s Fisher and Wolfe were colleagues in the English department at New York University. The two men became close friends. *Passions Spin the Plot* is the second volume of a tetralogy of novels about Vridar Hunter. The first volume in the series, *In Tragic Life* (Caldwell, Idaho: Caxton Printers, 1932) concentrates upon Hunter's childhood. The last two works in the tetralogy, *We Are Betrayed* (117) and *No Villain Need Be* (147), follow Vridar to Chicago for graduate study, back to Wasatch College for his first teaching appointment, and then on to New York City where Hunter serves as a member of the faculty of "Manhattan College." In 1960 revised versions of these four novels, plus some additional concluding material, were brought together as *Orphans of Gethsemane* (322).

115.   Montross, Lois Seyster. *The Perfect Pair*. Garden City, New York: Doubleday, Doran and Co., 1934.

Howard Granville and Meredith Hazlitt are the most popular students at a Midwestern state university. Though

they are only good friends, various campus matchmakers
(and their parents) try to push them into a romance.
Eventually Howard and Meredith yield to social pressures
and announce their engagement. The university newspaper
headlines the upcoming marriage of "the perfect pair."
Both Howard and Meredith really love others, however, and
both elope with their respective hearts' desires on the
eve of their scheduled wedding. The ceremony is cancelled
when neither the prospective bride nor the prospective
groom appears, and the assembled guests leave the church
disappointed. Considering their job aspirations, one
assumes that the deviousness which Howard and Meredith
display with regard to their aborted wedding portends,
for both of them, successful careers. Howard wants to
become a politician. Meredith's intention is to become
a college president. The emphasis in this light, semi-
comic novel is on the social side of college life, but
there are a few glimpses of academic matters because
Meredith's actual husband-to-be is a graduate student in
chemistry and a future professor.

Lois Seyster Montross wrote *The Perfect Pair* after her
divorce from Lynn Montross. Two collaborative works by
Lynn and Lois Montross, *Town and Gown* (72) and *Fraternity
Row* (85), appear in this bibliography.

116.   Brown, Rollo Walter. *The Hilliken*. New York: Coward-
       McCann, 1935.

The Hilliken is the third volume of a four-volume family
saga which describes the experiences of the Dabneys, a
poor but honest coal mining family in Ohio. In *The Hilliken* Giles Dabney, the family's nineteen-year-old son,
enters Harvard. Because he is poor Giles must work his
way through college; thus he has little time for the normal run of extracurricular activities. Giles decides to
become a city planner. After graduation he obtains a
teaching appointment at "Steel City College," an institution near his homestead, and he begins to construct a plan
which promises to transform Steel City from a grimy indus-
trial town into an urban paradise. His plan meets significant opposition, but it is finally accepted. By the
end of the novel, Giles is well on his way to professional
fame and fortune. The first two novels in the Dabney
series are *The Firemakers* (New York: Coward-McCann, 1931)
and *Toward Romance* (New York: Coward-McCann, 1932). These
novels deal primarily with Giles' parents and grandparents.
The last novel in the series, *As of the Gods* (New York:
D. Appleton-Century, 1937), follows Giles into his middle
years.

Rollo Walter Brown received a bachelor's degree from
Ohio Northern in 1903 and an M.A. from Harvard in 1905.
He was a member of the English department at Wabash College from 1905 until 1920 and served on the faculty at
Carleton College from 1920 until 1923. After spending
the 1923-24 academic year as a visiting lecturer at Harvard, Brown deserted academe for full-time writing. In
addition to the series of novels about the Dabneys, he
wrote biographies, textbooks, and *Harvard Yard in the
Golden Age* (New York: A.A. Wyn, 1948), a book of profiles
of various turn-of-the-century Harvard figures.

117. Fisher, Vardis. *We Are Betrayed*. Garden City, New York:
 Doubleday, Doran and Co., 1935.

The third volume of Vardis Fisher's Vridar Hunter
tetralogy, *We Are Betrayed*, takes up Vridar's life story
at the point where *Passions Spin the Plot* (114) concludes.
After graduating from "Wasatch College" Vridar goes to
Chicago for further study at "Midwestern University." He
hopes that this renowned university will be the citadel
of intellectual vitality its reputation promises. He
finds, instead, that it is populated largely by people of
few ideas and little substance. Faced with financial
problems, and plagued by intellectual frustrations, Vridar
lapses into dark neurotic moods. At the end of the book
Vridar's wife, Neola, commits suicide. Like all the
books in the Hunter tetralogy, *We Are Betrayed* is both
autobiographical and stylistically reminiscent of the
novels of Fisher's friend Thomas Wolfe.

After obtaining his bachelor's degree from the University of Utah in 1920, Vardis Fisher did graduate work
at the University of Chicago. He received a Ph.D. from
Chicago in 1925.

118. Henderson, Robert. *Whether There Be Knowledge*. Philadelphia: J.B. Lippincott Co., 1935.

When the editor of the student newspaper at an unnamed
state university in the Midwest has a nervous breakdown,
Donnie Trevett is named as his replacement. Donnie is a
senior from Chicago. Visualizing himself a fearless
journalist, he launches an editorial crusade against the
school's administration. Donnie's issue is the dismissal
of six junior faculty members in a university economy
drive. The institution's president, not one of the leading advocates of free speech in college fiction, threatens
to expel Donnie if he continues his tirades. Properly

intimidated, Donnie spends the rest of his editorship
focusing the paper on routine campus social events. Serious in tone, the book offers considerable detail about
student life during the Depression.

Robert Henderson was born in Chicago in 1906. He attended the University of Illinois. *Whether There Be
Knowledge* was his first novel. At the time the book was
published Henderson was an instructor of English at Illinois.

119.   Ingham, Travis. *Young Gentlemen, Rise*. New York: Farrar
and Rinehart, 1935.

After opening with scenes from the 1934 reunion of the
Yale class of 1928, this novel flashes back to review
the life of Gene Davidson, one of the merrymakers. Gene
is the son of a New England bank cashier. Before Yale
he attends "Charlesgate Preparatory School." At Yale he
leads a fairly routine undergraduate existence. After
graduation he marries a Smith girl and takes a position
with a Boston advertising agency. But when the Depression
deepens Gene loses his agency job and, as he attends the
Yale reunion, he is reduced to working as a $20-per-week
gas jockey in a filling station. Gene's Yale years occupy
the middle third of the book. From the standpoint of
college fiction perhaps the most notable passage in the
novel comes when Gene and some Yale chums discuss Percy
Marks' *The Plastic Age* (75). All of them disagree with
Marks' contention that the major topic of undergraduate
conversation are sex and religion. Religion, according
to Gene and his friends, "is a dead issue." At the reunion Gene shares some of the disillusionment with higher
education felt by Hugh Carver, the protagonist of Marks'
novel. Upset over the loss of his advertising job, Gene
wonders if his Yale degree has equipped him for anything
better than manual labor. Nevertheless, he remains opti-
mistic about his long-range prospects. Indeed, the reader
is left with the clear impression that Gene will soon
return to the white collar ranks and, as he moves into
middle age, will become a stalwart of the Yale Club of
Boston.

120.   Byer, Herbert. *To the Victor*. Garden City, New York:
Doubleday, Doran and Co., 1936.

To the Victor is a bitter satire on high-pressure
intercollegiate football and a literary castigation of
those schools which promote the enterprise. The protagonist

of the piece is Jerry Fleet, the star running back for "Cranston University." Cranston is a small Midwestern school which gains fame and fortune through Jerry's gridiron exploits. After leading Cranston to victory after victory Jerry becomes an all-American. Yet after graduation he finds that life beyond Saturday afternoon heroics is cold and cruel. Having majored in such courses as "art appreciation," Jerry lacks a vocation. He stars in a quickie motion picture (which one reviewer calls the worst film ever made), tries his hand unsuccessfully at the stockbroker trade, becomes head football coach at "Jonathan and Josephine University" (where his pathetically inept team has a non-winning season), and then suffers crippling injuries in professional football. Totally broke, Jerry hops a freight to Cranston in order to see his old team play its arch rival. When he arrives at Cranston he is refused admission to the stadium because he lacks the funds to purchase a ticket. Though there are many villains in the book--all of whom exploit Jerry in one way or another--Walter Waters, the president of Cranston, is singled out for special condemnation. Waters, who harbors "a powerful urge to stroke (co-eds') breasts," uses Jerry's fame to raise the capital for a major campus building program and then publicly parades himself as a master fund raiser and organizational genius.

Herbert Byer was born in Cincinnati in 1899. After receiving an undergraduate degree from Ohio State University he entered the advertising business and eventually became a partner in the firm of Byer and Bowman in Columbus, Ohio. *To the Victor* was his first novel.

121. Linn, James Weber. *This Was Life*. Indianapolis and New York: Bobbs-Merrill Co., 1936.

This novel recounts the University of Chicago freshman year of Jerry Grant, a minister's son. The time is 1893-94. Sensitive, naive, and bursting with enthusiasm, Jerry finds the year both exciting and fulfilling. The author introduces Jerry, and the readers of the novel, to a host of campus characters. These include a Marxist student from Germany, an immoral co-ed, a former prize-fighter now an undergraduate, and a variety of faculty members. There is a plot, of sorts, to the book. But, in essence, the novel is the story of Jerry's self-awakening and each incident in the story serves to add another dimension to Jerry's developing outlook on life.

James Weber Linn produced two other novels included in this bibliography: *The Chameleon* (51) and *Winds Over the*

Campus (148). The latter picks up Jerry Grant's life in
late middle age, when Jerry is a veteran professor of
English. Linn graduated from the University of Chicago
in 1892 and spent his entire career as a member of Chicago's department of English.

122. Santayana, George. *The Last Puritan: A Memoir in the*
      Form of a Novel. New York: Charles Scribner's Sons,
      1936.

George Santayana, the preeminent philosopher of the
early twentieth century, received an A.B. from Harvard in
1886. After gaining his doctorate in 1889 he spent twenty-
three years as a member of the Harvard faculty. *The Last
Puritan* was written late in Santayana's life, after he had
left Harvard to live in Europe. It was his only full-
length work of prose fiction.

The Last Puritan takes place just before and during
World War I. The protagonist is Oliver Alden, a wealthy
boy from Connecticut. Oliver is the "puritan" of the
book's title. He is engaged in a continuing struggle to
find the proper ways to put his wealth and talent to good
moral purpose. During the course of the long (602-page)
narrative Oliver attends Williams College as an undergraduate and then does graduate work in philosophy at
Harvard. The college scenes in the book are both graphic
and fascinating. During one Harvard episode Oliver and
his cousin, Mario, discuss professors and courses. When
one of Santayana's courses comes up in the conversation
Oliver decides not to take it. Santayana, so it seems,
has told Mario to avoid the course because, in Mario's
words: "He (Santayana) says that it would be highly dangerous for me to become more civilized than I am." Although
part of *The Last Puritan* takes place in academic locales,
the plot carries Oliver to a wide variety of settings,
and Santayana explores a great many issues beyond those
found in conventional college novels.

Since its publication *The Last Puritan* has been the
subject of considerable literary and philosophical analysis. Some literary scholars have seen the novel as primarily a description of turn-of-the-century New England
character. Most philosophers, on the other hand, have
read the book as a fictive extension of the philosophic
premises which Santayana articulated in his many non-
fictive works.

123.   Cannon, Ralph. *Out of Bounds*. Chicago: The Reilly and
       Lee Co., 1937.

       Although *Out of Bounds* is primarily a conventional col-
       lege sports novel it has enough unusual twists and turns
       to merit inclusion in this bibliography. The protagonist
       of the story is Dick Martivani. The son of poor, Italian-
       American working people, Dick attends "Northern Universi-
       ty" strictly to play football. He becomes the star end
       on the Northern team, but thanks to his coach, Pat Dorgan,
       he discovers that Northern offers more than head-bashing
       on Saturday afternoons. Dorgan is impressed with Dick's
       intelligence and warns him against wasting his opportuni-
       ty for an education. Under Dorgan's urging Dick decides
       to become a lawyer. While Dick does not give up foot-
       ball, he comes to realize that studies must have top
       priority on his personal agenda. Much of the book is
       given over to play-by-play football narrative, and there
       are no classroom scenes. But the near father-son relation-
       ship which develops between Dick and Coach Dorgan is
       unique in college fiction.
       Ralph Cannon attended both James Milliken University
       and the University of Chicago. After graduating from
       Chicago in 1930 he entered the newspaper field and eventu-
       ally became a columnist for the *Chicago Evening Journal*.
       Out of Bounds was his third novel.

124.   Eaton, Geoffrey Dell. *John Drakin*. Milwaukee: Guten-
       berg Publishing Co., 1937.

       The title character of this fast-paced novel is a
       seeker of truth and purity. Unfortunately, he finds
       neither in high school, in the army during World War I,
       as an undergraduate at the University of Michigan, or
       during his post-college life as a newspaperman in New
       York City. John Drakin's experiences at Michigan take
       up approximately a quarter of the book. He receives
       straight A's in his courses at Ann Arbor, but his grades
       only disillusion him because he feels unchallenged by his
       intellectually tepid professors. Some idea of John's
       character can be gained by his solution to an unhappy
       campus love affair. John forgets his sorrow by studying
       German by himself for six hours a day.
       Geoffrey Dell Eaton was a journalist who died at the
       age of thirty-five, before *John Drakin* was published.
       The book includes a three-page posthumous tribute to the
       author by "one who knew and loved G.D. Eaton." This
       anonymous individual describes Eaton as "alone even in

the largest group of people" and notes that the novel is autobiographical.

125. Cushman, Clarissa White Fairchild [Mrs. Robert Eugene
      Cushman]. *The Other Brother*. Boston: Little, Brown
      and Co., 1939.

The "other brother" in this uniquely premised college novel is Everett Marbury, the older sibling of Anthony. Both young men are the sons of James Marbury, the distinguished president of an unnamed but high-status university in the East. As the novel begins Everett is an unenthusiastic graduate student in sociology at the school over which his father presides. He also is something of the family black sheep. Shy, and suffering from an inferiority complex, he has yet to discover a direction for his life. Anthony, on the other hand, is an immensely popular senior on the campus. Intellectually shallow, but devastatingly charming, he obviously is destined to follow his father into the ranks of university presidents. Most of the plot of the novel centers on Everett, as he drops out of graduate school to take a job as a high school teacher, and as he loves from afar one Alison Blake, a young lady who is presumably to become Anthony's bride. The climax of the story occurs when Everett plunges into the ocean in an attempt to save a girl from drowning. Although he gets caught on rocks, and must himself be saved by the ever-intrusive Anthony, he acquires a modicum of confidence. He enrolls in an out-of-town university for graduate work in English and in a quiet moment with Alison he tells her of his ardor. Alison then informs Everett that Anthony really is a boor and that it is he, the shy, quiet brother, whom she has loved all along. James Marbury, who seems to be aloof not only from his university constituents but from his family as well, makes few appearances in the story. His wife Laura, by contrast, pops up at frequent junctures and regularly chides Everett for lacking Anthony's winning ways.
      Clarissa White Fairchild Cushman was born in Oberlin, Ohio, in 1889 and graduated from Oberlin College in 1911. Her father, Charles Gradison Fairchild, was a member of the Oberlin faculty. Her husband, Robert Eugene Cushman, also was an academic and at the time *The Other Brother* was published he was chairman of the department of government at Cornell. *The Other Brother* was Mrs. Cushman's sixth novel. It represented a significant departure from her normal mode of writing. Before and after *The Other Brother*, Mrs. Cushman specialized in mysteries and suspense stories.

126. Lewis, Wells. *They Still Say No*. New York: Farrar and
     Rinehart, 1939.

The protagonist of this novel is Crane Stewart, an indifferent student at Harvard. Crane's major concern is
women, and he pursues them first as a freshman in Cambridge and then in Mexico where he spends a summer vacation. The writing wavers between satire and serious social commentary about the offspring of America's wealthy
business-elite. The Harvard scenes, most of which come
at the beginning of the book, concentrate upon extracurricular life.

Wells Lewis was the son of Sinclair Lewis. He was a
twenty-one-year-old Harvard senior when *They Still Say No*
was published. Despite (or perhaps because of) Lewis'
illustrious father, the book received singularly bad notices. The reviewer for *The New Republic* (April 26, 1939)
predicted that *They Still Say No* "will be an embarrassment
to (Wells Lewis) if he grows up to be a writer." Unfortunately, Wells Lewis did not live long enough to be embarrassed by the novel. He was killed in 1944 while
serving in the United States Army in France.

127. North, Sterling. *Seven Against the Years*. New York:
     Macmillan Co., 1939.

The protagonists of this novel are seven male friends
who graduate from the University of Chicago in 1929 and
then make their separate ways through the Depression. By
1939, when the novel concludes, the central characters'
occupations range from social worker to literary editor
of a major Chicago newspaper. Only the first chapter of
the novel is set entirely during the protagonists' college
years. The remaining chapters deal primarily with the
protagonists' post-graduation exploits, but many of these
chapters include flashbacks to the chums' days on the
Chicago campus. Robert Hutchins makes a brief appearance
in Chapter One, as he presides over Chicago's 1929 graduation exercises.

Sterling North attended the University of Chicago in
the late 1920s. He then became a newspaper reporter and,
subsequently, literary editor of the *Chicago Daily News*.

*128. Stewart, George Rippey. *Doctor's Oral*. New York: Random
     House, 1939.

Doctor's Oral is generally regarded as the classic
novel about graduate education in America. The protagonist

is Joe Grantland, a young man who is studying for a Ph.D.
in English at an unnamed university. Joe's funds have
run out, his fiancée is pregnant, and he desperately needs
a job. Although he has an offer of employment at a junior
college, the invitation is contingent upon his passing
his upcoming oral examination. The exam, and the faculty
decision-session which follows it, occupy the last half
of the book. The initial ballot on Joe's candidacy ends
in a three-to-three tie, with one abstention. Only after
his examiners argue among themselves, and only after they
reveal all of their petty interests and jealousies, does
Joe receive enough votes to pass. The novel contains
merciless portraits of Joe's seven inquisitors and the
detailed recounting of the stress-laden examination is
among the most exacting pieces of description in college
fiction.

George Rippey Stewart received an A.B. from Princeton
in 1917 and a Ph.D. from Columbia in 1922. From 1923
until his retirement in 1962 he was a member of the department of English at the University of California at
Berkeley. During his career Stewart wrote novels, literary biographies, and social histories. *Doctor's Oral*
was his second novel. Stewart died in 1980.

129. Wolfe, Thomas Clayton. *The Web and the Rock*. New York:
     Harper and Brothers, 1939.

The Web and the Rock is the third of three Thomas Wolfe
novels to be set, in part, in academic locales. The first
two are *Look Homeward, Angel* (96) and *Of Time and the
River* (146). Like its predecessors, *The Web and the Rock*
is autobiographical. The protagonist of the story is
George Webber, a small-town boy from North Carolina who
attends a Southern institution which Wolfe calls "Pine
Rock College." Webber then moves to New York City where
he teaches English at "The School for Utility Cultures,"
has a tumultuous love affair with a wealthy theatrical
woman, and labors heroically to become a successful writer.
The college scenes in this book are considerably less extensive than those in Wolfe's two earlier novels.

The Web and the Rock was published after Thomas Wolfe's
death in 1938. With Maxwell Perkins' help, Edward C.
Aswell of Harper and Brothers wrested the book from a
massive uncompleted manuscript. *The Web and the Rock*
emerged from the first part of Wolfe's draft. The latter
portion of the manuscript was published, after extensive
editing, as *You Can't Go Home Again* (New York: Harper and
Brothers, 1940).

130. Lewis, Wilmarth. *Tutor's Lane*. New York: Alfred A.
      Knopf, 1922.

   Tutor's Lane is a brief (164-page) but elegant novel
of academic manners. The setting is "Woodbridge College,"
a small and ultra high-status institution in southern
New England. The plot has Tom Reynolds, a young instructor of English, courting and marrying the sister of a
faculty colleague. There are no particular obstacles to
the romance, hence the plot is virtually without tensions.
In lieu of an exciting story the author provides a series
of parties and get-togethers, many of them held in the
home of Woodbridge's acting president. At these soirees
faculty and administrators engage in learned and charming
conversation. Most of the characters in the novel are
portrayed as independently wealthy. Thus no one seems
unduly distressed over the fact that three years is the
shortest period of time anyone at Woodbridge has ever
served as an instructor before being promoted to assistant
professor.
   Wilmarth Lewis received an A.B. from Yale in 1920.
Tutor's Lane was his only novel. Employed by the Yale
University Press during much of his adult life, Lewis is
best known in literary circles for his unflagging scholarly attention to Horace Walpole and his works. His edited
anthology of Walpole's correspondence, published by Yale
University Press, will run to approximately fifty volumes
when completed.

131. Anonymous. *Grey Towers*. Chicago: Covici-McGee Co., 1923.

   Joan Burroughs returns to her alma mater, "Grey Towers,"
to teach English composition. A small Midwestern college
during Joan's student days, the institution has grown in
her brief absence to become a thriving university. Joan
finds that most of the positive aspects of the school have
been discarded. Grey Towers is now an academic assembly

line, a handmaiden to big business, and the epitome of
cold, impersonal higher education. Much of the plot concerns Joan's unsuccessful attempts to bring about curricular reforms: hence *Grey Towers* is one of only a few
college novels to offer a detailed examination of curriculum issues. Joan is also harassed sexually, bullied
by a mindless department chairperson, and otherwise abused
by most of the institution's staff. At the end of the
book she vents her spleen at a faculty meeting and thereby
ensures her non-reappointment.

The author of this book clearly was well acquainted with
whatever university he or she took as the model for Grey
Towers. Since the novel exposes so many of the school's
ills, and since most of the nefarious campus characters
were presumably drawn from real life, it is little wonder
that the saga was published anonymously.

*132.   Cather, Willa Sibert. *The Professor's House*. New York:
        Alfred A. Knopf, 1925.

Willa Sibert Cather received a B.A. from the University
of Nebraska in 1895 and went on to become one of the outstanding American novelists of the early twentieth century. *The Professor's House*, her ninth novel, was written
at the height of her career.

Set at a state university in the upper Midwest, *The
Professor's House* describes the adjustments and non-
adjustments of an aging professor of history as he faces
both the end of his career and the acquisition of newly
acquired wealth. The money, which comes from a prize
for an eight-volume work on Spanish explorers in America,
allows Professor Godfrey St. Peter to move to a new, more
opulent residence. Yet he retains his old home as a
workplace, and in the solitude of his familiar surround-
ings he reflects upon his past, present, and future. The
story includes a number of sub-plots. The most notable
of these focuses upon the barely ethical actions of St.
Peter's Jewish son-in-law. This individual exploits for
his own gain a scientific discovery made by a deceased
student of the professor. Although the book is slowly
paced, and although there are only a few scenes of St.
Peter in his classroom, *The Professor's House* is one of
the most sensitive studies of an academic in all of college fiction.

*133.   Johnson, Stanley. *Professor*. New York: Harcourt, Brace
        and Co., 1925.

   The protagonist of this satire--the first full-length,
intentional satire of on-campus professorial behavior--
is J. Tanksley Parkhurst. Dr. Parkhurst is a thirty-
five-year-old professor of English at "Thurston University" in Vermont. A bachelor, Parkhurst has a well-devel-
oped eye for the ladies but, although he squires them on
dates, he remains pure. In fact, in one scene he visits
a local doctor to inquire about the possible debilitating
side effects of prolonged sexual continence. Parkhurst
also is an inveterate name dropper, a pedantic classroom
instructor (Chaucer is his specialty), and a thief of
ideas. At a local civic club meeting, for instance, he
meets an uneducated insurance salesman who expounds a new
interpretation of Chaucer's works. Parkhurst immediately
writes an article, under his own name, which plagiarizes
the salesman's thesis. Despite his own outrageous actions Parkhurst demands propriety in others. He is
especially outraged when one of his students, named Tyson
Ware, writes a satirical college novel in which a Parkhurst-
like figure is the central character. Parkhurst buys up
all the copies of the book in the local bookstores and
engineers Ware's exit-without-degree from the university.
   Stanley Johnson received a B.S. from Vanderbilt University in 1917 and a M.A. from the same institution in
1921. At the time *Professor* was published he was a member of Vanderbilt's department of English.

*134.   Herrick, Robert. *Chimes*. New York: Macmillan Co., 1926.

   Literary scholars generally accord Robert Herrick
premier status in the ranks of America's "realistic"
novelists of the early part of this century. Herrick
received a B.A. from Harvard in 1890, taught English at
the Massachusetts Institute of Technology from 1890 until
1893, and then became a member of the English faculty at
the University of Chicago. Herrick remained at Chicago
until 1923 when, at the age of fifty-five, he resigned
because of repeated angina attacks and a chronic bron-
chial condition. He then lived in California, Florida,
and the Virgin Islands, where he died in 1938. When
Herrick left Chicago, after thirty years of service, the
university refused to grant him a pension because he had
not reached retirement age.
   Chimes is a thinly disguised fictional history of the
University of Chicago during Herrick's long tenure on

the campus. It is bitter in tone and unflattering to
many of its characters. The protagonist of the story is
Beamon Clavercin, a young Harvard-educated instructor of
English who arrives--at "Eureka University"--just before
the turn of the century. Through Clavercin's adventures
over a thirty-year span Herrick recounts Chicago's growth
into a major university and he offers many character
sketches of the university's personnel. Among the events
chronicled in the novel are the power struggles which
followed the death of President William Rainey Harper in
1905 and the rush of Chicago's faculty to enter government service during World War I. The latter phenomenon,
as Herrick makes clear, was motivated more by desire to
escape the boredom of teaching than by patriotism.

Although *Chimes* was the only one of Herrick's novels
which focused directly upon college life, others of his
many novels dealt peripherally with academe. In particular, *The Real World* (New York: Macmillan Co., 1901), has
as its protagonist a young lawyer named Jack Pemberton
who is shown, in a portion of the book, attending Harvard.

135.   Van Doren, Carl Clinton. *The Ninth Wave*. New York:
        Harcourt, Brace and Co., 1926.

This crisply written novel traces the life of Kent
Morrow, from his boyhood in a small Midwestern town,
through his education at a nearby university, and then
into late middle age as a professor of history at his
alma mater. A devoted family man and a diligent teacher-
scholar, Kent settles into a grey if pleasant existence.
Suddenly, toward the end of the story, he unexpectedly
wins the prestigious Ogden Prize for a book on the history
of the Northwest. Although the prize might facilitate
late-in-career upward academic mobility, Kent chooses to
remain at the university and to continue much as before.
The portraits of Kent and his spouse, Margaret--a woman
with penetrating insight into the human condition--are
among the most sensitive depictions of a faculty member
and his wife in American literature. And Kent's grateful
yet jaundiced reaction to a post-prize congratulatory
speech by the university's president is a classic piece
of college-fiction writing.

Carl Clinton Van Doren received an A.B. from the University of Illinois in 1907 and a Ph.D. from Columbia in
1911. Unlike Kent Morrow, Van Doren did not settle for
a placid academic life. Though he taught on a sometimes
basis at Columbia, he also was one of the founders of the
Literary Guild and for many years he was editor of the

Sunday literary supplement of the *New York Herald Tribune*. As a critic, essayist, and prodigious literary scholar, Van Doren was one of the most influential intellectuals of his time.

136. Imbs, Bravig. *The Professor's Wife*. New York: Dial Press, 1928.

The central character in this episodic novel of academic manners is Delia Ransom, the wife of Myron Ransom, a wealthy professor of English at an unnamed college in New England. Delia acts as the institution's matchmaker, gadfly, arbiter of social taste, and—above all—as its hostess for visiting dignitaries. In the course of the story Delia entertains a number of real-life famous names, including Robert Frost and Rebecca West. The book is narrated by Eric, a student at the college, who serves as a houseboy in the Ransom home. With good humor, but with a constant eye for Delia's many eccentricities and pretensions, Eric provides a running account of the events at the Ransom establishment. A great many college faculty and administrators appear in the book, as they attend one or more of Delia's many dinner parties, and some of them—after offending Delia in one way or another—find that their careers at the college have been ruined.

Bravig Imbs attended Dartmouth in the 1920s. While in Hanover he served as a houseboy in the home of a member of the faculty. After leaving college at the end of his sophomore year Imbs went to Paris where, until World War II, he mixed writing with schoolteaching, work as a newspaperman, and violin playing in cafes. He also was a member of the set of intellectuals which gathered around Gertrude Stein. After Germany's invasion of France, Imbs served the allied forces by broadcasting radio news and propaganda into the occupied portion of the country. He was killed in 1946 in an automobile accident. *The Professor's Wife* was his first novel.

137. Hoyt, Janet. *Wings of Wax*. New York: J.H. Sears, 1929.

The protagonist of this story is Victor Marston, the recently appointed, boy-wonder president of "Woban University." Woban is a state university somewhere in the Midwest. Only thirty-seven, and a chemist by training, Marston has high hopes of modernizing Woban's archaic academic policies, but he lacks both the sophistication and the tact to carry out his plans. The university treasurer embezzles funds. Parents complain about the

lack of discipline on campus. And Woban's female students nearly go on strike after Marston keeps the school's
co-eds, but not its male students, confined to campus
after a post-football game riot. Meantime, Marston is
dominated by his mother, suffers as the prisoner of a
deteriorated marriage, and is dangled on the end of a
very long string by a wealthy society woman whom he covets.
His administration and his personal life in shambles,
Marston is asked by Woban's trustees to vacate his office.
Shortly thereafter he is killed in an automobile accident.
Although the 1920s detail in this novel renders it dated,
modern-day president watchers will find the book still
makes for gripping reading.

John Lyons, in *The College Novel in America* (see footnote 3, Introduction), reports that Janet Hoyt was a dean
of women. Richard Boys (see footnote 3, Introduction)
states that *Wings of Wax* "allegedly has as the object of
its scorn a former president of the University of Michigan."

*138. Neff, Wanda Fraiken [Mrs. Emery Neff]. *Lone Voyagers*.
       Boston and New York: Houghton Mifflin Co., 1929.

This rich and insightful novel is set at "Chippewa
University" in the Midwestern city of St. Anthony. A
state institution, Chippewa gives every appearance of
being the University of Minnesota in fictive dress. The
protagonist of the story is Jane Norton, an instructor of
philosophy who retires from the classroom when she marries Keith Lamberton, an assistant professor of English.
The plot of the book takes Jane and Keith through a series
of personal and professional crises. But these incidents
are only vehicles for introducing the reader to a collection of troublesome academic issues, some of which
were rarely discussed inside or outside of fiction at
the time. Among the matters raised by *Lone Voyagers* are
the teaching versus marriage dilemma for female instructors, the (supposed) second-rate nature of higher education at state universities, and the distinction between
serious teachers and those showy professors who court
student popularity by offering more entertainment than
intellectual substance in their classrooms.

Wanda Fraiken Neff was born in Minneapolis in 1889.
She received a B.A. from the University of Minnesota in
1909 and a Ph.D. from Columbia in 1929. At various points
in her career she taught English at the universities of
Colorado and Minnesota, Vassar College, and Columbia.
Her husband, Emery Neff, was a long-time professor of
English at Columbia.

139. Cary, Lucian. *One Lovely Moron*. Garden City, New York: Doubleday, Doran and Co., 1930.

The "moron" in the title of this comic novel is Brenda Berenson, the daughter of the president of a large state university in the Midwest. Brenda, who has flunked out of several Eastern colleges, is a thorn in her father's side. When she returns home after her latest academic fiasco President Berenson calls in Michael Torr, a young professor of psychology at the university, and instructs Michael to test Brenda's IQ. Although previous IQ tests have shown Brenda to be of sub-normal intelligence, Michael finds her a near genius. Moreover, he falls in love with her. Brenda's problem, Michael finds, is that she is easily bored. Michael brings excitement to Brenda's life by squiring her to a speakeasy. The establishment is raided; Michael and Brenda escape; and during the subsequent chase Michael shoots out the radiator of a pursuing police car. President Berenson has no choice but to dismiss Michael from his faculty. With Brenda in tow, Michael leaves academe and triples his salary by accepting a position as a corporate psychologist with a New York City trucking firm. *One Lovely Moron* offers little insight into academe, but it is perhaps the only college novel to contain an extensive discussion of Stanford-Benet tests.

Two other Lucian Cary novels, *The Duke Steps Out* (93) and *Second Meeting* (153), are included in this bibliography.

140. Hull, Helen. *The Asking Price*. New York: Coward-McCann, 1930.

This serious, sometimes bitter novel recounts the first twenty years in the academic career of Oliver Gilbert, a member of the English department of "Drummond College." Drummond is a small, private institution in the Midwest. Although Oliver harbors great ideas—one of which is to leave academe and become a farmer—he is continuously repressed by his wife, whose aim is to acquire status in Drummond society. Only once, when he takes leave of his family to teach a summer course at NYU, does Oliver become more of a man than a mouse. At NYU he meets Kate, a free-lance writer, with whom he has an exhilarating clandestine affair. But at the end of the summer Oliver and Kate agree to part forever in the interest of Oliver's three children. Eventually Oliver becomes chairman of his department, but neither he nor the readers of this

novel feels that his ascendancy to administrative eminence
has been worth the "price."

Helen Hull attended Michigan State and the University
of Michigan before receiving a Ph.B. from the University
of Chicago in 1912. She taught English literature and
creative writing at Wellesley from 1912 until 1914, and
at Columbia from 1914 until her retirement in 1958. A
popular and prolific novelist, Hull also wrote a number
of books on the techniques of fiction writing.

141. [Coonradt, Paul Talbot]. *Dance Out the Answer*. By David
     McCloud (pseud.). New York: Longman's Green and Co.,
     1932.

     Dance Out the Answer is a gentle novel of academic
     manners set at "Adams College," a small and exclusive
     institution in the East. The protagonists of the piece
     are the Frisbys--Alfie and Deborah. Alfie is a pleasant
     professor of music whose hobby is growing irises. Deborah
     is an aspiring social lioness. Holding what seems to be
     a perpetual open house, she entertains an endless parade
     of Adamsites. Everyone in the book is fiscally comfort-
     able and the talk in the Frisbys' "music room"--where
     Deborah holds court--runs to discussions of Proust, re-
     capitulations of travels to London, and mild gossip about
     those college personnel who have yet to arrive for their
     tea and macaroons. Tragedy enters the story briefly when
     the Frisbys' son, Jamie, is killed in a traffic accident.
     A student at Adams, Jamie was the light of his parents'
     life. But even Jamie's death puts only a temporary halt
     to the Frisbys' entertaining. A few weeks after his
     funeral the get-togethers begin once again.

     Paul Talbot Coonradt was born in Cold Brook, New York,
     in 1897. He received an A.B. from Hamilton College.
     Dance Out the Answer was his second novel.

142. Aldrich, Bess Streeter [Mrs. Charles Sweetzer Aldrich].
     Miss Bishop. New York: D. Appleton-Century Co., 1933.

     This exercise in academic sudsmanship chronicles the
     career of Ella Bishop, long-time faculty dogsbody at
     "Midwestern College." For fifty years Ella teaches
     English composition, advises students, supervises campus
     extracurricular activities, and gives most of her money
     away to ne'er-do-well relatives who take advantage of
     her good nature. Ella's one big romance, with a faculty
     colleague, is aborted when her swain is killed in an auto
     accident. At the end of the book Ella is past seventy

but still active and alert, and she hopes to continue
teaching indefinitely. But the new president of Midwestern has other ideas. In hopes of giving Midwestern
a youthful image, he summarily fires Miss Bishop by letter,
thereby assigning her to an empty and penurious old age.
This book has two major virtues. It offers detailed insight into turn-of-the-century higher education on America's prairies. And it makes a fine, implicit case for
mandatory pension plans. In 1941 the novel was transformed into a motion picture, entitled "Cheers for Miss
Bishop." The film starred Martha Scott in the title role
and the screen adaptation was by Stephen Vincent Benet.
    Another of Bess Streeter Aldrich's novels, *A White Bird
Flying* (101), is included in this bibliography.

143. Childers, James Saxon. *God Save the Duke*. New York:
      D. Appleton and Co., 1933.

    Lord Peter Duncaster, a wealthy Briton from Oxford,
arrives at the "State University of Mittewanga"--somewhere
in the South--to spend a year teaching English literature.
Lord Peter brings with him his valet and his dog. The
latter is named Sir John Falstaff. At first Lord Peter
makes grievous errors. He wears his academic robes to
class, practices cricket with his valet on the campus,
and even fails the star of Mittewanga's football team.
But Lord Peter eventually becomes the university's most
popular professor and as his reward he takes an American
bride back to Great Britain. *God Save the Duke* is the
first American college novel to chronicle the exploits of
a visiting British professor at an American institution
of higher learning. It also contains one of American
fiction's relatively few favorable portraits of a college
president. Dr. Charles Hoskins, president of the university, is described as a sensitive intellectual. Indeed, other than Lord Peter, he is the only real intellectual on the Mittewanga campus.
    James Saxon Childers received a B.A. from Oberlin in
1920. He then studied at Oxford as a Rhodes Scholar.
From 1925 until 1942 Childers was a member of the English
department at Birmingham Southern University. After
service as a colonel with the U.S. Army Air Force in
World War II, he entered the publishing business. At
his death in 1965 he was president of Tupper and Love,
an Atlanta book publishing firm. *God Save the Duke* was
Childers' fourth novel. His first novel, *Laurel and
Straw* (New York: D. Appleton and Co., 1927), deals with
the exploits of an American Rhodes Scholar at Oxford.

*144. Vermorcken, Elizabeth Moorhead. *The Forbidden Tree.*
       Indianapolis: Bobbs-Merrill Co., 1933.

Charles Maynard, the central character of this episodic
novel, is one of the more ill-fated faculty members in
American college fiction. Fresh from Harvard, Charles is
instructor of English at a large Midwestern university.
The novel begins with the death of the kindly department
chairperson who recruited him. This worthy is replaced
by one Dr. Perkins, a repugnant bureaucrat whom Charles
detests and who detests Charles in return. Then, even
as things are going badly in the department, Charles loves
and loses three women. These women, in order of their
disappearance from his love life, are a faculty colleague,
a co-ed (who commits suicide), and the wealthy daughter
of a university trustee. Finally, in what may be the
most dismal of all Charles' misadventures, our hero invests his meager savings in the stock market, acquires a
paper fortune, but delays selling his shares until most
of his winnings evaporate with a sudden downturn in their
price. The novel is rich in academic atmosphere. It is
particularly effective in detailing the frustrations of
poorly paid and overworked junior faculty.
For many years prior to the publication of this novel
Elizabeth Moorhead Vermorcken was a professor of English
at the Carnegie Institute of Technology.

145. DeVoto, Bernard. *We Accept with Pleasure.* Boston:
      Little, Brown and Co., 1934.

One of America's outstanding twentieth-century men of
letters, Bernard DeVoto received a B.A. from Harvard in
1920. During the early 1920s he combined creative writing
with schoolteaching, newspaper reporting, and work as a
ranchhand. In 1927 he joined the English department at
Harvard, where he remained until 1936 when he became
editor of *The Saturday Review of Literature.*
We Accept with Pleasure was DeVoto's fourth novel. It
deals with a group of World War I veterans who experience
varying degrees of success in their post-war lives. The
central characters all were students at Harvard before
entering military service. One of the protagonists, Ted
Grayson, is first seen as a struggling assistant professor of history at Northwestern. When Ted speaks at a
League of Nations rally in Chicago he is accused of being
a Communist and is fired by the university's administration. This prompts a nervous breakdown and his former
Harvard classmates rush to his rescue. They move Ted,

his wife Libby, and their infant child to Boston so that Ted may recuperate. Eventually Ted becomes a successful and affluent Broadway playwright but, in the process, he grows estranged from Libby. She wants to return to academe. When Ted is offered a teaching position at Ohio State he turns his back on fame and riches. At the end of the novel, he and Libby are packing for their move to Ohio.

146. Wolfe, Thomas Clayton. *Of Time and the River*. New York: Charles Scribner's Sons, 1935.

Of Time and the River takes up the life of Eugene Gant at the point where *Look Homeward, Angel* (96) ends. It describes Gant's experiences as a graduate student at Harvard and then moves on to his unhappy days as an instructor of English at a large university in New York City. In both of these sequences the book provides copious and often devastating portraits of faculty and students.

Thomas Wolfe's own three years at Harvard were filled with frustration and disillusionment. He studied playwriting under Professor George Pierce Baker at the Harvard 47 workshop. But after initially lionizing Baker, Wolfe subsequently found him to be shallow and naive. In *Of Time and the River* Baker appears as Professor James Greaves Hatcher. Wolfe's experiences as a faculty member at New York University also were dismal. He felt overwhelmed by New York City and both feared and disliked the Jewish students who populated his classes in large numbers. His negative portrayals of these students in *Of Time and the River* led some critics to accuse him of anti-Semitism. Wolfe resigned from the NYU faculty in February of 1930 and spent the next year in Europe. *Of Time and the River* was begun while Wolfe was in Europe, and at the end of the novel Wolfe depicts Eugene Gant on an extended European odyssey.

147. Fisher, Vardis. *No Villain Need Be*. Garden City, New York: Doubleday, Doran and Co., 1936.

No Villain Need Be is the final volume in Vardis Fisher's Vridar Hunter tetralogy. The novel continues Vridar's story from the end point of *We Are Betrayed* (117). Vridar leaves Chicago to teach at his alma mater, "Wasatch College," in Salt Lake City. As a student Vridar found Wasatch a disappointing intellectual environment. As a faculty member he finds little reason to alter his earlier

impression. *No Villain Need Be* is liberally laced with
portraits, most of them decidedly negative, of Wasatch
faculty, administrators, and students. While at Wasatch
Vridar writes fiction and, after many rejection notices,
he finally has a novel accepted for publication. At this
point he resigns his post at Wasatch and goes to New
York City, where he teaches English at "Manhattan College." In New York he meets Robert Clark, a fictive
version of Thomas Wolfe. At the conclusion of the novel
Vridar returns to his native Idaho to pursue writing on
a full-time basis.

Vardis Fisher taught English at the University of Utah,
his own alma mater, from 1925 until 1928. From 1928 until
1931 Fisher was an assistant professor of English at New
York University where, during much of the period, he and
Thomas Wolfe were faculty colleagues.

*148.   Linn, James Weber. *Winds Over the Campus*. Indianapolis
        and New York: Bobbs-Merrill Co., 1936.

        Jerry Grant, the protagonist of this novel, was first
        seen as a freshman at the University of Chicago in James
        Weber Linn's *This Was Life* (121). In *Winds Over the
        Campus* Grant reappears as a grizzled, about-to-retire
        professor of English at an unnamed university in the Mid-
        west. *Winds Over the Campus* follows Jerry through a
        series of sometimes traumatic experiences. One of his
        students is shot at an anti-capitalism protest rally.
        Another student, a Black girl named Olivia, tries to
        seduce him and commits suicide after he rejects her.
        And a former student--now a playwright--has one of his
        dramas produced on Broadway. Jerry enthusiastically
        travels to New Haven for a tryout performance and is
        saddened, some weeks later, when the show is panned by
        New York critics. All the while, Jerry offers reflec-
        tions on his life, on academe, and on American society.
        Written with injections of humor, and with a minimum of
        sensationalism despite the nature of some of its epi-
        sodes, the book is a reasoned look at an aging professor
        nearing the end of his career.

        James Weber Linn was a member of the department of
        English at the University of Chicago from 1896 until his
        death in 1939. In addition to *This Was Life*, an earlier
        Linn novel titled *The Chameleon* (51) also appears in this
        bibliography.

149. McConnaughey, James Parker. *Village Chronicle*. New York: Farrar and Rinehart, 1936.

Set in "Churchill," North Carolina, just a few miles down the road from Durham, this often angry novel describes the happenings at a Southern state university. The protagonist is Joel Adams, an instructor of English at the university and the son of the editor of the town's weekly newspaper. Joel is a liberal in a hotbed of conservatism. When a student is expelled from the university because he is one-eighth Negro, Joel takes over his father's newspaper and begins to fill its pages with scathing editorials. Needless to note, Joel becomes Churchill's resident pariah and the paper nearly goes out of business. All is forgiven, however, when Joel's wife becomes critically ill and the forgiving Churchill community rallies to the Adams' aid. The book contains many generally unflattering portraits of university faculty and administrators. Read as a piece of historical fiction, the novel is a grim reminder of the racial barriers which once prevented Blacks from attending state universities in the American South.

James Parker McConnaughey was born in Dayton, Ohio, in 1908. During the 1920s he attended Ohio Wesleyan and Yale. He left both schools before graduating. In an autobiographical passage on the book's dust jacket, McConnaughey notes that he left Yale after failing a Latin examination. "I believe I can state very positively," he writes, "that I got the lowest final examination and term grade ever given at that institution." McConnaughey then spent a brief period of time in the advertising business. He was a free-lance writer when *Village Chronicle*, his first novel, was published.

150. Moody, Minnie Hite. *Towers with Ivy*. New York: Julian Messner, Inc., 1937.

Towers with Ivy is a warm, sentimental chronicle of one hundred years in the life of the Winfield family. Josiah Winfield, the patriarch of the clan, is an Ohio banker who founds a college in his hometown. His heirs retain fiscal and emotional interests in the institution—though academic control passes into the hands of others—and thus the college serves as the backdrop for the entire saga. A great number of professors appear in the story. Many of them court and some occasionally win Winfield women. There are countless passages which deal with changing campus dress codes, sexual mores, and

intellectual fashions at various stages of the school's
development. The time span of the book is from the 1830s
until 1933. The college begins as an institution for
men, but it becomes coeducational in the 1870s.

Minnie Hite Moody was born in Granville, Ohio, in 1900.
She did not attend college. Married to a high school
athletic director in Atlanta, Georgia, she combined child-
rearing with writing. *Towers with Ivy* was her third
novel. From 1938 until 1942 Mrs. Moody wrote a popular
literary and local chit chat column for the *Atlanta
Journal*.

*151. Ward, Mary Jane [Mrs. Edward Quayle]. *The Tree Has Roots*.
New York: E.P. Dutton and Co., 1937.

This highly unusual novel has as its focus the lives
and times of a set of behind-the-scenes college workers.
Included in the cast are an aging janitor, a young dining
hall waitress, a stenographer, a food service manager,
and a superintendent of buildings and grounds. The setting is "Elm University," somewhere in the Midwest, and
the time is the Depression. With low pay, and with low
institutional status as well, the various characters in
the book all face monumental personal crises. The plot,
which often meanders as the author stops to offer in-depth
and sympathetic character sketches, has the principals
interacting with each other, sometimes in amorous relationships, as they attempt to cope with their dilemmas.

Mary Jane Ward attended Northwestern University for
four semesters between 1923 and 1926. After her brief
college experience she worked in various fields, including
commercial art, before turning to writing. *The Tree Has
Roots* was her first novel. A later Ward novel, *The Snake
Pit* (New York: Random House, 1946), is generally considered to be one of the most insightful works about the
problems of institutionalized mental patients. After
The Snake Pit, Ward turned her attentions to a novel
about a college faculty member. That book, *The Professor's Umbrella* (223), appears in this bibliography.

152. Wilder, Isabel. *Let Winter Go*. New York: Coward-McCann,
1937.

Let Winter Go is an involved but eventually heart-
warming academic romance. The protagonists are Francis
Hyatt, a professor of English, and Alicia Rowe, a graduate student. The setting is "Newton University," an
institution snuggled in deepest New England. The affair

between Francis and Alicia is made difficult by Enid Hyatt, Francis' shrewish wife. Only when Enid dies in an automobile accident at the end of the book are the central characters free to love without harassment. But even though they plan to marry, they know that they will be eternally stigmatized by the Newton community. Thus Francis accepts a post as professor of English at Cornell. The story pays very little attention to the academic aspects of Newton.

Isabel Wilder studied at the Yale Art School and at Oxford before graduating from the Yale Department of Drama in 1928. During a varied work career she was a puppeteer with a marionette company, a costume designer, a book reviewer for *The New Haven Journal Courier*, an instructor of drama, a librarian, and a museum curator at the Connecticut College for Women. The sister of novelist Thornton Wilder, she was encouraged to write fiction by Professor George P. Baker, who moved his 47 Play Shop from Harvard to Yale in the 1920s. *Let Winter Go* was her third novel.

153. Cary, Lucian. *Second Meeting*. Garden City, New York: Doubleday, Doran and Co., 1938.

When Mary Carr was a student at the "University of Minnewaska" she saved a young professor of political science from drowning after a boating accident. Some years later she returns to the Midwestern university to stay with friends. She meets the professor again, but now he is the famous Arthur Bennett, the youthful, bachelor president of the institution. Mary is in the final stages of a divorce from her New York-architect husband, and she and Arthur fall in love. The only problem is that local Minnewaska society frowns upon Arthur's intention to marry a divorcee. But Arthur and the rescue-prone Mary bravely extricate two students from the wreckage of an automobile accident, and the community gives its blessings to Mary as a prospective presidential wife. Perhaps Minnewaskians feel that marriage, even to Mary, will help Arthur concentrate on his presidential duties. Totally absorbed in his romance, Arthur spends very little time on university business during the course of this light, frothy story.

Two earlier novels by Lucian Cary, *The Duke Steps Out* (93) and *One Lovely Moron* (139), also appear in this bibliography.

154.   Shuster, George Nauman. *Brother Flo: An Imaginative*
       Biography. New York: Macmillan Co., 1938.

       Told in the first person by a picture restorer who is
       plying his trade at "Merrymount College"--a Catholic
       college for men--this unique novel focuses upon the ex-
       ploits of Brother Florian, a college porter. Brother
       Flo, as he is called by everyone at Merrymount, diligently
       watches over his "boys," as well as the faculty, and with
       puckish good humor he is the real power behind the Merry-
       mount scene. The book consists of a series of incidents.
       In one, Brother Flo tricks the school's overzealous presi-
       dent, Father Davidson, into believing that a murder has
       been committed on campus. But, in fact, Flo has poured
       red paint on a drunken passerby and the "corpse" sits up
       just after the president calls the police. Flo dies in
       the last chapter. His last wish is that he be included
       in any written histories of the college.
       George Nauman Shuster received an A.B. from Notre Dame
       in 1915 and an A.M. from that institution in 1920. He
       was chairman of the department of English at his alma
       mater from 1920 until 1924 before embarking upon a peri-
       patetic academic career which was to see him become, in
       1939, president of Hunter College.

*155.   Stribling, Thomas Sigismund. *These Bars of Flesh*.
       Garden City, New York: Doubleday, Doran and Co.,
       1938.

       These Bars of Flesh is a highly amusing satire set at
       the "University of Megapolis," a world-famous institution
       in New York City. The protagonist is Andrew Barnett, a
       Georgia superintendent of schools who lacks a college
       degree. In order to obtain a diploma Andrew enrolls in
       the university for a summer term. However, since Andrew
       has been a state legislator as well as a school official
       the university immediately makes him a professor of po-
       litical science. Although the novel includes a great
       many digs at "progressive" education, and at faculty
       charlatanism, the main thrust of the satire is directed
       at the interplay between liberalism and conservatism on
       university campuses. Andrew, a conservative, is eventu-
       ally fired after locking horns with a liberal economist.
       The pettyfogging dean of the university tells Andrew that
       "materialistic collectivism" is currently in vogue and
       that the institution's reputation will be damaged ir-
       reparably if it harbors advocates of "individualism."
       The university's students are depicted as mindless

agitators. Though they usually take to the streets for liberal causes, when Andrew is dismissed they stage a spirited demonstration in his behalf.

Born in 1881 in Clifton, Tennessee, Thomas Sigismund Stribling received an undergraduate degree from the Alabama Normal School in Florence and a law degree from the University of Alabama. After practicing law for a brief period Stribling went into newspaper work, an activity which he combined with creative writing. One of Stribling's many novels, *The Store* (Garden City, New York: Doubleday, Doran and Co., 1932), won the 1933 Pulitzer Prize.

*156. [Coffin, Mrs. Harrison Cadwallader]. *Beer for the Kitten*. By Hester Pine (pseud.). New York: Farrar and Rinehart, 1939.

This book consists of a series of character sketches and interconnected incidents. The characters are all part of the community of "Quincy College," a small and reasonably high-status institution in the East. The incidents take place during one year of the college's existence. The Quincy personage followed most closely is Frederick Trainor, the school's president. Often harassed, but seldom without composure, Trainor copes with a host of problems caused by the book's other characters. Trainor is unique among fictive college presidents in that he secretly writes his own college fiction. His forte is the academic mystery, through which he vicariously murders especially obstreperous members of his faculty and administrative staff. Other notable Quincyites in the novel are an unpopular dean, a male assistant professor of English who is accused of homosexual forays into the student body, and a junior member of the biology department who falls in love with a local beautician.

The name "Hester Pine" was a pseudonym employed by Mrs. Harrison Cadwallader Coffin, the wife of a long-time professor of Greek at Union College in Schenectady, New York.

The American College Novel
1940–1959

157. Atkins, Elizabeth Mary. *Holy Suburb*. New York: E.P.
      Dutton and Co., 1941.

    Holy Suburb is an academic period piece set in turn-of-
the-century Nebraska. The Admire family move from a farm
to the town of "University Place" because Papa Admire
wants to provide his adolescent son and daughter with
higher education. University Place, a suburb of Lincoln,
is the site of "Epworth College." Epworth is a fundamentalist church institution. Much of the plot deals
with the Admire children's growing awareness of Epworth's
cultural restrictiveness. The most dramatic incident
occurs when Ernest Leslie, a young, Harvard-trained professor of English, is dismissed from the college for
smoking cigarettes. Professor Leslie is a special favorite of Addison, the Admire daughter, and Addison cannot
quite understand why pipes, cigars, and chewing tobacco
are permissible for Epworth faculty members while cigarettes are taboo. Throughout the book the various characters compare Epworth with the nearby University of
Nebraska. The latter is generally acknowledged to be a
center of sin.
    Elizabeth Mary Atkins was born in Sterling, Nebraska,
in 1891. Her undergraduate education was at Nebraska
Wesleyan University and she received a Ph.D. from Radcliffe. She was an assistant professor of English at
the University of Minnesota when *Holy Suburb*, her first
novel, was published.

158. Carrick, Gertrude. *Consider the Daisies*. Philadelphia
      and New York: J.B. Lippincott Co., 1941.

    The protagonist of this quiet, temperate novel is
Frances ("Flippy") Flippen, an undergraduate at Vassar.
The story covers Frances' junior and senior years. A
serious student and an aspiring writer, Frances develops
a crush on Brooks Creighton, a middle-aged bachelor

professor of English. Brooks constantly praises Frances'
writing but he is too busy with research--he is writing
a monograph on Coleridge's last years--to respond to her
romantic overtures. As graduation approaches Frances
half-expects Brooks to break out of his professorial shell
and propose. When she presses the point, at their last
meeting, Brooks tells her he is "a dried-up, old scholar"
and advises her to go out in the world and find a suitable
young man. Since the novel ends at this point the reader
must assume that Frances follows his suggestion. The book
contains an enormous amount of detail about Vassar student
life in the 1930s, and the celibate Professor Creighton,
who is seen as romantically desirable not only by Frances
but by most of Vassar's nubile young ladies, emerges as
one of the most stolid devotees of scholarship in college
fiction.

Gertrude Carrick attended Vassar in the 1930s. After
graduation she worked as a copywriter for Sears, Roebuck
while writing *Consider the Daisies*, her first novel.

159.   Stegner, Wallace Earle. *Fire and Ice*. New York: Duell,
       Sloan, and Pearce, 1941.

This brief (218-page) novella covers a few days in the
life of Paul Condon, an undergraduate at a Midwestern
state university. Paul is working his way through the
university by posing as a male model for art classes, by
washing dishes, and by serving as the night manager of a
poolhall which caters primarily to students. Paul is
also a fervent activist in the university's chapter of
the Communist Party. He is not an especially disciplined
member of the party, however, and he runs afoul of its
leadership when he violates orders by staging an unauthor-
ized disturbance at a campus defense-bond rally. The
climax of the story comes when Paul is interviewed by
Miriam Halley, a wealthy co-ed who is writing about working students for the school newspaper. After the interview Paul attempts to rape Miriam, whom he sees as embodying the evils of capitalism. Miriam does not press
charges but Paul leaves the university. As he makes his
exit, for parts unknown, Paul realizes that his life to
that point has been in error. His future goal will not
be to destroy the capitalistic system but to exploit it
for his own personal gains. The novel deals only tan-
gentially with the academic aspects of Paul's aborted
undergraduate career, but it includes many detailed
portraits of his leftist student compatriots.

Wallace Earle Stegner received an A.B. from the

University of Utah in 1930 and a Ph.D. from the University of Iowa in 1935. He taught at Augustana College, the University of Utah, and the University of Wisconsin before becoming a member of the English composition staff at Harvard in 1939. Stegner remained at Harvard until 1945, when he became professor of English at Stanford. *Fire and Ice* was his fourth novel. Although this book received only modest critical approval, Stegner's earlier and later novels earned him acclaim as one of America's foremost writers. *Sports Car Menopause* (411), a novel by Page Stegner, Wallace Stegner's son, is included in this bibliography.

160. Amrine, Michael. *All Sons Must Say Goodbye*. New York: Harper and Brothers, 1942.

Roger Wendell, Jr., the son of a domineering, fundamentalist-Christian attorney, enters "Watertown Agricultural College" in Kansas. Watertown is a public institution across the state from the small town in which Roger has been raised. At Watertown Roger learns to smoke cigarettes, to drink beer, and to espouse various "liberal" philosophical positions. When he returns home at the end of his freshman year Roger angers his father by behaving in accordance with his newly acquired outlook on life. After one particularly stressful late-night argument with his son, the elder Roger Wendell suffers a stroke and dies. At this point, which comes at the end of the book, Roger Jr. experiences a mixture of sadness and exaltation. On the one hand, he has a sudden realization of the love his father was trying to express through his moralistic dictates. On the other, he now finds himself free to forge his own future without his father's interference. Although the basic plot of this book is relatively routine in American college fiction, the story is written with unusual force and sensitivity. The on-campus scenes focus upon both social and academic matters and several Watertown professors are portrayed as important influences upon Roger's intellectual development.

Michael Amrine was born in 1919 in Council Grove, Kansas. He attended Kansas State Teacher's College and Columbia University. Early in his professional career he worked as a staff member on William Allen White's *Emporia Gazette*. After World War II Amrine became a public relations officer for the Federation of Atomic Scientists and in this role he authored numerous pamphlets, articles, and books about scientific matters. At the time of his death from cancer, in 1974, Amrine was on the staff of the National

Heart and Lung Institute and was organizing a public relations campaign to warn the public of the dangers of
unrecognized hypertension. *All Sons Must Say Goodbye*
was his first novel. A later Amrine novel, *Secret* (Boston: Houghton Mifflin Co., 1950), deals with the ethical
issues which surrounded the development and use of America's first nuclear weapons.

161. Huie, William Bradford. *Mud on the Stars*. New York:
    L.B. Fisher, 1942.

The protagonist of this novel is Peter Garth Lafavor.
Garth, as he is known to his friends, is a wealthy South-
erner whom the story follows through the University of
Alabama, into the newspaper business, on an in-search-of-
himself trip to the West Coast, and then into the army at
the beginning of World War II. Garth's sojourn at Alabama
is covered in the first third of the 341-page book. In
many respects Garth is a typical fictive undergraduate.
He joins a fraternity and is initiated into the wonders
of both sex and liquor. But Garth also has some decidedly
atypical experiences. On a psychology field trip to a
mental asylum he is startled to find that "Case No. 4864,"
being questioned by a psychiatrist for the edification of
the class, is his grandfather. And, back on the Alabama
campus, he befriends a number of Jewish students from New
York from whom he gains insight into Southern social in-
justices. Written with attention to detail, that portion
of *Mud on the Stars* which deals with Garth's student days
at Alabama provides considerable insight into undergraduate life at Southern state universities in the 1930s.
    William Bradford Huie was born in Hartselle, Alabama,
in 1910. He received an A.B. from the University of
Alabama in 1930. After completing his degree Huie was
a reporter on the *Birmingham Post* before becoming an
associate editor of *The American Mercury* in 1941. After
service in the Navy during World War II, he turned his
full attention to writing. Known during the 1950s and
1960s as a voice of Southern liberalism, particularly on
racial issues, Huie's literary output includes such
diverse works as *The Revolt of Mamie Stover* (New York:
Duell, Sloan and Pearce, 1951), *The Americanization of
Emily* (New York: E.P. Dutton and Co., 1959), and *He Slew
the Dreamer* (New York: Delacorte Press, 1970), a biography
of James Earl Ray. *Mud on the Stars* was Huie's first
novel.

162. Miers, Earl Schenck. *Big Ben*. Philadelphia: The West-
     minster Press, 1942.

   Big Ben is a fictionalized version of Paul Robeson's
   early years. The heart of the book describes Robeson's
   undergraduate days at Rutgers. Robeson is called Ben
   Jackson in the novel and Rutgers is the "State University." The only Black student on campus, Ben overcomes a
   series of racially inspired obstacles to become an all-
   American football player and a member of Phi Beta Kappa.
   There is a preface to the book in which the author states
   that the novel is true "in spirit, if not always in fact"
   to Robeson's experiences. The author also states that
   he hopes the book will "be the story of a struggle for a
   high goal in our own America--the right of a member of
   any minority to be treated with the dignity which God
   bequeathed to all men."
   Earl Schenck Miers received a B.Litt. from Rutgers in
   1933 and an A.M. from the same institution in 1943.
   During a long and productive writing career he published
   adult novels, mysteries, and fiction for juveniles. Some
   of Miers' fiction was issued under the pseudonym David
   William Meredith. Miers also edited many compendia of
   Civil War papers and wrote a number of historical books
   about the Civil War. Another of Miers' novels, *The Ivy
   Years* (170), is included in this bibliography.

163. Farrell, James Thomas. *My Days of Anger*. New York: Van-
     guard Press, 1943.

   This novel, the fourth in James T. Farrell's Danny
   O'Neil series, has Danny attending the University of
   Chicago as a commuter student. The time is the late
   1920s. Danny's initial aspiration is to become a lawyer
   but thanks to the encouragement he receives from Professor Paul Morris Saxton, his crusty English composition
   instructor, he decides to become a writer. There are
   some effective classroom scenes in the novel and Farrell
   pays special attention to the struggles of poor, hard-
   working, nonresident students.
   James T. Farrell never graduated from college but attended the University of Chicago on an on-again, off-
   again basis from 1925 to 1929. In *The League of Fright-
   ened Philistines* (New York: Vanguard Press, 1945), a
   book of essays, Farrell reviews his days at Chicago and
   attributes part of his own desire to write to the help
   he received in college from professors Robert Morse
   Lovett and James Weber Linn. Three of Linn's own novels,

The Chameleon (51), *This Was Life* (121), and *Winds Over the Campus* (148), are included in this bibliography. Another of Farrell's novels, *The Silence of History* (274), also is included in the bibliography.

164.   Saxton, Alexander Plaisted. *Grand Crossing*. New York: Harper and Brothers, 1943.

Although this "realistic" novel is set, in part, at Harvard and at the University of Chicago, it is as much an ideological exploration of youthful dissatisfaction with pre-World War II American society as it is a college novel. The protagonist, Michael Reed, is a young man of wealth who identifies with the downtrodden working class. Michael leaves Harvard when his elite classmates and his course work become irrelevant to his social concerns. He then transfers to Chicago in order to join a friend with whom he hopped freights the previous summer in the Pacific Northwest. The friend is a Jewish socialist student who helps Michael refine his political orientations. As the novel progresses Michael marries a well-heeled Smith graduate, drops out of Chicago, and takes up a solidly non-bourgeois career as a railroad yardman.

Alexander Plaisted Saxton spent two years at Harvard in the late 1930s and then transferred to the University of Chicago. He received a B.A. from Chicago in 1940. The reviewer for *The New Yorker* (August 1, 1943) characterized *Grand Crossing* as "a competently written first novel by a young man who recently went to Harvard and still seems sore about it."

*165.   Shulman, Max. *Barefoot Boy with Cheek*. Garden City, New York: Doubleday, Doran and Co., 1943.

Barefoot Boy with Cheek is generally regarded as the classic modern satire on undergraduate life. The book follows the exploits of Asa Hearthrug during his freshman year at the University of Minnesota. Through a series of comic situations and a barrage of one-line gags the author describes and devastates freshman advisement, fraternity life, student government elections, and a host of other undergraduate phenomena. No precis can begin to indicate the range or mischievousness of the book's satirical commentaries but, perhaps, one example will be suggestive. The first class Asa attends at Minnesota is introductory sociology. The professor, wearing a pince-nez, looks out over the assembled students and muses to no one in particular: "Jeez, they get crumbier every year." He

then announces eight mandatory textbooks, all of which
he authored. In his next breath he dismisses the class
early so his pupils can run to the bookstore in order to
buy his tomes. "Don't try to get them secondhand, because
you can't," he adds as an afterthought. "I just wrote
them this summer."

Max Shulman graduated from the University of Minnesota
in 1942. *Barefoot Boy with Cheek* was his first novel.
Shulman touches upon the absurdities of higher learning
in some of his later works. In *The Many Loves of Dobie
Gillis* (Garden City, New York: Doubleday and Co., 1953)
and *I Was a Teen-Age Dwarf* (New York: Bernard Geis, 1959)
Shulman's protagonist, Dobie Gillis, spends time as an
undergraduate at a state university. And, in *The Zebra
Derby* (Garden City, New York: Doubleday and Co., 1946),
Asa Hearthrug returns from World War II military service
and tries to resume his studies at Minnesota. Unfortunately, the school's admission counselors diagnose him
as psychologically disturbed. Rather than accept the
therapeutic courses in handicrafts and community singing
which they insist be part of his re-entry program, Asa
gives up the idea of continuing his formal education.

*166.   Champagne, Marian Grosberg [Mrs. Herbert Champagne]. *The
        Cauliflower Heart*. New York: Dial Press, 1944.

This well-written novel follows a set of Smith College
students through their four undergraduate years and then
into the uncertain world beyond college during the Depression. The first two-thirds of the book is set at
Smith. In contrast to most stories of women's colleges,
The Cauliflower Heart pays considerable attention to the
protagonists' intellectual development as well as to their
acquisition of social and sexual graces. While the Smith-
ies in the story go on dates (and some of them marry after
graduation), most of the novel's central characters also
study and the more energetic of them even become campus
activists in anti-fascist causes. The book is laden with
minutiae about Smith in the 1930s and the author offers
much detail about the liberal idealism with which many
college students of the period were infused.

Marian Grosberg Champagne received an A.B. from Smith
in 1936. Married to an attorney, Mrs. Champagne entered
Albany Law School in her late thirties and graduated in
1955. She then went into the general practice of law in
Albany, New York. *The Cauliflower Heart* was her first
novel.

167. Corrigan, Barbara. *Voyage of Discovery*. New York: Charles
      Scribner's Sons, 1945.

      Cornelia Ross, only seventeen but sophisticated beyond
      her years, enters "Pacific State University," an insti-
      tution which bears a remarkable resemblance to the Uni-
      versity of California at Berkeley. As one of her sorority
      sisters puts it late in the novel, Cornelia "majors in
      sin." She has affairs with a variety of male students
      and faculty members. Finally, perhaps out of sheer ex-
      haustion, she settles upon one young man as her life's
      companion. The novel is written as satire. It is note-
      worthy for its unflattering depictions of sorority life
      and, considering the date of its publication, for its
      relatively explicit treatment of Cornelia's sexual esca-
      pades.

168. Kehoe, William. *A Sweep of Dust*. New York: E.P. Dutton
      and Co., 1945.

      A Sweep of Dust is a meandering novel about the Fahrner
      family, a working-class clan in the city of "Graceville."
      Curt Fahrner, the oldest son, is sent to "Ames University."
      Curt is an introspective young man who spends much of his
      time being strong and silent. At Ames he studies art,
      joins a fraternity, and discovers the joys of consorting
      with the opposite sex. While there are many scenes of
      college life in this book, the plot moves Curt back and
      forth between Ames and his Graceville home. The novel is
      set in the early 1940s. It ends in 1942 when Curt drops
      out of college to await his "greetings" from Uncle Sam.

*169. Maxwell, William. *The Folded Leaf*. New York: Harper and
      Brothers, 1945.

      The Folded Leaf is a masterful story of two high school
      chums from Chicago--Lymie Peters and Spud Latham--who
      attend a small university in Indiana. As the boys wend
      their way through college, and as they develop separate
      interests and identities, their once-solid relationship
      is shaken. When they become rivals for the affection of
      the same girl, the daughter of a philosophy professor,
      Spud emerges victorious and Lymie attempts suicide. Ly-
      mie's near self-destruction convinces both lads of their
      undying affection for each other and, at the end of the
      novel, they are reconciled. *The Folded Leaf* is an extreme-
      ly sensitive exploration of love between two heterosexual
      males. Literary scholars generally rate the book as one

of the best of all student-centered college novels, and
as one of the best American novels about male adolescents
as well.

William Maxwell was born in Lincoln, Illinois, in 1908.
He received a B.A. from the University of Illinois in
1930. *The Folded Leaf* was his third novel. Most of
Maxwell's professional career was spent as fiction editor
of *The New Yorker*.

170.   Miers, Earl Schenck. *The Ivy Years*. New Brunswick, New
      Jersey: Rutgers University Press, 1945.

Earl Schenck Miers received a B.Litt. from Rutgers in
1933 and *The Ivy Years* is a frankly autobiographical novel
about his experiences as a Rutgers undergraduate. The
protagonist of the story is called Jeremy Baxter but, as
Miers notes in a preface, "buildings and places are named
as they exist; and members of the faculty are presented
by name." The fast-moving plot takes Jeremy through four
generally pleasant years on the Rutgers campus. During
these years Jeremy has a series of benign escapades and,
of more significance, he finds intellectual stimulation.
As graduation approaches, Jeremy harbors ambitions to
become a writer.

An earlier Miers novel, *Big Ben* (162), appears in this
bibliography. *Big Ben* is a fictionalized account of Paul
Robeson's days as a Rutgers student. Robeson makes a
cameo appearance in *The Ivy Years* when he returns to
Rutgers to give a concert.

171.   Parsons, Peryl Wade. *My Love is Young*. Philadelphia:
      MacRae, Smith Co., 1945.

Set at a small, private coeducational college in
California, this romantic novel deals with the growing
love of Frances "France" Ferrell, a wealthy undergraduate,
for Leo Pussard, a young professor of music. France's
parents oppose the match, in part because Leo is a brilliant pianist and, in their view, "genius is a dangerous
disease." For her part, France sees Leo as "something
unreal in the line of men." At the end of the book France
accepts Leo's proposal of marriage despite her parents'
objections. The book is written with a minimum of com-
pound sentences. While it contains a few classroom scenes
and many passages about co-ed gossip sessions, it is perhaps more valuable as an exemplar of 1940s' grade-B romantic fiction than as a college novel.

172. Abelson, Ann. *Angel's Metal*. New York: Harcourt, Brace
     and Co., 1947.

     Angel's Metal is a serious first novel about Helen
     Bianchi, who is first seen as an ambitious and inquisi-
     tive student at the "College of St. Regina," a Catholic
     college for women. Through her discussions with faculty
     members, with other students, and--most of all--with an
     iconoclastic nurse in the college infirmary, Helen achieves
     a series of personal intellectual breakthroughs and begins
     to see the world in new and exciting ways. Eventually
     Helen marries the college physician. The latter portion
     of the book follows Helen and the doctor through the some-
     what rocky first years of their marriage. Although the
     novel is fundamentally a romance there is considerable
     attention paid to life in Catholic women's colleges in
     the early 1940s.

173. Grafton, Cornelius Warren. *My Name is Christopher Nagel*.
     New York: Rinehart and Co., 1947.

     The year is 1926 and Christopher Nagel, a brawny lad
     from a small town in South Carolina, plans to attend
     nearby "Brewster College." However, when Christopher
     pitches a no-hit high school baseball game, he is re-
     cruited to "Stanley University," a Southern sports power-
     house. In part, Christopher agrees to attend Stanley
     because he wants to be a surgeon and its recruiters tell
     him that the institution has an excellent pre-med program.
     Once on the Stanley campus, Christopher is persuaded to
     try football and he immediately becomes a star running
     back. His head begins to swell along with his collection
     of press clippings and, fortified by liberal ingestions
     of bootleg alcohol, he has a dalliance with the dean's
     daughter. This leads to a shotgun marriage. At the end
     of the book Christopher drops his pre-med course--he
     barely passes introductory biology--and is trying to de-
     cide between physical education and business administra-
     tion as his new major. Although this book certainly must
     be counted among the many anti-big-time-sports novels in
     college fiction, its tone is more ironic than bitter.
     Christopher is portrayed as fundamentally well-meaning
     but not overly cerebral. Indeed, the reader is left with
     doubts that he would ever have become a doctor, even
     without his involvement in athletics.
        Cornelius Warren Grafton, the son of an American mis-
     sionary, was born in Kiangsu Province, China. During
     the 1920s he attended Presbyterian College (in Clinton,

South Carolina), Columbia University, and Northwestern. From 1930 until 1932 he taught English at Presbyterian. In 1932 he entered law school in Louisville, Kentucky, and was admitted to the Kentucky bar in 1935.

174. Wetherell, June Pat [Mrs. Daniel Frame]. *Run Sheep Run.* New York: E.P. Dutton and Co., 1947.

This melancholic novel follows two co-eds through the University of Washington in the early 1930s and then traces their interlocking lives until the end of World War II. Pat Reed, the more headstrong of the two women, enjoys the sexual attentions of several male students before settling upon Chuck Clark as her marriage partner. Chuck is a wealthy Seattle aristocrat with "beautiful white teeth." Suzie McGill, an aspiring novelist, has an affair with a married professor. When the professor returns to his wife, Suzie marries Ken Morrison, a student without money but with a kind, understanding nature. The first quarter of the story takes place on the Washington campus and includes abundant information about college dating and mating customs at the dawn of the Depression. During the remainder of the novel Pat and Suzie struggle to protect their respective husbands from various extramarital temptations. In Suzie's case one of the threats to family bliss is Pat, who has designs upon the good-hearted Ken. Pat's comeuppance occurs in 1945 when her own hubby, Chuck, is killed in the war. Ken survives infantry duty in Europe, and he and Suzie presumably live happily ever after. At one juncture during World War II Suzie returns to the University of Washington for graduate study. Her renewed interest in academic work is prompted, in part, by her lack of success as a creative writer. She labors for four years to complete her first novel, a Civil War epic. But just as she is editing the final draft she discovers that Margaret Mitchell has usurped much of her plot in the just-published *Gone with the Wind*.

At the time *Run Sheep Run* was published June Pat Wetherell was serving as a member of the English department at Michigan Normal College (now Eastern Michigan University) while her husband was enrolled as a graduate student at the University of Michigan. An earlier Wetherell novel, *But That Was Yesterday* (211), also appears in this bibliography.

175. Willingham, Calder. *End as a Man*. New York: Vanguard
      Press, 1947.

    End as a Man is an angry ethnographic novel about stu-
dent life in a Southern military academy. The protagonist
is Robert Marquales, a freshman cadet. At the academy
Marquales encounters a set of bullies, homosexuals, and
simpletons as his fellow undergraduates. The worst of
the bad lot--though the race for this honor is very close--
is Jocko DeParis, a wealthy, psychopathic upperclassman.
Jocko and his friends make Robert's life miserable until,
at the end of the book, they are expelled from the academy
by General A.L. Draughton, the school's commandant.
General Draughton is portrayed as pompous but fair. The
author offers many of General Draughton's speeches and
memoranda in their entirety and the General emerges as
one of the best delineated academic administrators in
student-centered college fiction.

    Calder Willingham was born in Atlanta in 1922. He
attended The Citadel during the 1940-1941 academic year.
He then transferred to the University of Virginia. *End
as a Man* was his first novel. Willingham later became
a successful screen writer. Among his film credits are
"Paths of Glory" (1959), "The Graduate" (1967), and "The
Strange One" (1957), a film adaptation of *End as a Man*.

176. Winther, Sophus Keith. *Beyond the Garden Gate*. New York:
      Macmillan Co., 1947.

    Forrest Bailey, a junior at the University of Oregon,
has his initial sexual experience with a slow-witted,
seventeen-year-old farm girl. The girl becomes pregnant
and Forrest is arrested for statutory rape. Then, to
complicate matters, the girl lapses into catalepsy and
must be sent to a mental hospital. The girl's parents
decide to raise the infant, and Forrest is released from
jail when they decide not to prosecute him. Shaken by
all of this, Forrest flees Oregon forever. Although the
plot of this novel would do credit to the most heart-
wrenching of soap operas, the writing is polished and
the ethical issues are handled with considerable sensitivity. Most of the story takes place off-campus, but
there is one particularly interesting scene at the university in which a sorority girl laments the fact that
Oregon, in contrast to other institutions of higher
learning, has only two years' worth of "snap courses."

    Sophus Keith Winther was born in Denmark in 1893. He
received a B.A. from Oregon in 1918 and a Ph.D. from the

University of Washington in 1925. He spent his entire professional career as a member of the Washington department of English. *Beyond the Garden Gate* was his fourth novel.

177. Barber, Elsie Oakes. *The Trembling Years*. New York: Macmillan Co., 1949.

When Kathy Storm, a freshman at "Windsor College," is stricken with paralytic polio, she reacts with self-pity. But Kathy is made of strong stuff. As the plot of this novel unfolds Kathy pulls herself together, sheds her wheelchair, and returns to a reasonably normal co-ed life. Windsor is a private institution just north of Boston. There are a great many Windsor scenes in the book, and *The Trembling Years* is one of very few American college novels to explore the inner workings of a college infirmary.

Elsie Oakes Barber received a B.A. from Tufts in 1936 and did graduate work at Smith and Northwestern. *The Trembling Years* was her second novel. As a freshman at Tufts Barber contracted polio.

178. Graves, Ralph Augustus. *Thanks for the Ride*. Philadelphia and New York: J.B. Lippincott Co., 1949.

Jerry, Bob, and Greg, three former high school buddies, attend "Rutherford University" after military service in World War II. Rutherford is a high-quality institution in the East. Most of the story centers upon Jerry's efforts to keep the old gang together despite the lads' various campus romances and the widening differences in their intellectual performances. Toward the end of the book it is clear that Jerry is headed toward an academic career. Dr. Wood, Rutherford's president, calls him into his office and offers him a fully paid scholarship to Harvard on condition that he return to Rutherford to teach English after receiving his M.A. The story includes a number of portraits of professors, but the best descriptive line in the book is directed toward President Wood. Appointed during the war, and not especially popular in the Rutherford community, Wood is thought of by the university's populace as "[a wartime] aftermath, a displaced person, one of the unsolved problems of peacetime education."

Ralph Augustus Graves received a B.A. from Harvard in 1948. *Thanks for the Ride* was his first novel. After graduating from Harvard, Graves joined the staff of *Time*. He eventually became a senior editor of the magazine.

179. Lampell, Millard. *The Hero*. New York: Julian Messner,
      Inc., 1949.

      Steve Novak, an all-state high school halfback from
      northern New Jersey, is recruited to play football for
      "Jackson University." Jackson is located in Virginia.
      Steve becomes the star of the team but midway through
      his sophomore season he incurs a shoulder separation
      which ends his athletic career. Hurting in mind as well
      as in body, Steve leaves Jackson. He returns to New
      Jersey and plans to continue his education through night
      classes at New York University. In terms of its funda-
      mental message, *The Hero* is a denunciation of big-time
      college football. But because Novak is portrayed as a
      budding intellectual as well as a football hero the book
      follows him into his classes. In one intriguing classroom
      scene Steven astounds his cynical English professor by
      actually having memorized a poem assigned to be read as
      homework. "You don't understand, Novak," says the pro-
      fessor, "you [football players] are not supposed to be
      like this."
      Millard Lampell was born in Patterson, New Jersey, in
      1919. He received a B.S. from the University of West
      Virginia in 1940. *The Hero* was his first novel. Lampell
      is best known as a dramatist, film writer, and song
      lyricist. Early in his career he performed as a folk
      singer in a group known as "The Almanacs." This group
      included Pete Seeger, Woody Guthrie, and Lee Hays.

*180. [Manfried, Frederick Feikema]. *The Primitive*. By Feike
       Feikema. Garden City, New York: Doubleday, Doran and
       Co., 1949.

       Thurs Wraldson, a strapping orphan lad from the
       prairies, seeks higher education at Zion College, a
       fundamentalist church institution in Michigan. During
       the four Depression-era years covered by the novel Thurs
       loves and loses, plays basketball and wins, and gradu-
       ally becomes aware of Zion's cultural insularity. Par-
       ticularly distressing to Thurs is the dismissal of Mr.
       Menfrid, an aging instructor of music and Thurs' advisor.
       Menfrid is fired because he is suspected of harboring
       deviant religious beliefs. *The Primitive* is a serious,
       intense novel, and it is reminiscent of the novels of
       Thomas Wolfe and Vardis Fisher.
       Frederick Feikema Manfried was born Feike Feikema in
       Rock Rapids, Iowa. He received an A.B. from Calvin
       College in 1934. *The Primitive* is the first volume in

a trilogy of novels about Thurs Wraldson. The other two
novels in the series are *The Brother* (Garden City, New
York: Doubleday, Doran and Co., 1950) and *The Giant*
(Garden City, New York: Doubleday, Doran and Co., 1952).
Manfried called the trilogy his "World's Wanderer" series.
It carries Thurs through World War II. In *The Giant*,
Thurs is killed in an automobile accident.

181. Goodin, Peggy. *Take Care of My Little Girl*. New York:
      E.P. Dutton and Co., 1950.

      Written in simple prose, *Take Care of My Little Girl*
was intended both for older girls and for their parents.
It is a direct attack on the sorority system. The protagonist, Liz Erickson, comes from a small town to a
large Midwestern state university. Pledged to an exclusive sorority known as "The Queens," she spends the
first half of her freshman year totally engrossed in
the sorority's frivolous activities. Unhappily, Liz'
classwork suffers to the extent that she finds herself
on both academic and social probation at the end of her
first semester. Shocked by this turn of fortune, Liz
begins to question the value of sorority life. Figuring
largely in her calculations is The Queens' policy against
Jews and Catholics as members. Liz befriends a Jewish
girl and begins to develop empathy with those whom The
Queens exclude from their company. Moreover, Liz finds
romance with a virile, non-fraternity man at a nearby
college. By the end of her freshman year Liz has raised
her grade average to a B-level and she then shocks her
sorority sisters by becoming the first co-ed in twenty
years to voluntarily depledge from The Queens.
      Peggy Goodin was born in Kansas City, Missouri, in
1923. She received a bachelor's degree from the University of Michigan and an M.A. from McGill. *Take Care of
My Little Girl*, Goodin's second novel, was written in
Collioure, a village in the French Pyrenees, where she
was recuperating from tuberculosis. The novel was adapted
for a 1951 motion picture of the same title. The film
starred Jeanne Crain and Dale Robertson.

182. Stillwell, Hart. *Campus Town*. Garden City, New York:
      Doubleday, Doran and Co., 1950.

      "Lefty" Mason, the protagonist of this novel, is a
student at a state college in the South. The time is
1946. A part-time reporter for the town newspaper, Lefty
has more insight than does the usual undergraduate into

the political workings of the college. He is also aware
of, and unhappy with, the power of the local Ku Klux Klan.
When the college yields to Klan pressures, and fires a
liberal Jewish professor, Lefty takes action. Modern-day
students and faculty alike may take vicarious pleasure
in the climactic scene in which Lefty enters the college
president's office and punches him in the mouth. At the
end of the book Lefty is no longer a student. The book
has a number of chilling scenes of Klan activities, including one in which Lefty is kidnapped and almost killed
by Klansmen.

Born in 1902, Hart Stillwell graduated from the University of Texas in 1924. A newspaperman and free-lance
writer during most of his career, Stillwell produced many
books on hunting and fishing as well as novels about the
South and Southwest. *Campus Town* was his third novel.

*183.   Jackson, Shirley [Mrs. Stanley Edgar Hyman]. *Hangsaman*.
        New York: Farrar, Straus, and Young, 1951.

In *The College Novel in America* (see footnote 3, Introduction), John Lyons calls *Hangsaman* "the most impressive
novel about an undergraduate's experience at a woman's
college." The protagonist of the story is Natalie Waite,
the daughter of a domineering writer-father. Natalie
attends a progressive women's college in rural New England.
She is shy and sensitive and lives primarily in a brooding world of her own fantasies. Not until she meets Tony,
a vibrant fellow student, does Natalie find someone with
whom she can relate. But her association with Tony comes
to a sudden, dramatic conclusion when, as the two girls
take a long and frightening walk through the woods, Tony
reveals herself as a lesbian. Through this experience,
which occurs at the end of the novel, it is clear that
Natalie has been shocked into a new ability to cope with
reality. In addition to the portraits of Tony, Natalie,
and Natalie's father, the book also includes a sympathetic and poignant depiction of Elizabeth Langdon, a
faculty wife. Elizabeth, who befriends Natalie midway
through the story, is a mentally disturbed alcoholic.
In one singularly effective scene Natalie watches as two
other students ply Elizabeth with liquor in a deliberate
attempt to propel her into a stupor.

Shirley Jackson received a B.A. from Syracuse University in 1940. Although she left a varied literary
oeuvre at her death in 1965, she is best known for such
dark, mysterious works as *The Lottery* (New York: Farrar,
Straus, and Young, 1949). Married to Stanley Edgar

Hyman, a member of the English department at Bennington
College, Jackson was a resident of North Bennington,
Vermont, when *Hangsaman* was published.

184. Ellison, Ralph Waldo. *Invisible Man*. New York: Random
House, 1952.

Ralph Waldo Ellison was born in 1914 in Oklahoma City.
He attended Tuskegee Institute from 1933 to 1936 before
moving to New York City, where he became associated with
the Negro Federal Writer's Project. One of America's
most respected men of letters, Ellison taught at Bard
College, the University of Chicago, Rutgers, and Yale
before becoming Albert Schweitzer Professor of Humanities
at New York University in 1970.

Invisible Man, seven years in the writing, was Ralph
Ellison's first novel. The protagonist-narrator of the
story is an unnamed young Black man who, during the first
third of the book, attends a college for Blacks in the
South. The college was founded by an illustrious Black
statesman whose history, which is recounted briefly, is
very much like that of Booker T. Washington. A promising
student, the narrator is entrusted to chauffeur Mr. Norton,
a visiting White trustee. When he makes the mistake of
driving Mr. Norton through the poorest Black area of the
nearby countryside, the school's Black president, Dr.
Bledsoe, dismisses him from the institution. The protagonist has violated Dr. Bledsoe's strategy of shielding
White benefactors from the grimness of Black life just
beyond the school's idyllically beautiful campus. A
despot, feared by his students, Dr. Bledsoe then unchar-
acteristically promises to write a favorable letter of
recommendation for the narrator to a prospective White
employer in New York. In fact, Dr. Bledsoe's letter
turns out to be a vengeful attack on the narrator's
character. The last two-thirds of the novel deals with
the protagonist's continued self-awakening, as he experiences the realities and contradictions of Harlem. *Invisible Man* won the 1953 National Book Award.

185. Hall, Oakley. *The Corpus of Joe Bailey*. New York:
Viking Press, 1953.

This grim, negative novel follows Joe Bailey through
the University of California at Berkeley, into the Marines
during World War II, and then through the early post-war
years. Joe is from a poor San Diego family and he never
is able to adjust to the middle-class fripperies of

college life. Although he stars in football, is elected
president of his fraternity, and even marries a girl from
"the Cadillac set," he constantly questions the meaning
of it all. As the novel concludes Joe has purchased a
gravel pit and plans to make an honest living in the
construction business.

Oakley Hall received a B.A. from the University of
California at Berkeley in 1943 and an M.F.A. from the
State University of Iowa in 1950. Much of this novel,
his second, was written while he was an instructor at
the Iowa Writers' Workshop from 1950 to 1952. After *The
Corpus of Joe Bailey*, Hall turned to writing westerns and
mysteries, some of them under the pseudonym Jason Manor.
In 1968 Hall became a professor of English and director
of the graduate program in creative writing at Berkeley.

186. [Lumbard, Charles Gillis]. *Senior Spring*. By C.G.
      Lumbard. New York: Simon and Schuster, 1954.

      Senior Spring is a serious and vaguely existential novel
about a male undergraduate's intellectual and sexual coming of age. The protagonist is Steven Burnett, an archi-
tectural student in his senior year at a state university
in California. Steve has an affair with an aggressive
co-ed named Cassy Kane. Cassy soon announces she is
pregnant. Steve is skeptical and refuses to marry her.
After Cassy attempts suicide, however, Steve begins to
undertake his responsibilities. As all of this is happening Steve starts to doubt his abilities as an architect.
His confidence is restored when he has a long talk with
an elderly visiting architect who is presumably modeled
after Frank Lloyd Wright. The novel, told by Steven in
the first person, offers many extensive descriptions of
California student life in the years just after World War
II.

      Charles Gillis Lumbard was born in Sacramento, Cali-
fornia, in 1928. He attended the University of California at Berkeley where he was editor of the campus
humor magazine. *Senior Spring* was his first novel.

187. Miller, Nolan. *Why I Am So Beat*. New York: G.P. Putnam's
      Sons, 1954.

      Set at and around an unnamed city university, this
sometimes funny satire describes a long and frenetic
weekend in the life of Mark Gillis, a bright but ingenuous
undergraduate who aspires to be a poet. Most of the
story involves Mark in close association with Marty

Feldman, a free-thinking and uninhibited classmate, and
with Monica Satterfield, the sexually liberated editor
of the campus literary magazine. Joining this trio in
some of its frolics is a young woman of the streets
named Jane, who brings along her infant son. One of
the group's activities is attendance at a houseparty
given by Professor Kempthorne, a teacher of literature
who likes his out-of-class relationships with students
to be as informal as possible. Kempthorne begins his
party with a showing of pornographic movies and then
offers a second unreeling of the films for latecomers.
The novel is told in the first person by Mark, whose cool
manner of speech clearly stems from intensive study of
Holden Caulfield's monologues in J.D. Salinger's *Catcher
in the Rye* (Boston: Little, Brown and Co., 1951).

Nolan Miller was a member of the department of English
at Antioch College when *Why I Am So Beat* was published.
The Merry Innocents (219), another Miller novel, also
appears in this bibliography.

188.   Scott, Glenn. *A Sound of Voices Dying.* New York: E.P.
       Dutton and Co., 1954.

This conventional novel of student awakening is set at
"Philips-Whitehead University," a small, private institution located in "Concord Bridge," Virginia. The protagonist, Reid Carrington, is followed through his freshman year. Reid comes to Philips-Whitehead from a small
Virginia town. Initially shy and naive, he matures in
college after an affair with the wife of a fraternity
brother and after another member of the frat is killed in
an automobile accident. Much of the story is taken up
with drinking bouts. The book includes a few lengthy
dormitory bull sessions but passages about Reid's classroom experiences are held to a minimum. Perhaps as
testimony to Reid's newfound maturity, the author por-
trays Reid as unenthusiastic about attending Philips-
Whitehead as a sophomore. At the end of the book, as
summer vacation approaches, a classmate asks Reid if he
will be back in the fall. "Yeah," says Reid, "I suppose
so."

Glenn Scott was an undergraduate at Washington and Lee
when this novel was published.

189.   Breckling, Grace Jamison. *Walk in Beauty.* New York:
       Charles Scribner's Sons, 1955.

This novel takes place in the 1920s at "St. James
College," an exclusive institution for women in

Pennsylvania. Narrated by Marcia Kane, a young instructor
of French, the story centers upon two half-sisters from
Memphis, Tennessee, who are students at the school. The
older sister, Denise Tallentyre, is a dark, brunette beauty and the most popular girl in the senior class. Courtney Tallentyre, a recently arrived sophomore--she has
just transferred to St. James from a Southern "finishing
school"--is a light blonde. Courtney is jealous of
Denise's social success. In particular she is distressed
because Denise has recently become engaged to Giles West-
over, a handsome professor. The climax comes when Courtney destroys Denise's popularity, and jeopardizes her
engagement, by revealing that her dusky half-sister is,
in fact, part Negro. When Denise finds that Courtney has
made this secret public she steals away to a nearby river
and drowns herself. In the last chapter, a postscript,
narrator Marcia castigates the students, faculty, and
administrators at St. James for fostering an atmosphere
in which such a tragedy could occur.

Grace Jamison Breckling was born in Stillman Valley,
Illinois, in 1900. A graduate of Rockford College she
spent most of her career as an English teacher in Cleveland, Ohio, high schools. She had published many short
stories and several novels before *Walk in Beauty* appeared
in 1955.

190. Halevy, Julian. *The Young Lovers*. New York: Simon and
      Schuster, 1955.

Eddie Slocum, known affectionately to his friends as
"The Groper," meets Pam Oldenburg, an art student, on a
New York City subway platform. The two young people fall
in love. Eddie is an undergraduate at New York University. Unfortunately, Eddie's romance cuts into his study
time and his grades fall to the point where his draft
board is no longer willing to grant him a student defer-
ment. Meanwhile, Pam becomes pregnant. The book ends
with Eddie and Pam marrying, but by this time Eddie already has been drafted into the army. The novel contains
some interesting classroom scenes at NYU and some in-
depth portraits of NYU students.

There is no information about Julian Halevy in any of
the standard biographical reference books. But an insert
on the last page of *The Young Lovers* describes him as a
native New Yorker who served in World War II and then
"worked intermittently in the entertainment industry."
In the early 1950s Halevy "traveled in Europe and Latin
America, seeing the world and trying to decide what to
do with it." *The Young Lovers* was his first novel.

191. Irving, Clifford Michael. *On a Darkling Plain*. New York:
      G.P. Putnam's Sons, 1956.

> *On a Darkling Plain* recites the interwoven emprises of
> Mike Donnenfeld, Joe MacFarlane, and Pete Reed. The
> three protagonists of the piece are undergraduates at
> Cornell during the first half of the book. They then
> transport themselves to New York City for post-graduate
> adventures. Though not without their introspective mo-
> ments, Mike, Joe, and Pete search primarily for social
> and sexual gratifications throughout the story, hence the
> collegiate portions of the narrative emphasize the extra-
> curricular side of student life in Ithaca.
> Clifford Irving received a B.A. from Cornell in 1951
> and then went on to a literary career which eventually
> saw him imprisoned after he accepted a publisher's ad-
> vance for a bogus autobiography of Howard Hughes. *On
> a Darkling Plain* was his first novel. While a student
> at Cornell Irving was a compatriot of Robert Thompson,
> the author of *Halfway Down the Stairs* (197), and Robert
> Gutwillig, who wrote *After Long Silence* (198). Reviewing
> Gutwillig's work in *The Ithaca Journal* (May 24, 1958),
> William G. Andrews noted that Irving, Thompson, and Gut-
> willig all included in their novels a fictive character
> modeled after Ken Hutchinson, a real life Cornell student
> from 1948 until 1953. Hutchinson, a high-living under-
> graduate whose pre-college record was highlighted by an
> undesirable discharge from the air force, was killed in
> an automobile accident on August 1, 1953. In the novels
> of Thompson and Gutwillig, the Hutchinson-based character
> meets a violent death. In *On a Darkling Plain* Joe Mac-
> farlane, Irving's fictive tribute to Hutchinson, survives
> to the end of the book, but his girlfriend is killed when
> the sports car she is driving crashes near the George
> Washington Bridge in New York.

192. Shulman, Irving. *Good Deeds Must Be Punished*. New York:
      Henry Holt and Co., 1956.

> The protagonist-narrator of this serious, polished
> novel is a young, Italian-American veteran of the Korean
> War who enrolls at "Gresham College." Gresham is an un-
> distinguished private institution in West Virginia. The
> narrator, who is from the New York City area, finds that
> the Gresham student body segregates itself according to
> religious and ethnic heritage. There are separate frater-
> nities and sororities for Italians, Jews, Irish, and
> various other student clusterings. Moreover, each

fraternity and sorority constructs its own world, and a
Gresham undergraduate attempts to cross ethnic and religious boundaries only at considerable social peril.
Much of the story centers on the Catholic protagonist's
successful effort to win the affections of a Protestant
girl. As the plot unfolds the author probes the prejudice and bigotry which underlie the Gresham scene. The
book pays relatively little attention to academic matters,
but it offers some detailed descriptions of life inside a
fraternity for Italian-Americans.

Irving Shulman was born in Brooklyn, New York, in 1913.
He received an A.B. from Ohio University in 1937 and an
M.A. from Columbia in 1938. He was a member of the English department at George Washington University from 1943
until 1947. After the publication of his best-selling
first novel, *The Amboy Dukes* (Garden City, New York:
Doubleday and Co., 1947), Shulman left academe to devote
his full energies to writing. *Good Deeds Must Be Punished*
was Shulman's sixth novel.

193. Frede, Richard. *Entry E.* New York: Random House, 1957.

The protagonist of this ironic saga is Ed Bogard, a
junior at "Hayden University." Hayden is a high-status,
Ivy League institution. An introspective sort, Ed calcu-
lates all of his actions in terms of personal gain, and
he is generally indifferent to the frivolous behavior of
his classmates. When the boys down the hall mass-rape a
drunken girl, however, Ed rescues the young woman and
takes her to the hospital. Though he is subsequently
exonerated of taking part in the rape, he is asked to
resign from the university because he failed to report
the incident to campus security. Most of the characters
in the book, other than Ed, are fictional campus stereotypes. Reviewers tended to treat *Entry E* with kindness.
Some saw it as a commentary on the 1950s' "silent gener-
ation."

Richard Frede received a B.A. from Yale in 1955. *Entry
E* was his first novel. His second novel, *The Interns*
(New York: Random House, 1960), was a best-seller.

194. Ham, Roswell Gray, Jr. *Fish Flying Through Air.* New
      York: G.P. Putnam's Sons, 1957.

This semi-comic novel follows three male pranksters
through prep school, Yale, the army during World War II,
and then into their adult lives. The protagonists are
Charlie Baxter, George McGough, and "Spook" McDonald.

Their Yale experiences are told in the middle third of the book. While at Yale the lads behave in a fashion which was pioneered by those incorrigible, turn-of-the-century fictive Yalies who always disappointed and sometimes terrorized their mentors. The Yale administration asks the three boys to leave, without degrees, but not before one of McGough's professors gets in a last word. "After each class with you," says the professor to George, "I return to my office in despair and seriously contemplate suicide."

Roswell Gray Ham, Jr., was born in Alameda, California, in 1920. His father was president of Mount Holyoke College from 1937 until 1957. Roswell Jr. attended Yale. *Fish Flying Through Air* was the second of four novels he produced during his lifetime. At the time of his death in 1967 he was editor and publisher of *Seaside Topics*, a weekly specialty newspaper published in New York City.

195. Kaufmann, Myron S. *Remember Me to God*. Philadelphia and New York: J.B. Lippincott Co., 1957.

This long (640-page) and sober novel focuses upon a Jewish undergraduate at Harvard who tries to deny his heritage. The protagonist, Richard Amsterdam, cuts himself off from his family and from other Jewish students in an effort to rise socially. He becomes engaged to a wealthy gentile, but neither his family nor hers approves of the match. Toward the end of the book the girl permanently breaks off the relationship. The novel is set during the early days of World War II. Distraught over his broken romance Richard fails his senior examinations and is drafted. The novel ends with Richard, now a private in the infantry, embarking for combat duty overseas. Although much of the book takes place off-campus there are a number of finely etched views of Harvard.

Myron S. Kaufmann graduated cum laude from Harvard in 1943. After World War II service in the army he became a journalist. *Remember Me to God* was his first novel.

196. Sourain, Peter. *Miri*. New York: Pantheon Books, 1957.

The title character of this story is a Greek girl who immigrates to the United States, comes under the protection of her wealthy uncle in New York City, and then is sent to an unnamed college in Boston. There, beside the Charles River, she develops romantic leanings toward her male cousin, Lexy, a fellow student. Lexy is in intellectual rebellion against his father, Miri's

benefactor, though his extravagant life-style suggests
that he has not spurned parental financial support.   The
novel is essentially a saga of burgeoning young love, and
the academic aspects of college life seldom intrude in
the plot.

Peter Sourain was born in Boston in 1933.   He received
a B.A. from Harvard in 1955.   *Miri* was his first novel.

197.   Thompson, Charles.   *Halfway Down the Stairs*.   New York:
Harper and Brothers, 1957.

The protagonist of this rapid-fire novel of adolescent
revelry is Dave Pope.   During the middle third of the
book Dave is a student at Cornell.   His time in Ithaca
is spent principally in marijuana parties, three-day
drunks, and sexual escapades.   After Cornell Dave moves
to New York where, eventually, he becomes a businessman.
The story is told in the first person.   Of Cornell Dave
observes: "A lot of people there have big inferiority
complexes about not being at Yale or Princeton--but it's
a damn good thing they aren't because they just wouldn't
make it at Yale or Princeton."   Considering Dave's
aversion to studying one wonders how he manages to graduate even from lowly Cornell.

One of Dave's hard-drinking college buddies is Hugh
Masters.   Toward the end of the story Hugh drowns after
going for an inebriated midnight swim.   The character of
Hugh is modeled after Ken Hutchinson, an actual Cornell
student from 1948 until 1953.   Under other fictive names
Hutchinson appears in Clifford Irving's *On a Darkling
Plain* (191) and in Robert Gutwillig's *After Long Silence*
(198).   Hutchinson, Irving, Gutwillig, and Thomson were
undergraduate compatriots at Cornell.   *Halfway Down the
Stairs* was Charles Thompson's first novel.

198.   Gutwillig, Robert.   *After Long Silence*.   Boston: Little,
Brown and Co., 1958.

This fast-paced first novel begins in the senior year
of Tom Freeman at "Arden University."   Arden is an Ivy
League institution high atop a hill in upstate New York.
Tom, his free-spirited crony Chris Hunt, and a collection
of other Arden seniors spend their time in a continuous
round of parties broken only by sexual interludes.   Midway through the book the action shifts to New York where
Tom and some of his Arden friends obtain entry-level jobs
in the mass media.   Near the close of the story Chris is
killed in an automobile accident and Tom, recently married, enters graduate school.

As an undergraduate at Cornell Robert Gutwillig was a member of a student clique which included Clifford Irving, the author of *On a Darkling Plain* (191), and Robert Thompson, the author of *Halfway Down the Stairs* (197). Also in this social set was Ken Hutchinson, a master of collegiate debauchery, who was killed in an automobile accident in 1953. The character of Chris Hunt in this novel is patterned after Ken Hutchinson. Hutchinson appears, in other fictional guises, in *On a Darkling Plain* and in *Halfway Down the Stairs*.

199. Kozol, Jonathan. *The Fume of Poppies*. Boston: Houghton Mifflin Co., 1958.

Told in the first person by an unnamed Harvard undergraduate, this brief (181-page) story chronicles the narrator's romance with Wendy Allen, a Radcliffe student. The two meet in the lecture hall of Professor Putnam's English 163 course, and their amorous adventures take them to New York, Paris, and Geneva as well as to a furnished room in Cambridge.

Jonathan Kozol received a B.A. from Harvard in 1958, the year in which *The Fume of Poppies* was published. Kozol subsequently became well known as a critic of American public education. His nonfiction work *Death at an Early Age* (Boston: Houghton Mifflin Co., 1967) won the 1968 National Book Award. Based in large part upon Kozol's own experiences as a teacher in Boston, it is generally regarded as a classic expose of American urban public schools.

200. [Miller, Warren]. *The Bright Young Things*. By Amanda Vail (pseud.). Boston: Little, Brown and Co., 1958.

The Bright Young Things is a comic novel about two undergraduates--Emily and Amy--at "Northcliffe College," an institution for women in New England. Emily has an affair with a young businessman in New York City. Amy marries Henry Salem, an instructor of English at the college. Although the book is primarily a study of the girls' love lives and their family relationships, it does contain some interesting academic scenes. On several occasions Henry is depicted in his classroom attempting to acquaint reluctant Northcliffe students with the wonders of literature. And one of the book's ancillary characters, a middle-aged local landlady, is depicted as a font of knowledge about sundry academic subjects since she reads all of the professional journals which her faculty tenants discard.

Warren Miller was born in Stowe, Pennsylvania, in 1921.
He received B.A. and M.A. degrees from the University of
Iowa. The author of eight adult novels and (with Edward
Sorel) three children's books, Miller served during the
late 1950s and early 1960s as literary editor of *The Na-*
tion. Two of his novels, *The Bright Young Things* and
Love Me Little (New York: McGraw-Hill, 1957), were written
under the pseudonym Amanda Vail. *Love Me Little* deals
with the preparatory school exploits of Emily and Amy.
Miller died of lung cancer on April 20, 1966.

201. Mitchner, Stuart. *Let Me Be Awake*. New York: Thomas Y.
       Crowell Co., 1959.

This novel was published after the manuscript won a
"college novel contest" sponsored by the Thomas Y. Crowell
Company. Set at "Allen University," a private institution in Pennsylvania, the book has as its protagonist a
freshman named Vincent Reed. The story tells of Vincent's
gradual self-awakening and of his simultaneous deepening
disillusionment with college life. At the end of his
first year at Allen Vincent leaves for his Indiana home
doubting that he will return. In most respects *Let Me Be*
Awake is a conventional student Bildungsroman. It is
distinguished, however, for including among its characters
one of the best described practitioneers of sexual harassment in American college fiction. Clifford Hartman, a
professor of geography, insists on having co-eds come to
his office for long advisement sessions, during which he
probes their sex lives. He also makes obscene phone
calls to his female students. When the young ladies show
signs of unhappiness over his attentions, Hartman gives
them failing grades and publicly abuses them by offering
sarcastic oral evaluations of their work in class.
     Stuart Mitchner was born in 1938 in Hutchinson, Kansas.
His father was a member of the English department at the
University of Kansas. *Let Me Be Awake* was begun when
Mitchner was a freshman at the University of Indiana.
He received a B.A. from Indiana in 1960. Before he under-
took graduate work at Rutgers in 1968, Mitchner worked
as a college traveler for W.W. Norton.

202. Offord, Lenore Glen. *Angels Unaware*. Philadelphia:
     Macrae, Smith Company, 1940.

The Stevenages, who comprise a faculty family in Berkeley, are happily pursuing their various middle-class
interests when Roland Perry and his teenage son, Victor,
arrive for a weekend visit. Roland is a famous playwright
who was a high school friend of Marion, the lady of the
household. Unknown to the Stevenages, however, Roland
is now dead broke, and he and Victor stay on, and on, and
on. As their guests adopt various ploys to extend their
rent-free sojourn, the Stevenages begin to quarrel among
themselves. Moreover, the family's three children begin
to detest Victor, and Bennet Stevenage, a professor of
history at the University of California, finds Roland so
repulsive that he begins retreating to his campus office
"to outline lectures." Eventually, Roland and Victor
depart, but only after Roland receives a $1,000–per–week
offer of employment from a Hollywood movie studio. The
book contains no on-campus scenes but, on occasion, Bennet Stevenage and the truculently sophisticated Roland
engage in acrimonious discussions about higher education.
Some uncharitable reviewers thought the plot of the novel
more than vaguely reminiscent of the story line of Moss
Hart and George S. Kaufman's 1939 Broadway show, *The Man
Who Came to Dinner*.

Lenore Glen Offord was born in Spokane, Washington,
in 1905. She received a B.A. from Mills College in 1925
and then did graduate work at the University of California
at Berkeley during the 1925–1926 academic year. *Angels
Unaware* was her third novel. Later in her career Ms.
Offord became a book reviewer for *The San Francisco
Chronicle* and a writer of mystery novels. Some of the
latter were published under the pseudonym Theo Durrant.

203.   Ross, Nancy Wilson [Mrs. Stanley Young]. *Take the Light-
       ning*. New York: Harcourt, Brace and Co., 1940.

       Set at a university in the West, this novel deals with
       the tortured efforts of Dalton Errol to retain the affec-
       tions of his wife Corwyn. Dalton is a psychiatrist who
       teaches in the university's psychology department. On
       a part-time basis he also counsels disturbed students.
       Corwyn is a beautiful but neurotic artist who married
       Dalton after living in Paris with Stephen Aldrich, an
       expatriate American painter. After her Paris escapades
       Corwyn finds the university, and Errol, dull and unsatis-
       fying. The plot thickens when Stephen pays the Daltons
       an unexpected visit. But just when it seems as though
       Corwyn is about to leave with Stephen, she contracts
       severe pneumonia. During her long recuperation she
       realizes that her place is with Dalton. At the close of
       the story, Stephen has gone and Corwyn is preparing for
       happy and contented faculty wifedom. Though the book
       concentrates on the Errols' convulsive domestic affairs,
       there are many passages about the academic side of Dal-
       ton's life. In particular, the story includes a sub-
       plot which focuses upon the problems of a therapeutically
       oriented psychiatrist in a psychology department domin-
       ated by theorists.
       Nancy Wilson Ross was born in Olympia, Washington, in
       1910. She attended the University of Oregon. Married
       to the noted playwright Stanley Young, she was a prolific
       author of both fiction and nonfiction. *Take the Lightning*
       was her second novel.

*204.   Watkin, Lawrence Edward. *Geese in the Forum*. New York:
       Alfred A. Knopf, 1940.

       Set at "Beauregard University," an up-and-coming insti-
       tution in the South, this often satirical novel follows
       the attempts of John Burgess, a Yankee professor of his-
       tory, to adjust to academic life below the Mason-Dixon
       Line. Although the North versus South aspects of the
       book are pervasive, they by no means monopolize the
       plot. Another major theme is the attempt by the insti-
       tution's president, "Burkeyboy" Burkholder, to bring
       Beauregard into the modern corporate age. An assiduous
       reader of higher education journals, President Burkholder
       continually diverts resources from the liberal arts in
       order to develop "schools" of business, architecture,
       and engineering. The latter is particularly distinguished.
       Five years after its inception one of its graduates actu-
       ally "gets a job on a Warner Brothers' soundtruck in

Hollywood." When Burkholder tries to start a "school of citizenship," to "train men to lead the mob in the right direction," the remnants of his liberal arts staff rebel and after considerable furor Burkholder is forced to relinquish his office.

Lawrence Edward Watkin received an A.B. from Syracuse University in 1924 and an A.M. from Harvard in 1925. From 1926 until he entered the navy in 1942 he was a member of the English department at Washington and Lee. After the war Watkin became a Hollywood screenwriter, working principally for Walt Disney Studios. In 1965 he became a professor of English at the University of California at Fullerton. He remained at Fullerton until his retirement in 1970. *Geese in the Forum* was his second novel. His first novel, *On Borrowed Time* (New York: Alfred A. Knopf, 1937), won extensive critical praise and was later adapted for the stage by Paul Osborn.

205. Basso, Hamilton. *Wine of the Country*. New York: Charles Scribner's Sons, 1941.

Tait Ravenwill, a young anthropologist, returns to "Chadhurst College" after more than a year of research in Polynesia. Chadhurst is a picturesque institution in New England. Tait stays at Chadhurst long enough to marry Ellen, the orphaned niece of Anthony Prescott, his department chairman. Then he obtains yet another year's leave, this one to write a book about his research. Tait takes Ellen to his rural South Carolina home where he spreads out his notes and begins the great opus. Poor Ellen attempts to adjust to the heat, and to Tait's rustic relatives, but she yearns for the year to end. One broiling day, just as Ellen's spirits have reached their nadir, Tait announces that he has resigned from Chadhurst and intends, henceforth and forever more, to stay in South Carolina and become a farmer. Ellen commits suicide by drowning herself in a nearby swamp. Only the first third of the novel takes place at Chadhurst, but because Ellen continually pines for the cool, invigorating air of New England there are many references to the college in the latter portions of the story. Anthony Prescott, Ellen's uncle, is portrayed as a dedicated scholar whose office and home are filled with skulls, native ceremonial masks, and other mementoes of "red-eyed half-men growling in evolutionary ooze." Tait Ravenwill, though not especially interested in teaching, is an indefatigable researcher. Just as Ellen begins to loathe his South Carolina domicile, Tait forces her to accompany him on nocturnal trips in the woods where he studies the sounds of the local natives' "voodoo drums."

Hamilton Basso was born in 1904 in New Orleans. He
attended Tulane University from 1922 until 1926 but left
without graduating. Much of his adult life was spent in
the magazine business. At the time *Wine of the Country*,
his sixth novel, was published, Basso was an associate
editor of *The New Yorker*.

206. Kempton, Kenneth Payson. *So Dream All Night*. New York:
     G.P. Putnam's Sons, 1941.

Set at Harvard, this quiet, poignant novel spans eighteen years in the life of Oliver Richmond and his wife,
Kent. Oliver is a member of the Harvard department of
English. The book is divided into three sections. The
first describes Oliver's early days at Harvard. Brimming
with youthful enthusiasm, he does battle with his obnoxious department chairman, loses, and is marked as a
non-promising young man. The second section, which takes
place approximately a decade later, deals with Oliver's
brief romance with a young woman who soon dies of cancer.
The third section, which brings the action to 1938, focuses primarily on Oliver's search for Carol, the Richmond's teenage daughter, who runs away in rebellion
against her parents. The Depression is making inroads
into Harvard's fiscal viability during this section, and
the university is dismissing many of its less distinguished
faculty. Without a strong publication record, Oliver
fears for his job. At the end of the novel he receives
a long, official envelope marked with the Harvard seal.
He does not open the envelope before the book ends, but
readers have few doubts about its contents.
    Kenneth Payson Kempton received a B.A. from Harvard in
1912. From 1912 until his death in 1955 he was a member
of the Harvard department of English. *So Dream All Night*
was his third novel.

207. Walworth, Dorothy [Mrs. Merle Crowell]. *Feast of Reason*.
     New York: Farrar and Rinehart, 1941.

The protagonist of this unusual academic story is Susan
Laird, the fortyish, all-purpose dean at "Future Junior
College." Future Junior is an ultra-progressive institution for young ladies. A cheerful individual, despite
a crippled foot which causes her to walk with a permanent
limp, Susan runs afoul of Lily Pardee, the school's
domineering president. One of very few women presidents
in college fiction, Lily raises sexual harassment to a
high art. Widowed and lonely, she attempts to seduce

Silas Brown, an instructor of English. By way of in-
centive, Lily offers Silas an administrative post if he
will yield to her charms. But Silas has eyes only for
Susan and he declines Lily's invitation. Lily then
terminates Silas' contract and that of Susan as well.
At this point the students of Future Junior, unhappy over
the loss of a popular teacher and a popular dean, threaten
to leave the school en masse. The trustees rescind Lily's
firings, dismiss her, and offer the presidency to Susan.
Feast of Reason is primarily a satire but there are some
semi-serious passages in the text about curriculum matters. And, in addition to her characterizations of
Susan, Lily, and Silas, the author offers portraits of a
number of other Future Junior faculty and staff.

Born in 1900, Dorothy Walworth graduated from Vassar
in 1920. Married to a senior editor of *The Readers Di-
gest*, she published nine novels before her death in 1953.
Walworth made one adult foray into academe. During the
1937-1938 academic year she served as dean of curriculum
at Briarcliff Junior College in Briarcliff Manor, New
York.

208.   Wilson, William Edward. *Yesterday's Son*. New York:
       Farrar and Rinehart, 1941.

Twenty years before the start of this epic John Corey,
then a twenty-one-year-old graduate of "Conrad University,"
had an affair with Jessica Pindar, the young wife of a
wealthy banker. As *Yesterday's Son* opens John, now an
associate professor of English at Conrad, is reading the
class roll for a section of freshman English. Right
between Peterson and Prosser on the list is Pindar, L.J.,
who turns out, of course, to be John's son from the now
nearly forgotten liaison. Most of the book consists of
denouements, wherein everyone of consequence finds out
everything of importance. But academic readers will
appreciate the fact that John plays no favorites and
fails L.J. (Lawrence Jewitt) when he turns in an abysmal
end-of-term examination. And they may appreciate, as
well, the rich streams of irony which run throughout the
book. John, once tabbed by his mentors a budding genius,
is now a man struggling to avoid professional stagnation
while his son L.J., who is bright but uninterested in
scholarship, shows great promise of leading an exciting
and profitable life outside of academe.

William Edward Wilson was born in Evansville, Indiana,
in 1906. He received an A.B. from Harvard in 1927 and
an A.M. from Harvard in 1930. *Yesterday's Son* was his

first novel. At the time the book was published Wilson
was chairman of the English department at the Rhode
Island School of Design. In later years Wilson became
a professor of English at Indiana University and a well-
respected writer of historical novels and nonfiction
works about the American Midwest.

209.   Baker, Dorothy. *Trio*. Boston: Houghton Mifflin Co.,
       1943.

       Janet Logan, a twenty-three-year-old graduate student
at a Western university, is torn between her love for
Ray Mackenzie, another graduate student, and her fear of
Pauline Maury, a middle-aged lesbian professor of French
who demands Janet's full devotion. A victim of sexual
harassment, Janet knows that Pauline will ruin her career
if she reverts to heterosexuality and marries Ray. It
is all resolved neatly, however. Pauline, it seems, has
plagiarized her most recent book. When this becomes
known and her own career is destroyed, Pauline commits
suicide. The portrait of Pauline as a desperate female
academic trying frantically to hold her young student
lover is especially well drawn.
       Dorothy Baker received an A.B. from the University of
California at Los Angeles in 1929 and an M.A. from the
same institution in 1934. Her first novel, *Young Man
with a Horn* (Boston: Houghton Mifflin Co., 1938), won
wide critical acclaim. *Trio*, her second novel, was
generally praised by reviewers but the book was banned
from some libraries because of its lesbian theme.

210.   Seifert, Elizabeth [Mrs. Elizabeth Seifert Gasparotti].
       Bright Banners. New York: Grosset and Dunlap, 1943.

       The time is World War II and Liz Arnette, a new Ph.D.
in psychology, joins the faculty of "Bethel University."
Liz' job is to counsel army officer candidates in training on the campus. Possessed of considerable beauty,
Liz soon marries Greg Adams, famous young professor of
chemistry. No sooner is the honeymoon over, however,
than Greg's neurotic sister-in-law falsely accuses him
of fathering her child. Then Greg has a near fatal
accident in his laboratory. By the end of the book the
sister-in-law has been sent packing, Greg has recovered,
and Liz has retired from the university to become a
faculty wife. The book's secondary characters include
a Neanderthal dean who, in the interests of academic
purity, tries to keep Greg from doing war-related

research, and a prudish old-maid professor of music whose
cranky disposition acts as a counterweight in the plot to
Liz' youthful vitality.

Born in 1897, Elizabeth Seifert Gasparotti received a
Ph.D. in 1918 from Washington University of St. Louis.
After her graduation she took a position as a clinical
secretary in a hospital. Married, with four children,
she did not begin writing professionally until 1938.
Bright Banners was her ninth novel. Despite her late
start as a writer she compiled an extensive oeuvre. She
published more than fifty novels, most of them light romances about doctors and other medical personnel.

211. Wetherell, June Pat [Mrs. Daniel Frame]. *But That Was
    Yesterday*. New York: E.P. Dutton and Co., 1943.

Jinx and Stephen Ferris are a faculty couple at "Danville College," a small, private institution in Minnesota.
Stephen is a plodding professor of English and Jinx sometimes questions the wisdom of her choice of mate. Jinx
is startled to learn that Mike Logan, famous foreign
correspondent and author, is scheduled to deliver a
lecture at the college. A decade earlier Jinx and Mike
were sweethearts during their undergraduate days at
"Kulshan College" in the Pacific Northwest. Will Mike
remember Jinx? Will he, perhaps, try to carry her away
from academe and into his glamorous life? In fact, Mike
doesn't get the chance to rekindle the old romance. His
lecture--a laudatory review of Adolph Hitler's accomplish-
ments in Germany--revolts Jinx. Moreover, since Mike's
talk is given on the night of December 6, 1941, his
ideas have even less appeal for Jinx by mid-afternoon of
the next day. After Jinx sees the kind of man Mike has
become, Stephen doesn't seem so bad after all. The first
and last parts of this novel are set at Danville. The
central portion flashes back to Kulshan. The Kulshan
section includes some negative depictions of sorority
life.

June Pat Wetherell was born in 1909 in Bellingham,
Washington. After beginning her studies at the Western
Washington College of Education she received a B.A. from
the University of Washington. She then entered newspaper
work in Seattle and began to produce a steady stream of
romantic novels, some of which were published under the
name Patricia Frame. *But That Was Yesterday* was her
third novel. A later Wetherell novel, *Run Sheep Run*
(174), also is included in this bibliography.

*212. Guerard, Albert Joseph. *The Hunted*. New York: Alfred
       A. Knopf, 1944.

       The Hunted is a dark, brooding novel which probes the
       insularity, status-striving, and rumor-mongering of small
       college life. John Richmond, a professor of English at
       "Hollis College" in New England, marries Claire, a wait-
       ress from a local restaurant. Although both attempt to
       bridge the gap in their social and intellectual back-
       grounds, the local faculty ladies make the former wait-
       ress' life unbearable. Eventually John and his wife be-
       gin to distrust each other's marital fidelity. The
       climax occurs when Claire offers assistance to a badly
       hurt prison escapee who breaks into their home. Thinking
       that Claire's actions are prompted more by sexual attrac-
       tion than by humanitarianism, John turns the escapee over
       to the police. On that note Claire and John permanently
       part company. All the action in the second half of the
       book takes place during a violent rainstorm and flood.
       The year is 1940, and the whole novel transpires against
       the backdrop of worsening war news from Europe.
       Albert Joseph Guerard received a B.A. from the Uni-
       versity of California in 1934, an M.A. from Harvard in
       1936, and a Ph.D. from California in 1938. He was a
       member of the English department at Harvard when *The
       Hunted* was published. In 1961 he became a professor of
       literature at Stanford.

213.   Gessner, Robert. *Youth is the Time*. New York: Charles
       Scribner's Sons, 1945.

       This sometimes farcical satire is set at "Metropolitan
       University," an institution located in New York City.
       The protagonist is Christopher Nash, a young man who
       comes fresh from Harvard to join the university's English
       department. At first, Christopher finds his students
       bellicose and uncontrollable. He thinks of quitting.
       But then he thinks again, stays on, and eventually wins
       the students' confidence. The problem, Christopher dis-
       covers, is Metropolitan's outdated "medievalist" cur-
       riculum. He tears up the reading list of "97 great
       books" he is supposed to inflict upon his classes and,
       instead, leads his charges on trips through Gotham in
       search of useful knowledge. Christopher's Deweyesque
       teaching methods bring him into conflict with his faculty
       colleagues and he is fired. At the end of the story
       Christopher moves on, presumably to a more progressive
       bastion of higher learning. His former students, one

assumes, will now begin their study of the classics under someone else's tutelage. The book is one of few college novels to deal intensively with curricular matters. It contains many classroom scenes and a great number of derogatory characterizations of Metropolitan's faculty members and administrators.

Robert Gessner was born in Escanaba, Michigan, in 1907. He received an undergraduate degree from the University of Michigan and an M.A. from Columbia. A screenwriter as well as a novelist, Gessner was a professor of motion pictures at New York University when *Youth is the Time* was published. He died in 1968.

*214.   Howe, Helen [Mrs. Alfred Reginald Allen]. *We Happy Few*. New York: Simon and Schuster, 1946.

The protagonist of this bitter, sometimes satirical novel is Dorothea Calcott, the scheming wife of John Calcott, a professor of history and literature at Harvard. An inveterate hostess, Dorothea tries to maneuver her reluctant husband into the position of master of Bromfield House. But when World War II breaks out in Europe, John joins the British navy and goes down with his ship. Dorothea begins to comprehend the shallow nature of her former life, takes a volunteer job in a hospital, and has an unsatisfactory affair with an old flame from her girlhood. Late in the book, and late in World War II as well, Dorothea's son, John Jr., enlists in the American navy. Her hair rapidly whitening, the sad-but-wiser Dorothea hopes that John Jr. will not be killed. The first portion of the novel, during which Dorothea acts as Harvard's social lioness, contains many well-itemized portraits of various Harvard faculty and their wives. And the party scenes, during which Dorothea is a font of snobbish good cheer, are among the most graphic descriptions of faculty social gatherings in American college fiction.

Helen Howe was born in Boston in 1905. She attended Radcliffe for one year. A monologist as well as a writer, Howe appeared throughout the United States in a one-woman show of character sketches of famous personages. She performed twice at the White House. *We Happy Few* was her second novel. Helen Howe died in 1975.

215.   Beresford-Howe, Constance. *Of This Day's Journey*. New York: Dodd, Mead and Co., 1947.

The protagonists of this especially intriguing academic romance are Camilla Brant, a beautiful, twenty-five-year-old

instructor of English from Canada, and Andrew Cameron,
the thirty-eight-year-old president of "Blake University."
Cameron is married to a woman who has become paralyzed
from the waist down through some unspecified misfortune.
He maintains physical contact with his wife by giving her
nightly backrubs, but these do little to relieve his
sexual tensions. When Camilla arrives at Blake, she and
Cameron fight a growing mutual attraction until one day
they meet on a deserted country road and consummate their
passion. Camilla begs Cameron to go away with her. After
giving agonizing debate to the matter, Cameron declines.
The fact which tips the balance in his decision-making is
not the prospect of deserting his crippled wife. Rather,
Cameron finds he cannot bear the thought of leaving his
presidency. The novel concludes with Camilla departing
Blake forever. She leaves on an evening train. Alone in
his presidential office, brooding in the dark, Cameron
listens forlornly to the sound of the train's whistle
fading in the distance.

    Born in Montreal in 1922, Constance Beresford-Howe re-
ceived a B.A. from McGill University in 1945 and a Ph.D.
from Brown in 1950. At the time *Of This Day's Journey*
was published she was a lecturer in English at McGill.
Of This Day's Journey was her second novel. A later
Beresford-Howe novel, *The Book of Eve* (Boston: Little,
Brown and Co., 1974), won the Canadian Booksellers' annual
award. After more than twenty years on the McGill faculty, Beresford-Howe moved to Toronto in 1970 to become a
professor of English at Ryerson Polytechnical Institute.

216.   DeCapite, Michael. *The Bennett Place*. New York: The
        John Day Co., 1948.

    This fine spun novel is set in "Sparta," Ohio, the site
of the "University of Sparta." Katherine Bennett, the
last direct descendant of the university's founder, is an
aging, reclusive spinster who lives alone in the old
family homestead. One lovely autumn day Katherine retreats to her bedroom, raises a pistol to her head, and
blows out her brains. Katherine's suicide occurs in the
first chapter. The remainder of the book deals with six
members of the Sparta community as they attempt to explain
and/or adjust to her self-destruction. Among the mourners
are George Mather and Paul Brown, two professors. George,
a historian, once had a romance with Katherine. Paul, a
professor of English, admired Katherine for the poetry
which she wrote and read to him for criticism during
secret meetings in her home. George and Paul are both

academic mediocrities. Once a promising scholar, George
is now professionally static. Paul is an unsuccessful
creative writer. Katherine's death has no significant
impact upon the day-to-day operations of the university.
But for George and Paul, and for the other, non-university
characters upon whom the author focuses, her demise serves
as a forceful reminder of their own failures.

Michael DeCapite was born in Cleveland in 1915. He
received a B.A. in 1938 from Ohio University in Athens,
Ohio. After graduating from Ohio University, DeCapite
entered newspaper work and eventually became a press
officer for the United Nations. *The Bennett Place* was
his third novel.

217. Hedden, Worth Tuttle. *The Other Room*. New York: Crown
Publishers, 1947.

Nina Latham, a White girl from the rural South, graduates from Columbia in the late 1920s. Through an employment agency she obtains a teaching post at "Willard College" in New Orleans. When Nina arrives at Willard she
finds, to her horror, that it is an institution for
Blacks. She is tempted to leave on the first train but
decides, instead, to stay until she can acquire another
position. From that point the novel deals primarily with
Nina's growing empathy with her Black students and with
her romantic attraction to a Black faculty colleague.
The Other Room is steeped in moral messages. One of the
author's aims, among many, is to demonstrate that Blacks,
if given the opportunity, can be as cultured as Whites.
Hence most of the Black characters in the novel speak in
what would now be called "perfect standard English" while
many of the Whites, particularly those in the community
around the Willard campus, converse in heavy redneck
dialect.

Worth Tuttle Hedden was born in 1896 in Raleigh, North
Carolina. She received an A.B. in 1916 from Trinity
College (now Duke University) and then did graduate work
for a year at Columbia. After leaving Columbia she became an active worker for women's rights and an assistant
to Norman Thomas, the Socialist Party's perennial candi-
date for president. *The Other Room*, her second novel,
was praised by most reviewers, though more for its moral
intentions than for its execution.

218.   MacRae, Donald. *Dwight Craig*. Boston: Houghton Mifflin
         Co., 1947.

         This novel could well have been subtitled "The Making
of a College President." The title character is followed
from his childhood in a small Midwestern town to his ac-
cession to the presidency of "Western State University."
An orphan, Dwight is raised by an eccentric aunt, and he
finds it difficult to establish meaningful relationships
with his peers. After majoring in English at a local
college he obtains a teaching post in a high school, but
he finds that he detests students. When his aunt dies
Dwight does not visit her on her deathbed because he has
better things to do. Nonetheless, she leaves him a small
legacy which he uses to attend graduate school. He takes
a doctorate in education at "a great prairie university,"
and then stays on after graduation as a member of the
university's faculty. An accomplished amateur actor,
Dwight puts showmanship to work in his college classes
and becomes a popular instructor. He also writes a book
propounding the virtues of "dynamic totalism" in education. Whatever that philosophy may be--it is not explained
at any great length in the narrative--critics denounce it
as "phony liberalism." His book brings Dwight notoriety.
He moves to Western State as a full professor, marries
a socially prominent local lady, and by utilizing his
social connections he quickly manages to be named president. The last chapter offers a glimpse of Dwight a year
or so after he has become Western's chief executive. He
is visited in his home by an old graduate-school friend,
now a professor at another institution. The friend intends to stay for a few hours. But after observing
Dwight's wife, now in a perpetual state of hysteria from
her husband's constant browbeatings, and after listening
to Dwight's incessant egocentric prattle, the friend makes
a hasty exit.
         At the time *Dwight Craig* was published Donald MacRae
was a member of the English department at Reed College
in Oregon. The book won the 1947 Houghton Mifflin Literary Fellowship Award.

219.   Miller, Nolan. *The Merry Innocents*. New York: Harper
         and Brothers, 1947.

         The "merry innocents" in this novel are the Lowrys, a
relentlessly pleasant academic family. Papa Lowry, a
professor of English at "Holtby College" in Michigan,
presides over a household made up of a wife, four

adolescent children, and a Black maid named Julia. The action takes place over a Christmas vacation. Professor Lowry vows to catch up on his writing but various domestic harassments intervene. Wife Lillian constantly runs out of cigarettes, his children experience various upheavals in their social lives, and Julia runs afoul of racial bigotry in the town. Then, too, there are those obligatory faculty parties which fill the Lowrys' Christmas calendar. Through it all Julia remains the family's pillar of strength. Although the book is written as a cheerful study of academic domestic life, some readers may find that it contains an element of mystery. How can a professor of English with a large family afford a maid?

Nolan Miller received an A.B. from Wayne State University in 1929 and an M.A. from the same institution in 1940. *The Merry Innocents* was his second novel. At the time the book was published Miller was a member of the English department at Antioch College. Another novel by Miller, *Why I Am So Beat* (187), also appears in this bibliography.

220.   Mitchell, Ronald Elwy. *Design for November*. New York: Harper and Brothers, 1947.

The first half of *Design for November* is a conventional novel of academic manners. Set at "Creston University" in the Midwest, the story has as its protagonists Sam and Catherine Forrester. Sam is a graduate assistant in the art department, at a salary of $750 per year, and his wife is pregnant. Dr. Smithson, chairman of the art department, implies that Sam will soon be promoted to instructor at double his current salary. However, a recently arrived European emigre, one Dr. Konopka, is given the post instead. At this point the book is transformed from a study of manners into an academic morality tale. Catherine murders Dr. Konopka by secretly slipping poison into his drink. Sam gets the instructorship, but only a few months after does Catherine inform him that it was she who killed Konopka. Not a man to turn his back on a loyal spouse, ·Sam keeps silent. Shortly thereafter Catherine falls down a flight of stairs and both she and her unborn child are killed. At the end of the book Sam accepts a job with a decorating firm in New York, where he hopes to forget about his dismal experiences in academe.

Ronald Elwy Mitchell was born in London, England, in 1905. He received his undergraduate training at Kings

College, University of London. He also studied at Yale.
At the time *Design for November* was published Mitchell was
a professor of speech and theater at the University of
Wisconsin. Although *Design for November* was his first
novel, Mitchell had previously published a number of
dramas. *Design for November* was based upon *The Kindest
People*, one of Mitchell's early plays.

*221.   Nathan, Robert Gruntal. *Mr. Whittle and the Morning
        Star*. New York: Alfred A. Knopf, 1947.

This brief (175-page) and whimsical novel is among the
most entertaining and best-written studies of male faculty
middle-age identity crisis in college fiction. The protagonist is Robert Whittle, a fortyish professor of history at "Caraway College" in "Rivertown." Henpecked by
his wife, embarrassed by his low salary, and disgusted
by Dr. Amaders Thirkel, the school's bombastic president,
Whittle suddenly comes to the conclusion that the world
is about to end. One night, after a short and unplanned
dalliance with a co-ed, Whittle walks down to the river
to wait for the big event. It begins to rain; Whittle
catches cold; and in semi-delirium he has a long philosophical discussion with God, who resembles Dr. Thirkel.
Stumbling home the next morning, Whittle reluctantly
realizes that the world will continue. He goes to bed
with pneumonia, survives a fevered crisis, and awakes
to hear his wife scold: "Can't you wear your rubbers,
at least, when you go out in the rain?" No precis can
capture the full flavor of this book. Through epigrammatic passages the author comments on college administrators, the frustrations of teaching, genteel poverty, and
many other matters of relevance to academics.
        Robert Nathan entered Harvard in 1912 but left after
three years. He then worked for a brief period in the
advertising industry. During the 1924-1925 academic
year he was a lecturer in journalism at New York University. Most of his career, however, was devoted to
writing. A master of satirical fantasy, Nathan wrote
more than fifty books of fiction, poetry, and stories.
His first novel, *Peter Kindred* (65), is included in this
bibliography.

222.   Redinger, Ruby Virginia. *The Golden Net*. New York:
        Crown Publishers, 1948.

When beauteous Marcia Anderson arrives to teach English
at "John Willard College" in Ohio she immediately comes

to the attention of John Willard himself. The son of the
school's founder, John is chairman of Willard's board of
trustees and a multi-millionaire. John asks Marcia to
marry him, but he demands that she leave teaching to become a housewife. Though tempted by his offer, Marcia
refuses to give up her career, and John looks elsewhere
for female companionship. This disconcerting experience
behind her, Marcia agrees to marry a colleague in the
Willard English department. He may be poor, but he has
no objection to her staying on in the classroom. *The
Golden Net* fairly bursts its bindings with engaging, if
stereotypic portraits of various academic types. And
its many sub-plots deal with issues such as prejudice
against Jewish faculty members, trustee-administration
relationships, and the influx of officer candidates to
college campuses during World War II.

Ruby Virginia Redinger received a B.A. from Fenn College
in 1936 and a Ph.D. from Western Reserve University in
1940. She was an associate professor of English at Fenn
College when *The Golden Net*, her first novel, was published.

223. Ward, Mary Jane [Mrs. Edward Quayle]. *The Professor's
      Umbrella*. New York: Random House, 1948.

Set at "Tamarack University," a private institution
in the Midwest, this curious novel begins as a rather
conventional story about an assistant professor's quiet
professional life. As the book continues, however, we
find that the protagonist, Gregory Kitner, is Jewish
and that Tamarack's president, George Norton, dislikes
Jews. After Kitner is unjustly accused of consorting
with a co-ed, Norton seizes upon the opportunity to fire
him. Though Norton justifies his action on the grounds
of Kitner's "immorality," readers (and Kitner) know that
the act really is prompted by anti-Semitism. The title
of the book refers to the umbrella which Kitner carries
when he courts Harriet Hough, a faculty colleague, during rainstorms. Kitner's discipline is English. At the
end of the book he is about to marry Harriet and, even
though he has been offered an extremely lucrative position with a publisher, he is planning to take up a new
teaching position at a small college in Kansas.

Another novel by Mary Jane Ward, *The Tree Has Roots*
(151), appears in this bibliography.

224. Moon, Bucklin. *Without Magnolias*. Garden City, New
      York: Doubleday and Co., 1949.

      Set in Citrus City, Florida, during World War II, this
      novel describes the anger and frustration of Blacks in
      a Jim Crow environment. The book is kaleidoscopic in
      format. The plot touches upon the lives of a great number
      of Citrus City's Black citizens, but the largest portion
      of the story centers on members of the administration and
      faculty at a local college for Blacks. The administrator
      who is followed most closely is Ezekial Rogers, the insti-
      tution's Black president. Although Rogers is outwardly
      obsequious to the school's White trustees, he suffers
      great internal anguish over the racial injustices with
      which he must contend. The faculty member given most
      attention is Eric Gardner, a Black sociologist educated
      at the University of Chicago. Although Gardner is hardly
      a radical, even by the standards of the 1940s, he is less
      willing than Rogers to turn the other cheek. The story
      has its climax when Gardner writes a letter to the local
      newspaper. The letter implies that America's dropping
      of atomic bombs on Japan was prompted by racism. Under
      pressure from his White overlords, President Rogers re-
      luctantly fires Gardner. The book ends with Gardner re-
      turning to the North and with Rogers tendering his resig-
      nation. *Without Magnolias* offers considerable detail
      about the rituals and coping strategies of Southern Black
      colleges in the 1940s, and scholars interested in the
      history of higher education for Blacks in America will
      find the book to be of significant interest.
          Bucklin Moon was born in Eau Claire, Wisconsin, in
      1911. After graduating from Rollins College in Florida
      he went to New York City where he entered the publishing
      business. *Without Magnolias* was his second novel. At
      the time the book was published Moon was an editor at
      Doubleday and Co.

225. Wilson, Mitchell. *Live with Lightning*. Boston: Little,
      Brown and Co., 1949.

      This fast-moving, panoramic novel follows the life and
      times of Erik Gorin, a physicist, from his graduate
      school days at Columbia in the 1930s through his rise
      to prominence as an atomic scientist during World War II.
      Along the way Erik stops off at a number of universi-
      ties, research laboratories, and private industrial con-
      cerns. He also marries and, while remaining loyal to
      his wife, has an additional amorous relationship with a

female colleague at the University of Chicago. The book
contains portraits of a variety of academic scientists.
These include an evil department chairman, an over-the-
hill but benevolent big-name physicist, and Erik's afore-
mentioned female workmate whose professional advancement
is thwarted because of rampant sexism in America's scientific community. The novel also deals with anti-
Semitism on campus, the exploitation of research assis-
tants, and the moral implications of work on atomic
weaponry.

Mitchell Wilson received a B.A. from New York University
in 1934 and an M.A. from Columbia in 1938. Early in his
career he taught physics at Columbia and at City College
of New York. Wilson then became a physicist in private
industry until deciding, in 1954, to devote his full
energies to writing. *Live with Lightning* was his sixth
novel. The book was a selection of the Literary Guild
and, published in both hardbound and paperback editions,
it sold more than one million copies.

226. Taylor, Robert Lewis. *Professor Fodorski*. Garden City,
New York: Doubleday, Doran and Co., 1950.

The title character of this pleasant farce is Stanislaus
Fodorski, a refugee professor of engineering who arrives
in the United States with $140, an ability to speak frac-
tured English, and an eternally sunny disposition. Through
his one American friend Fodorski obtains a job at the
"Southern Baptist Institute of Technology" ("SBIT"), in
South Carolina. There he puts his engineering knowledge
to use designing plays for the school's football team.
With Fodorski's help, the SBIT Unicorns have an unbeaten
season and defeat Notre Dame in the Finger Bowl. At the
end of the book the institute offers Fodorski a ten-year
contract as head coach at half again his professorial
salary. Fodorski refuses the job, on the naive grounds
that football coaches should not earn more money than
faculty members. In order to induce Fodorski to take the
position, the institute gives all of its faculty a fifty-
percent raise.

Robert Lewis Taylor received an A.B. from the University
of Illinois in 1933. After a brief career in the newspaper business he became a profile writer for *The New
Yorker* in 1939. He was on the staff of *The New Yorker*
when *Professor Fodorski* was published. A later Taylor
novel, *The Travels of Jamie McPheeters* (Garden City, New
York: Doubleday and Co., 1958), won the 1959 Pulitzer Prize
for fiction.

227.   Gies, Joseph Cornelius. *A Matter of Morals*. New York:
       Harper and Brothers, 1951.

       A Matter of Morals is an academic freedom novel set in
       1938 at a Midwestern state university. The protagonist
       is Victor Townsend, an assistant professor of history.
       Victor rises to a mild and belated defense of three left-
       of-center students who are expelled from the university
       for organizing a rally to protest Hitler's invasion of
       Czechoslovakia. As Victor finds to his sorrow, the uni-
       versity's administration fears domestic leftists more
       than European fascists, and he loses out on an impending
       promotion. Upgraded to associate professor instead is
       Arthur Wheeler, Townsend's friend and colleague, who
       takes no particular stand on anything of consequence.
       Indeed, not long afterward Wheeler is made chairman of
       the history department. The book contains a number of
       sub-plots--including a brief and unhappy romance between
       the married Victor and the departmental secretary--and
       it contains many effective portraits of faculty and
       administrators. It also touches upon academic anti-
       Semitism. The three students expelled from the university,
       from among many the administration could have selected
       for dismissal, are all Jewish.
           Joseph Cornelius Gies received a B.A. from the Uni-
       versity of Michigan in 1939. *A Matter of Morals* was his
       second novel. At the time the book was published Gies
       was copy chief of *This Week* magazine. In 1965 Gies be-
       came a senior editor at Doubleday and Co.

228.   Pember, Timothy. *Swanson*. New York: Harcourt, Brace
       and Co., 1951.

       This novel chronicles the decline and fall of Humphrey
       Swanson, a bachelor professor of English at a university
       in California. A native of Great Britain, Humphrey has
       been in America for more than a decade and, by publishing
       extensively, he has become the star of his department.
       The only cloud in his otherwise sunny life is his land-
       lady, with whom he carries on a running feud. One day
       the landlady unexpectedly enters his room while he is
       in an incipient stage of dressing, and she publicly ac-
       cuses him of exposing himself in her presence. The uni-
       versity president immediately dismisses Humphrey, and
       when he goes to jail for his "crime" only Margot Rich-
       mond, the wife of one of his departmental colleagues,
       risks public censure by visiting him. Margot and Hum-
       phrey then have a post-prison romance, which Humphrey

supports by bagging groceries in a supermarket. At the
end of the book Humphrey tries to stop a robbery at the
store, but confusion reigns and he is arrested as an
accomplice in the holdup. The book is written with utmost
seriousness. Reviews were mixed. Some critics considered
it an insightful character study. Others thought it a
tepid, humorless satire.

Born in Great Britain, Timothy Pember was widely ac-
claimed for his first novel, *The Needle's Eye* (New York:
Reynal and Hitchcock, 1947). *Swanson* was his second
novel.

*229. Brace, Gerald Warner. *The Spire*. New York: W.W. Norton
and Co., 1952.

This well-constructed novel is set at "Wyndham College,"
a high-status institution in upper New England. The protagonist, Henry Gaunt, is recuited to teach English at
the college and the story covers his one eventful year
on the Wyndham campus. Henry is in his late thirties,
has already acquired a scholarly reputation during a
decade as a member of the faculty at Columbia, and is a
longtime friend of Wyndham's president, David Gidney.
When Wyndham's dean submits a sudden resignation, Gidney
asks Henry to assume the post. Henry reluctantly agrees
to do so and much of the book deals with his problems as
an administrator. Of more significance to the plot,
however, is Henry's romance with Lizzie Houghton, President Gidney's secretary. Lizzie is something of the community pariah. In her checkered past she gave birth to
an illegitimate child--now dead--and both she and Henry
know that Wyndham will never accept her as a dean's wife.
Thus, when Lizzie and Henry agree to be married, Henry
immediately accepts a new position in Oregon. *The Spire*
is written with a sympathetic concern for its characters
and with serious attention to academic detail.

Gerald Warner Brace received a B.A. from Amherst in
1922 and a Ph.D. from Harvard in 1930. During a long
and distinguished academic career he taught English at
Williams, Dartmouth, Mount Holyoke, Harvard, and Boston
University. At the time *The Spire* was published Brace
was professor of English at Boston University. *The Spire*
was Brace's sixth novel. One of his later works, *The
Department* (371), also is included in this bibliography.
Henry Gaunt appears as a young man growing up in rural
Vermont in an earlier Brace novel, *Light on the Mountain*
(New York: G.P. Putnam's Sons, 1941).

230. Macauley, Robie Mayhew. *The Disguises of Love*. New
      York: Random House, 1952.

      The Disguises of Love is centered upon an affair be-
      tween Howard Greame, a married professor of psychology,
      and Frances Mitchell, a seductive student in one of his
      classes. Although the book's premise is routine, the
      writing is well above average for illicit-professorial-
      romance novels and the work has an unusual format. The
      four principal characters--Howard, Frances, Howard's
      aggrieved wife Helen, and the Greames' precocious sixteen-
      year-old son, Gordon--take turns narrating the story.
      The setting is "Creston University," a private institution
      in Michigan which is supported in large part by funds
      from the Creston automobile empire. Creston University
      is noteworthy for the efficiency of its gossip network.
      Almost before Helen is aware that her husband is suffering
      from wanderitis her friends are providing her with details
      about Frances' height, mode of dress, and hairstyle.
      Toward the end of the book Frances decides that it "won't
      work," and she abruptly ends her relationship with Howard.
      He returns to Helen and Gordon, but none of the Greames
      is especially thrilled about the reconstitution of their
      family.
          Born in 1919, Robie Mayhew Macauley was an assistant
      professor of English at the Women's College of the Uni-
      versity of North Carolina (now the University of North
      Carolina at Greensboro) when *The Disguises of Love* was
      published. *The Disguises of Love* was his first novel.
      In 1966 Macauley became fiction editor of *Playboy* maga-
      zine.

*231. McCarthy, Mary Therese. *The Groves of Academe*. New
      York: Harcourt, Brace and Co., 1952.

      The Groves of Academe is a delicious satire on academic
      pretensions, and one of the best known of all American
      college novels. Set at "Jocelyn College," a small, pri-
      vate, and "progressive" institution, the plot revolves
      around President Maynard Hoar's attempts to discharge
      Henry Mulcahy, a much-traveled instructor of English.
      In order to stave off his dismissal Mulcahy pretends to
      be a Communist. Afraid of forfeiting his credentials
      as a liberal, President Hoar grudingly offers Mulcahy a
      new contract. Hoar then learns that Mulcahy is not and
      has never been a member of the party. Confused and em-
      bittered, Hoar offers his own resignation to the Jocelyn
      board of trustees.

Mary Therese McCarthy received an A.B. from Vassar in
1933. She taught at Bard College during the 1945-1946
academic year and at Sarah Lawrence in 1948-1949. *The
Groves of Academe* was her fourth novel. A later Mary
McCarthy novel touches upon college life. *The Group*
(New York: Harcourt, Brace and World, 1963) follows a
set of Vassar students, class of 1933, from graduation
into middle age.

232.   Larson, Martin Alfred. *Plaster Saint: A Novel of Heresy
       on the Campus*. New York: Exposition Press, 1953.

Plaster Saint is a bitter satire which features, in its
lead role, the most fulsomely described, evil department
chairman in college fiction. The mini-administrator at
the center of the book is Justin Homer Ashman (known to
one and all as "Assman"), chairman of the English department at a Western state university. Thirty-eight years
old, and destined for bigger things, Ashman forces his
faculty to assign an inane composition textbook he has
written, takes kickbacks in his position of chairman of
the university's finance committee, and ruins the careers
of junior faculty who oppose him. Henpecked by a shrewish
wife, Ashman also has affairs with female graduate students. Ashman is so nefarious that one might reasonably
ask how he can get away with his outrageous behavior.
The answer is that the institution's higher administrators are even more corrupt. Dean Aloysius Day, for example, offers to let various faculty join him in his
systematic raiding of the university treasury, and he
then blackmails these same individuals into supporting
him for a vacant presidency elsewhere in the state system.
When Day leaves to become a chief academic officer, Ashman is made dean.

Martin Alfred Larson received an A.B. from Kalamazoo
College in 1920 and a Ph.D. from the University of Michigan in 1923. He taught English at Eastern Michigan University from 1923 until 1925 and at the University of
Idaho from 1925 until 1927. He then went into private
business and at the time *Plaster Saint* was published he
was the owner-operator of the Larson Paint Company in
Detroit. A sometimes lecturer for Americans United for
Separation of Church and State, Larson wrote extensively
on religious topics. *Plaster Saint* was his first novel.

*233. Morrison, Theodore. *The Stones of the House*. New York:
        Viking Press, 1953.

        Students of college novels generally agree that *The
        Stones of the House* offers the most sympathetic, full-
        length portrait of a college president in American fiction.
        Andrew Aiken, the protagonist of the story, is president
        of "Rowley University," a private institution somewhere
        in New England. At the beginning of the book Aiken is
        acting president. But by conducting his office with wit
        and grace he is asked, at the novel's close, to take the
        post on a permanent basis. A host of academic characters
        appear in the plot. There is, for example, a paranoid
        professor of psychology who claims that persons unknown
        are spying on his research. And there is a wealthy,
        opinionated trustee whose son, a Rowley student, is
        killed in an automobile accident. During the course of
        the episodic story Aiken deals skillfully with the prob-
        lems which these individuals, and others, present him.
        He is helped throughout by Connie, his attractive and
        efficient wife. Her portrait, like that of her husband,
        is especially well drawn.
        Theodore Morrison received an A.B. from Harvard in
        1923. At the time *The Stones of the House* was published
        he was a professor of English at Harvard and a director
        of the Bread Loaf Writers' Conference at Middlebury
        College. Although Morrison had previously published a
        considerable amount of poetry *The Stones of the House*
        was his first novel. Two of Morrison's later novels,
        To Make a World (247) and *The Whole Creation* (335), also
        appear in this bibliography. Both of these novels are
        set at Rowley University, and in both of them President
        Aiken appears in ancillary roles.

234.   Fast, Howard Melvin. *Silas Timberman*. New York: The
        Blue Heron Press, 1954.

        The title character of this bitter novel about the
        abridgement of academic freedom is a historian at "Clem-
        ington University," an institution in the Midwest. Silas
        Timberman refuses to take part in a campus civil defense
        program and thereby incurs the wrath of Anthony C. Cabot,
        the school's president. When a committee of the United
        States Congress probes Communist inroads into American
        higher education, Cabot gratuitously gives Silas' name
        to the investigators. Though Silas is not a Communist
        he refuses to answer the committee's questions and, at
        the end of the book, he is sentenced to three years in

prison. In addition to Silas, many other Clemington
faculty appear in the story. A few of them, like Silas,
take strong stands against Cabot and the congressional
committee. Most, however, either support the forces of
darkness or remain apathetic while Silas is hurtling
toward personal and professional destruction.

Howard Melvin Fast was born in New York City in 1914.
He did not attend college. His first novel, *Two Valleys*
(New York: Dial Press, 1933), was published when he was
nineteen years old. During the next fifteen years Fast
combined creative writing with newspaper reporting,
service with the Office of War Information during World
War II, and overt political activity on behalf of the
American Labor Party. In 1947 Fast was sent to prison
for his failure to cooperate with the House Un-American
Activities Committee. After his release, publishing
blacklists forced him to create his own press, The Blue
Heron, in order to have an outlet for his works. In
The Naked God: The Writer and the Communist Party (New
York: Praeger, 1957), Fast notes that he wrote *Silas
Timberman*, his seventeenth novel, while a member of the
then-underground Communist Party. The book was written
to please his party superiors. Fast broke with the party
in 1956. During the 1960s Fast published with commercial
publishers under the pseudonym E.V. Cunningham. He began
using his own name on his writings once again in the 1970s.

*235.   Jarrell, Randall. *Pictures from an Institution*. New
        York: Farrar, Straus and Giroux, 1954.

Pictures from an Institution is often regarded as the
paramount satire on academic life. The novel takes place
at "Benton College," a progressive Southern institution
for women. The book has little plot. Instead, it consists
primarily of a series of incidents and character sketches.
Jarrell's pen drips a subtle mixture of honey and acid
as he describes, often through the jaundiced eyes of his
characters, a large roster of Benton faculty and administrators. Two individuals singled out for special treatment are Gertrude Johnson, a malevolent visiting writer
who is spending her year in residence slyly gathering
material for a college novel, and Dr. Dwight Robbins,
Benton's youthful but vacuous president. Robbins does
not have a Ph.D. His doctorate is an honorary one awarded
in 1947 by "Menuire College." Robbins suffers from over-
weening loquaciousness. In fact, the only way he can be
silenced is to mention that Menuire, in 1948, gave its
honorary doctorate to Milton Berle.

Randall Jarrell received an A.B. from Vanderbilt in
1935 and an A.M. from the same institution in 1938. A
giant among modern American poets, he was professor of
English at the Women's College of the University of North
Carolina (now the University of North Carolina at Greensboro) when this book was published. *Pictures from an
Institution* was Jarrell's only novel. He died in 1965.

236.   Marston, Everett Carter. *Take the High Ground*. Boston:
       Little, Brown, and Co., 1954.

Giles Harmony comes to "Chase College" to teach English.
Chase is a hard-pressed, private, coeducational institution in the East. With a Ph.D. from the University of
Chicago, Giles maintains high teaching standards and is
soon criticized by the Chase administration for failing
too many students. In fact, at one point President Elihu
Cousens drops into Giles' classroom to monitor his peda-
gogy. It takes time, but Giles gradually begins to adjust
to life in the academic little leagues. The process is
helped along by the wife of his department chairman. The
campus nymphomaniac, she eases Giles' tensions by taking
him to her bed. Then, when this affair ends, Giles finds
real romance with Maria, a young instructor of Spanish.
Despite the mundane nature of its plot and the stereotypic qualities of many of its characters, *Take the High
Ground* includes some well-written passages and it touches
upon a few academic issues which escape most other college
novels. Giles, for example, is considerably more confident than is the Chase administration that the school's
intellectually unwashed students are capable of serious
scholarship. And the book speaks to the status of a
publishing professor in an institution where publication
is not the norm. Though the faculty at Chase constantly
talk about their work "in progress," very little of this
phantom scholarship ever sees print. When Giles actually
publishes an article, the administration is so impressed
that he is offered a new contract with a $300 raise!
    Everett Carter Marston was educated at Colby College
of Maine and at Harvard. At the time *Take the High Ground*
was published he was a professor of English at Northwestern University.

237.   Morris, Wright. *The Huge Season*. New York: Viking
       Press, 1954.

The Huge Season is a deep and sensitive novel in which
the protagonist, Peter Foley, is depicted both as an

exuberant undergraduate and, thirty years later, as an
intellectually and morally exhausted professor of English.
The author's writing strategy is to alternate these per-
spectives. Each chapter about Foley's undergraduate days
is followed by a chapter about Foley in his mature years.
The plot has Foley entering "Colton College" in southern
California during the 1920s. He and many of his classmates worship another undergraduate, named Charles Lawrence, who seems to be the epitome of perfection. Foley
and his friends are devastated when Lawrence commits suicide, and neither Foley nor any of his college chums are
then able to make successes of their own lives. The book
contains a number of penetrating scenes of college life
but, in the last analysis, it is a study in human psychology. No precis of the novel can do it justice.

Wright Morris attended Pomona College from 1930 until
1933. After serving as a lecturer at various American
colleges and universities he became a professor of creative writing at San Francisco State in 1962. Morris is
generally regarded as a major American novelist. *The
Huge Season* was his ninth novel. A later Morris novel,
What a Way to Go (New York: Atheneum, 1962), deals peripherally with academe. The protagonist is Arnold Soby,
a middle-aged professor of English. Soby pursues his
lost youth when, on a cruise to Greece, he has an affair
with a sensous teenage girl.

238. Birney, Earle. *Down the Long Table.* Toronto: McClelland
      and Stewart, 1955.

Gordon Saunders is a professor of English at an unnamed
American university. He is called before an investigatory committee of the United States Senate and asked about
his political history. While being bullied by a McCarthy-
ish inquisitor, Saunders reflects upon his youthful left-
wing activities and upon his subsequent disillusionment
with Communism. As the flashbacks unreel, Saunders reviews his graduate school days at the University of
Toronto and his experiences at "Wasatch College" in
Salt Lake City, where he began his teaching career.

Earle Birney was born in Calgary, Canada, in 1904. He
received a B.A. from the University of British Columbia
in 1926 and a Ph.D. ten years later from the University
of Toronto. He began his own teaching career at the
University of Utah in 1930. From 1946 until 1963 he was
a member of the English department at the University of
North Carolina.

239. Dodd, Martha Eccles. *The Searching Light*. New York:
      Citadel Press, 1955.

      The Searching Light is a wordy yet effective novel about
      the loss of academic freedom during the McCarthy era.
      The regents of "Penfield University," a state institution,
      decide to have their faculty sign an anti-Communist loyal-
      ty oath. At first nearly all of the faculty refuse to
      comply, but as pressures are brought to bear most knuckle
      under. Finally, only John Minot and four others hold
      out. Minot, the chairman of Penfield's English depart-
      ment, is the character whom the novel follows most close-
      ly. Minot's wife has a near fatal heart attack at the
      height of the crisis. Eventually the five holdouts are
      fired and the Minots retire to a small farm which they
      have maintained as a summer residence. Minot and his
      four compatriots are depicted as lions of moral virtue,
      but most of the rest of the Penfield faculty emerge as
      poltroons.
      Born in 1908, Martha Eccles Dodd attended the University
      of Chicago, where her father, William Edward Dodd, was a
      professor of history. She left before graduating and
      entered newspaper work. In 1933 her father was appointed
      Ambassador to Germany, and Ms. Dodd accompanied her par-
      ents to Berlin. She stayed in Germany until 1937 and
      developed a deep hatred of fascism. Although she wrote
      a number of novels, her best known work is *Through Embassy
      Eyes* (New York: Harcourt, Brace and Co., 1939), a factual
      recapitulation of her experiences in Hitler's Third Reich.

240. Sarton, May. *Faithful are the Wounds*. New York: Rine-
      hart and Co., 1955.

      The setting for this novel is Harvard and the pro-
      tagonist is Edward Cavan, a professor of English. Cavan
      commits suicide by throwing himself under an elevated
      train. The story, told in part through flashbacks, re-
      views the events leading up to Cavan's self-destruction
      and then deals with the consequences of the tragedy for
      those whom Cavan leaves behind. *Faithful are the Wounds*
      is a complex novel and the precise reasons for Cavan's
      suicide are never fully explicated. Essentially, how-
      ever, Cavan kills himself because he sees "liberalism,"
      which he takes to mean passionate advocacy of free speech
      and humane justice, as a dying force in post-war America.
      As Cavan observes his Harvard colleagues equivocating on
      such issues as academic freedom and anti-Communist witch-
      hunts, his depression grows until he apparently loses his

mental balance. The cast of the novel includes many
Harvard faculty as well as a seventyish female radical
activist, the daughter of a former Harvard dean. This
character, named Grace Kinloch, is the only one of Cavan's
associates to remain as intractably liberal as Cavan himself. John Lyons, in *The College Novel in America* (see
footnote 3, Introduction), states that *Faithful are the
Wounds* is a fictionalized account of the suicide of F.O.
Matthiessen, a noted Harvard professor of English who
killed himself in April of 1950.

May Sarton, one of America's foremost novelists and
poets, was a member of the Harvard English department
from 1949 until 1952. *Faithful are the Wounds* was her
fifth novel. Another Sarton novel, *The Small Room* (331),
is included in this bibliography.

241. Goepp, Ada. *Small Pond*. Philadelphia: The Westminster
     Press, 1956.

This entertaining novel is set at "Warwick College," a
private institution in "West Amesbury," Massachusetts.
The plot revolves around the experiences of two new female recruits to the English department. One of the
women, a dazzling beauty named Virginia Butler, must re-
peatedly fight off the advances of her lustful male colleagues. The other, a somewhat less attractive young
lady named Anne Gordon, has a tumultuous romance with
the school's poet-in-residence. English department politics figure largely in the story. At one point, two
senior professors vie for the about-to-be-vacated chairmanship. The president of Warwick decides on his man,
and mollifies the loser--a bumbling, academic simpleton--
by arranging for him to become president of a college in
New Jersey.

Ada Goepp has disappeared into the recesses of literary
obscurity. *A Small Pond* would seem to have been her
first and only novel.

242. Johnson, Annabel [Mrs. Edgar Raymond Johnson]. *As a
     Speckled Bird*. New York: Thomas Y. Cromwell Co., 1956.

Curt Marin, an accomplished ceramic artist, returns to
his alma mater, "The Greenville Academy of Art," to teach
pottery-making. The academy, located in the upper South,
near the Kansas border, offers a fine arts degree in con-
junction with the nearby "University of Greenville."
Curt soon finds himself doing battle with Cole Brandt,
the well-meaning but morally weak president of the academy.

Brandt's overriding aim is to keep the school solvent, and at the climax of the story he rigs a student art competition so that the son-in-law of a potential bene-factor wins first prize. Curt, a strong-and-silent type, has a romance with a lady of the town and a teacher-mentor relationship with a talented young man from the Ozarks whom President Brandt cheats out of victory in the art contest. In addition to Curt, a host of other academy faculty members also appear in the story. In the interest of holding their jobs, most of these indi-viduals side with Brandt when Curt accuses him of per-verting the school's educational aims. At the end of the book, his integrity still intact, Curt leaves the academy to open a pottery business in the North.

Annabel Johnson was born in Kansas City, Missouri, in 1921. She attended the College of William and Mary during the 1939-1940 academic year and then left college to work as a librarian. In 1946 she moved to New York where she worked in the publishing business. She married Edgar Johnson, a ceramic artist and writer, in 1949. *As a Speckled Bird* was her first novel.

243.   Bassing, Eileen. *Home Before Dark*. New York: Random House, 1957.

This novel is set at a private college in rural New England. Charlotte Bronn, a faculty wife, returns home after two years in a mental hospital. Her husband, Ar-nold, is bucking for the chairmanship of the philosophy department. Arnold doesn't want to be embarrassed by Charlotte. Therefore, he contrives to keep her upstairs when colleagues call at their home, and in a variety of other ways he factors Charlotte out of as much of his life as possible. Arnold's callous behavior nearly drives Charlotte to another breakdown, but with the help of a few sympathetic friends she takes steps to resolve her problems. One of these steps, at the end of the book, is to sue Arnold for divorce. The plot of *Home Before Dark* focuses upon Charlotte's shaky psychological health and relatively little attention is paid to the normal routines of academic life.

Eileen Bassing attended Los Angeles City College. According to an "About the Author" page at the end of the book, Bassing married at sixteen and then "did ex-tensive reading in the fields of psychoanalytic, psychi-atric, and medical literature." In 1958 *Home Before Dark* was adapted for film. The motion picture, which bore the same title, starred Jean Simmons in the role of Charlotte Bronn.

244. Corbett, Elizabeth. *Professor Preston at Home*. Philadelphia and New York: J.B. Lippincott Co., 1957.

Can a disspirited professor of Greek find happiness
in retirement? He can in this cheery tale by Elizabeth
Corbett who was, during the 1940s and 1950s, one of
America's foremost purveyors of literary sunshine.
Charles Augustus Preston retires from "Gibson College"
in New England, remarries (he is a widower), and begins
to turn out all those books he dreamed of writing when
he was burdened by the cares of classroom teaching. His
books, on Greek mythology, are so good that he is able
to bypass university presses and have his works produced
by a major New York publishing house. In retirement
Charles also finds time to get on friendlier terms with
his once-estranged daughter. At the end of the book
Charles is anticipating his royalties and looking forward
to many more productive years.
Elizabeth Corbett received a B.A. from the University
of Wisconsin in 1910. Her many novels include *The Graper
Girls Go to College* (New York: D. Appleton-Century Co.,
1932) and *Growing Up with the Grapers* (New York: D.
Appleton-Century Co., 1934), two bubbly tales of undergraduate life intended for older girls.

245. Linn, Bettina. *A Letter to Elizabeth*. Philadelphia and
New York: J.B. Lippincott Co., 1957.

Sixteen-year-old Forresta Jordan is the illegitimate
daughter of Professor James Waterman and one of his
former students. Forresta now lives in the East with
her mother and stepfather. James, a famous anthropologist, lives in a Midwestern town where he teaches at a
high-status university. Forresta insists upon meeting
the man who sired her, and this novel describes her first
visit with her father. Most of the narrative focuses
upon Forresta and James as they go through the difficult
process of getting acquainted. The story ends when Forresta contracts polio and her mother comes to take the
girl home. The author provides flashback passages about
James' professional career, and when James' relationship
with Forresta becomes strained he is portrayed as behaving in proper professorial ways. Indeed, when the
trauma of Forresta's visit becomes especially pronounced
James retreats to his study and seeks solace in the
legends of a primitive people on whom he is an international expert. Although the author avoids the moralistic, cloying prose of turn-of-the-century fiction,

the book is in many ways reminiscent of those early-day
faculty novels in which professors were tragic, romantic
figures.

Bettina Linn received an A.B. from Bryn Mawr in 1926
and an M.A. from the same institution in 1929. In 1934
she joined the English department at Bryn Mawr and, at
the time of her death in 1962, she was the Margaret Kings-
land Haskell Professor of English Composition at her alma
mater. An expert in Russian literature, Professor Linn
served during World War II as a Soviet Union specialist
for the Office of Strategic Services. *A Letter to Elizabeth* won the Philadelpha Athenaeum Fiction Award in 1958.
Although many reviewers wrote that *A Letter to Elizabeth*
was Professor Linn's first novel, her initial novel was,
in fact, *Flea Circus* (New York: Smith and Haas, 1936), a
story of American city life.

246: Marbut, Ann Veronica [Mrs. F.B. Marbut]. *The Tarnished
      Tower*. New York: David McKay Co., 1957.

Although this story is told from the perspective of
Peg Scott, a faculty wife, the central character is Peg's
husband, Jerry, an ambitious assistant professor of political science. The setting is "Charleston State College." Part of the plot centers on Jerry's ultimately
unsuccessful attempt to make himself a nationally recog-
nized advocate of "transitional education," a catch
phrase he invents to describe a low-quality smorgasbord
of illiberal arts programs. More intriguing, however,
is that part of the plot in which Jerry tries to mold
Peg to his image of the loyal, supportive helpmate. He
fails in this attempt, as well, and at the end of the
book Peg exits the Charleston scene. There are a number
of detailed, if heavy-handed, portraits of academic character types in the novel. President Nielson is described
as a weak, vacillating chief executive, and Ross Adams,
his oily assistant, is one of the more repellent petty
administrators in college fiction. The novel also contains some protracted discussions about what does and
does not constitute a valid academic curriculum.

Ann Veronica Marbut was born in Aberdeen, South Dakota,
in 1912. A 1934 graduate of the Washington College of
Law, she combined marriage, law, and writing. *The Tarnished Tower* was her second novel.

247. Morrison, Theodore. *To Make a World*. New York: Viking
     Press, 1957.

   This novel is set, in large part, at "Rowley University," the same locale for *The Stones of the House* (233),
an earlier Morrison novel included in this bibliography.
The protagonist of *To Make a World* is Sam Norris, an
administrative assistant to Rowley's president, Andrew
Aiken. Sam is assigned to act as liaison between Rowley
and the Stoughton Foundation, a local research organization with which Rowley maintains financial links. Some
of the story focuses upon Sam's involvement in Stoughton
internal politics, but there are many scenes on the Rowley campus. President Aiken, portrayed favorably in *The
Stones of the House*, once again demonstrates his humane
wisdom, but his role in *To Make a World* is as a supporting
player. A third Morrison novel, *The Whole Creation* (335),
also is set at Rowley and it, too, appears in this bibliography.

*248. Nabokov, Vladimir. *Pnin*. Garden City, New York: Double-
      day and Co., 1957.

   Pnin is a classic college novel by a master of fiction.
The book's title character, Timofey Pnin, is an aging
assistant professor of languages at "Waindell College,"
a prestigious institution in the East. Pnin is a bumbling
but kindly Russian emigre whose conditions of life are
now sadly reduced from those he enjoyed in Europe. He
is the butt of student and faculty jokes at Waindell and,
at the end of the novel, he loses his academic appointment. Yet throughout the story Pnin perseveres, even
though he is haunted by his memories and confused by the
American world in which he finds himself. Despite the
melancholia which underlies the several episodes which
comprise the book, *Pnin* is written in large measure as
symbolic satire. For instance, the president of Waindell,
Dr. Samuel Poore, is both blind and pompous. Each day at
noon Dr. Poore is led into the university dining hall
where he eats his "invisible luncheon" alone under a
giant mural which shows him receiving scrolls of wisdom
from Richard Wagner, Dostoevski, and Confucius. Much of
Pnin appeared originally as stories in *The New Yorker*.
   Vladimir Nabokov was born in 1899 in St. Petersburg,
Russia. He left Russia with his family in 1919, graduated from Cambridge in 1922, and then lived in Berlin
where he wrote novels, plays, and stories in Russian.
In 1939 Nabokov accepted an invitation to lecture on

Slavic languages at Stanford. From 1941 until 1948 he
taught at Wellesley. From 1948 until 1959 Nabokov was
a member of the foreign language and literature faculty
at Cornell. Another of his many novels, *Pale Fire* (336),
appears in this bibliography.

249. Nemerov, Howard. *The Homecoming Game*. New York: Simon
      and Schuster, 1957.

Set at a large, coeducational liberal arts college, this
comic-satire has as its protagonist one Charles Osman, an
associate professor of history. When Charles fails Raymond Blent, the star of the school's football team, he
immediately comes under pressure from all quarters to
change Raymond's grade. He does so, but only after a
series of misadventures and misunderstandings which involve a gambler, a United States senator, the institution's vacillatory president, and a scheming co-ed.
Charles, a Jew, is portrayed as a faculty outsider, as
is Leon Solomon, a Jewish faculty colleague who, it turns
out, also gave Blent a failing grade. Considering the
comic nature of its plot, *The Homecoming Game* offers more
serious insights into academe than might reasonably be
expected. At times Charles, Leon Solomon, and President
Nagel seem to forget that they are players in a humorous
romp and they engage each other in academically sagacious
discussion. Under the title *Tall Story*, the novel was
adapted for both the stage and motion pictures. The stage
version was written by Howard Lindsay and Russel Crouse,
and was presented on Broadway in 1959. The movie version,
starring Jane Fonda in her film debut, was released in
1960. In both versions the plot was altered so that the
intercollegiate sport in question was basketball instead
of football.
       Howard Nemerov received an A.B. from Harvard in 1941.
A leading American poet, he was a member of the literature
faculty at Bennington College in Vermont when *The Homecoming Game* was published.

250. Schmitt, Gladys [Mrs. Simon Goldfield]. *A Small Fire*.
      New York: Dial Press, 1957.

The setting of this novel is a "second-rate" college
of fine arts near New York City. The central character
is Frieda Hartmann, a thirty-six-year-old, longtime
teacher of voice. A spinster, Frieda is attracted to
Arthur Sanes, a brilliant but neurotic concert pianist
who joins the school's faculty. The two have only a

sporadic relationship--Arthur's moodiness gets in the way
of a real romance--until one night Arthur has a breakdown
while giving a recital in New York. Arthur flees the
stage and Frieda, brimming over with compassion, traces
him to the uptown apartment of his parents. At the conclusion of the book it is clear that, as Mrs. Sanes,
Frieda will nurse the manic-depressive Arthur back to
some semblance of mental health. There are some interesting vignettes in the narrative about faculty life in
fine arts colleges, and the story is unusual for a 1950s
college novel in that the male protagonist is presented
as weak while the principal female character is portrayed
as harboring great inner strength.

Gladys Schmitt received a B.A. from the University of
Pittsburgh in 1932. She was a professor of English and
fine arts at the Carnegie Institute of Technology in
Pittsburgh when *A Small Fire*, her sixth novel, was published.

251.   Scribner, Robert Leslie. *Eggheads in the End Zone*. New
York: Exposition Press, 1957.

Eggheads in the End Zone is a satire on college football and, not incidentally, a satire on college administrators as well. The alumni of "Terranova College"
demand a winning football team but the institution lacks
the funds to purchase the necessary playing talent. In
a move of inspired desperation President Jonathan Dorsey
Tower proposes a "supersanity" rule to the NCAA. This
rule would limit participation in intercollegiate football to faculty members. The rule is adopted and Terranova, with a young faculty, achieves an undefeated season
and the national championship. As a result of its football notoriety, Terranova is flooded with student appli-
cations and President Tower launches a major building
program to turn his once struggling college into a university. *Eggheads in the End Zone* is narrated by James
Throgmorton, an assistant professor of history who receives
all-American honors as a halfback. Throgmorton's football career is short lived, however. Learning that other
schools are hiring faculty "goons" for the next season,
President Tower realizes that Terranova will not be able
to retain its number one ranking. Thus he proposes a
new, "superreality" rule to the NCAA, a plan which that
august organization promptly adopts. In the upcoming
year football will be limited to students with IQs of
eighty-five or less. Very few institutions, reasons the
wise President Tower, will be able to match Terranova in
its supply of these individuals.

*252.   Baker, Carlos Heard. *A Friend in Power*. New York:
        Charles Scribner's Sons, 1958.

        Set at "Enfield University," a high-status institution
        not far from New York City, this serious novel deals with
        a search for a new Enfield president. The protagonist is
        Ed Tyler, a forty-year-old professor of modern languages
        and an expert on the writings of Voltaire. A member of
        the faculty search committee, Ed has no designs on the
        job for himself. Yet, during the year the committee is
        in operation, Ed's goodness and humanity become apparent
        to the other committee members, and to the university's
        trustees, and in the end it is Ed who receives the ap-
        pointment. Though academic readers may question the
        optimistic view of presidential searches presented by
        the author, no one can claim that the book lacks an
        abundance of material about the rituals surrounding presi-
        dential selection.
        Carlos Heard Baker received an A.B. from Dartmouth in
        1932 and a Ph.D. from Princeton in 1940. A major scholar
        in the field of English literature, Baker was chairman of
        Princeton's department of English when *A Friend in Power*,
        his first novel, was published.

*253.   Barr, Stringfellow. *Purely Academic*. New York: Simon
        and Schuster, 1958.

        During the mid-portion of this century Stringfellow
        Barr was one of America's most prominent exponents of
        liberal arts curricula. A former Rhodes Scholar and pro-
        fessor of history at the University of Virginia, Barr be-
        came in 1937 president of St. Johns College in Annapolis,
        Maryland. At St. Johns he inaugurated the "great books"
        program, which did away with elective courses and required
        students to immerse themselves in classic writings. After
        leaving the presidency of St. Johns in 1946 Barr became
        president of the Foundation for World Government. *Purely
        Academic* was published when Barr was sixty-one years old,
        and after he had returned to academe--in 1955--as pro-
        fessor of humanities at Rutgers.
        Set at a small, private university (but not one with a
        great books curriculum), *Purely Academic* has as its pro-
        tagonist Henry Schneider, chairman of the school's depart-
        ment of history. Down at the heels, and a scholar of
        little distinction, Schneider is an academic gamesman.
        He attempts to get salary increases by flaunting mythical
        offers of higher paid employment, and he hides his writing
        of a textbook by claiming that he is doing secret

government research. Schneider also has a running feud
with a professor of economics and an affair with the
economist's wife. Eventually he is hired by a New York
foundation because the foundation director admires his
cynicism. Of particular note is Barr's portrait of
President Pomton, the institution's scheming chief executive. One of the more mockingly described academic presidents in college fiction, Pomton travels the country accepting donations from gamblers and, in the process, he
keeps one eye always open for bigger and better academic
jobs. Eventually he becomes president of a state-supported
multiversity. Reviewers generally found *Purely Academic*
lacking as a piece of literature but, nonetheless, a
sadistically funny satire on academics and on the American
academic scene. As S. Stephenson Smith noted in *Library
Journal* (January 1, 1958): "Stringfellow Barr has said
more about the plight of American higher education than
any dozen tomes or surveys."

254.   Barth, John. *The End of the Road*. Garden City, New
       York: Doubleday, 1958.

   If considered only in terms of its plot, *End of the
Road* is a black comedy about faculty life. The protagonist is Jacob Horner, a twenty-eight-year-old instructor of writing at "Wicomico State Teacher's College" on
Maryland's Eastern Shore. Jacob has an affair with the
wife of a colleague. The woman becomes pregnant and dies
following a botched abortion. Ridden with guilt, Jacob
flees Wicomico. But *The End of the Road* is, in fact, an
intricate metaphorical treatise on the modern human condition. Jacob, portrayed during most of the book as a man
who is unable to make decisions, is a sort of American
Everyman. The college, totally lacking in intellectual
distinction, is symbolic of a world without taste or
standards. Like all of Barth's novels, *The End of the
Road* furnishes much grist for the literary scholars'
mills.
   John Barth was born in 1930 in Cambridge, Maryland. He
received an A.B. from Johns Hopkins in 1951 and an M.A.
from the same institution in 1952. At the time *The End
of the Road*, his second novel, was published he was an
assistant professor of English at Penn State. Barth's
epic fiction, *Giles Goat-Boy* (362), also is included in
this bibliography.

255.   Elliott, George Paul. *Parktilden Village*. Boston:
       Beacon Press, 1958.

       On the back cover of the New American Library paper-
       back edition of this epic (1961), the publishers describe
       the work as "a novel of shattering impact ... (a study
       of) today's hard, alienated generation--the 'intellectu-
       als' and the 'hip' who hide their hopes and hungers be-
       hind a mask of cynical indifference." Despite the pub-
       lishers' hyperbole, *Parktilden Village* is perhaps better
       seen as a satire on sociology and on sociologists. The
       protagonist, Peter Hazen, is a young, hedonistic instruc-
       tor of sociology at Berkeley. Peter augments his uni-
       versity salary by drawing a syndicated comic strip. He
       also has an affair with a teenage girl. When the girl
       goes away to college Peter seduces her mother. Although
       humanists may well appreciate the negative implications
       about sociology contained in the story, most sociologists
       are likely to agree with Granville Hicks, who reviewed
       the book for *The Saturday Review* (May 31, 1958). *Park-
       tilden Village*, wrote Hicks, "leaves a bad taste in the
       mouth."
         George Paul Elliott received an A.B. from the Universi-
       ty of California at Berkeley in 1939 and an M.A. from
       that institution in 1941. *Parktilden Village* was his
       first novel. At the time the book was published Elliott
       was a lecturer at the Writers' Workshop at the University
       of Iowa. In 1963 Elliott joined the English department
       of Syracuse University. Since *Parktilden Village*, Elliott
       has published additional novels and many books of literary
       essays and criticism.

256.   Koch, Claude. *Light in Silence*. New York: Dodd, Mead
       and Co., 1958.

       This novel explores the reverberations which take place
       in an order of teaching brothers at a Catholic college
       immediately after the death of its longtime Prior. Cletus
       Paul, the beloved leader of the community, is replaced by
       Brother Eliphus Raymond, a much younger man who plans
       to modernize both the order and "St. Bardolph's College."
       St. Bardolph's is located atop a gorge overlooking Niag-
       ara Falls. The story covers only a week in the life of
       the community, hence it deals only with the short-term
       consequences of the old Prior's demise. Among these
       consequences are a series of visions which come to Brother
       Didymus, an aging member of the group who spends his spare
       time dressed in mufti viewing off-campus risque films,

and a feeling of vocational doubt which assails Brother
Finian Joseph, the director of the college art faculty.
Light in Silence treats all of its characters with respect, though not without touching upon their flaws.
Considered within its context, as a work about the teaching staff of a Catholic institution of higher education,
it is a penetrating exercise in faculty-centered college
fiction.

Claude Koch was born in Philadelphia in 1918. He received a B.S. from LaSalle College in 1940 and later did
graduate work at Niagara University in Niagara Falls, New
York. In 1947 he received an M.A. from the University of
Florida. *Light in Silence* was Koch's second novel. At
the time the book was published he was a member of the
department of English at LaSalle.

257. Angus, Douglas. *The Ivy Trap*. Indianapolis and New
York: Bobbs-Merrill Co., 1959.

The Ivy Trap is an unhappy tale of faculty-student sex.
Allan Hazard is an associate professor of English at an
Eastern university. He falls in love with Laurel Browne,
a beautiful co-ed and the granddaughter of a wealthy university benefactor. When their August-May affair is discovered by his wife--and by virtually everyone else on
the campus--Allan reluctantly tells Laurel that he can
no longer see her outside of class. Temporarily de-
ranged, Laurel goes to a fraternity party, imbibes freely
of liquid refreshment, and then entertains the entire
cadre of brothers in an upstairs bedroom. Laurel leaves
the university at the request of a disciplinary committee.
Allan, staggering under a host of emotional burdens of
his own, resigns his faculty position. The ruin of
Allen's career will be seen as particularly tragic by
academics because, after years of struggle, Allan has
just been informed that the university trustees have
approved his promotion to full professor. The book contains the usual compliment of secondary campus characters
and sub-plots.

Born in 1909 in Nova Scotia, Douglas Angus received a
B.A. from Arcadia University in 1934 and a Ph.D. from
Ohio State in 1940. At the time *The Ivy Trap* was published he was Professor of English at St. Lawrence University. The novel was published in Great Britain under
the title *The Descent of Venus* (London: Hodder and Stoughton, 1961).

258.   Engel, Monroe. *The Visions of Nicholas Solon*. New York:
       Sagamore Press, 1959.

       The title character of this lugubrious tragedy of man-
       ners is a professor of literature at "Banford College."
       Banford is a private institution in the East. Upon his
       arrival at Banford in 1938 young Nicholas has an affair
       with Clara Reed, the wife of his department chairman.
       He then switches allegiances to Hilda Greene, the wife
       of a local businessman. He and Hilda have an illegitimate
       daughter whom Hilda raises as her husband's child. Later,
       Nicholas marries Caddy, a student at the college. When
       Caddy learns about Nicholas' past peccadillos she becomes
       upset and, at the end of the book, she goes on an extended
       vacation to cogitate. A number of other faculty members
       and their wives appear in the story. Most of these char-
       acters, like Nicholas and his various women, are in the
       throes of domestic agonies.
       Monroe Engel received an A.B. from Harvard in 1942 and
       a Ph.D. from Princeton in 1954. He was an assistant pro-
       fessor of English at Harvard when *The Visions of Nicholas
       Solon*, his second novel, was published.

259.   Harris, Mark. *Wake Up, Stupid*. New York: Alfred A.
       Knopf, 1959.

       Wake Up, Stupid is a humorous epistolary novel which
       consists entirely of letters to and from Lee Youngdahl,
       a member of the English department at an institution of
       higher learning in San Francisco. An aspiring writer for
       television, part owner of a prize fighter, and in pur-
       suit of an appointment at Harvard, Youngdahl bombards
       his correspondents with lengthy and often sardonic mes-
       sages. They, in turn, generally offer laconic replies.
       Though much of Youngdahl's correspondence involves non-
       academic matters, some of it makes detailed reference to
       ongoing hearings on his tenure. Academic readers will
       be captivated by the inane, bureaucratic memoranda sent
       to Youngdahl from the chairman of his tenure committee.
       Mark Harris received a B.A. from the University of
       Denver in 1950 and a Ph.D. from the University of Minne-
       sota in 1956. He was a member of the department of
       English at San Francisco State College when this book
       was published. An accomplished dramatist and novelist,
       Harris is perhaps best known as the author of adult
       novels about baseball. The first of these novels, *The
       Southpaw* (Indianapolis: Bobbs-Merrill Co., 1953), is now
       a classic exemplar of American sports fiction.

260. Lipsky, Eleazar. *The Scientists*. New York: Appleton-
     Century-Crofts, 1959.

     David Luzzatto, a young professor of biology at "Haver-
     straw University," is enjoying the perfect academic life.
     Situated at a high-status institution, and becoming
     wealthy from a patent on a wonder drug which he developed
     while still a graduate student, David does his research
     and teaching amidst the finest of conditions. But his
     idyllic existence is suddenly threatened. Crotchety old
     Dr. Ullman, now retired from Haverstraw but once David's
     mentor, sues to gain control of the lucrative patent for
     himself. It is Dr. Ullman's contention that the drug was
     created in his laboratory, under his supervision, and
     that both the credit for the substance and the profits
     from it are rightfully his. In the end, a sort of compro-
     mise is arranged. David signs the income from his dis-
     covery over to the university. Before that occurs, how-
     ever, the author explores the legal and moral issues of
     the case and, through flashbacks, reviews David's rise to
     scientific prominence.
     Born in New York City in 1911, Eleazor Lipsky graduated
     from both Columbia College and Columbia Law School. A
     practicing attorney, as well as a writer, Lipsky at one
     point in his legal career served in the New York County
     District Attorney's Office. *The Scientists* was his fifth
     novel.

261. Taber, Gladys Bagg. *Spring Harvest*. New York: G.P.
     Putnam's Sons, 1959.

     This kaleidoscopic novel takes place in 1914 on the
     campus of "Westerly College," a small, private institu-
     tion in Wisconsin. The story follows the interlocking
     exploits of several Westerly students, faculty members,
     and administrators during the month preceding graduation.
     Featured in the large cast of characters are: Mike Hewitt,
     a Westerly football star who rejects an offer to transfer
     his gridiron talents to a "Big Ten" university; Alden
     Prescott, a frumpish professor of chemistry who opposes
     his daughter's engagement to Mike; and Mark Allingham,
     a frustrated professor of music who dreams in vain of
     discovering a world-class singing voice somewhere within
     the throats of his Westerly pupils. Richard Wallace,
     the youngish president of Westerly, also appears in a
     significant role. Married to Carol, a vain and heartless
     woman who eventually deserts him for a more exciting life
     in New York City, Richard has a secret crush on Louise

Richardson, Westerly's bachelorette dean of students.
Louise has a reciprocal secret crush on Richard. This
problem is resolved neatly when Carol is killed in an
automobile accident and Louise and Richard are left free
to declare their love, settle Carol's estate, and plan
for their wedding. The book includes considerable marginalia about pre-World War I academic life at a small,
Midwestern college. And its principal players, though
emotionally one-dimensional, are drawn in significant
detail.

The daughter of a college professor, Gladys Bagg Taber
was born in Colorado Springs, Colorado, in 1899. She
received a B.A. from Wellesley in 1920 and an M.A. from
Lawrence College in 1921. After teaching English and
creative writing at Randolph-Macon College during the
1920s, Taber became a professional writer and journalist.
At various points in her career she was an editor for
The Ladies Home Journal and a columnist for *Family Circle*.
She also taught English at Columbia University from 1936
until 1940. As a writer, Taber published children's
stories and works of nonfiction as well as novels. *Spring
Harvest* was her eleventh novel.

262. Tamkus, Daniel. *The Much Honored Man*. Garden City, New
      York: Doubleday and Co., 1959.

An unnamed professor of physics, in his youth the winner
of a Nobel Prize, hides behind his reputation to avoid
his responsibilities as a husband and father. The setting
is a high-status university. During the course of the
story the professor's spoiled daughter bears an illegitimate child by an especially obnoxious student, and the
professor's harassed wife stages an unsuccessful attempt
at suicide. The novel is told entirely in the form of a
revelatory letter from the professor to a young faculty
colleague who has proposed marriage to his daughter. The
professor is damned by his own words. From his letter he
emerges as pompous, without scruples, and devoid of moral
courage.

Daniel Tamkus graduated from Johns Hopkins University.
The Much Honored Man was his first novel.

The American College Novel
1960–1979

263. Johnson, Nora. *A Step Beyond Innocence*. Boston: Little,
     Brown and Co., 1961.

   Told in the first person by its protagonist, this sometimes buoyant, sometimes saturnine novel chronicles the
four Smith College years of Sally Fraits. A wealthy girl
from New York, Sally is uncertain how she will employ her
college education after graduation. She would like a
career, but the lure of post-graduation housewifery is
also strong. During the course of the story Sally turns
away three suitors, though not without soul-searching in
each instance. Compounding Sally's problem is her confusion over what career (if any) to follow. At the end
of the book she has accepted a position with a publishing
firm. The novel emphasizes the social side of Smith life
and it includes a number of portraits of Sally's classmates, many of whom are as confused as she is over the
career—versus—marriage dilemma.
   The daughter of novelist Nunnally Johnson, Nora Johnson
was born in Hollywood, California, in 1933. She attended
Smith College. *A Step Beyond Innocence* was her second
novel. Her first novel, *The World of Henry Orient* (Boston: Little, Brown and Co., 1958), won widespread critical
acclaim. Reviewers generally found *A Step Beyond Innocence* well written but thematically unexciting. Nora
Johnson's best-known work is *Pat Loud: A Woman's Story*
(New York, Coward, McCann and Geoghegan, 1974), a nonfiction recapitulation of Pat Loud's experiences before,
during, and after the filming of the television series
"An American Family" in the early 1970s.

264. Sherman, Susan Jean. *Give Me Myself*. Cleveland and
     New York: World Publishing Co., 1961.

   Nona Greene attends a summer session at "Masefield
College" and is enthralled by the lectures of Evelyn
Gordon McKenna. Nona is nineteen and Evelyn, a visiting

professor of literature from Ireland, is "an old thirty-
five." The two become friends and Evelyn takes Nona on
a long junket to New York City and then to Europe. But
Evelyn turns out to be an alcoholic and Nona comes to
regret her role as a travelling companion. When Evelyn's
boozing leads her to collapse on the floor of a flophouse
lavatory in Florence, Nona makes tracks for the American
Consulate, borrows air fare, and flies home alone. There
are undertones of lesbianism in the book but the major
thrust of the story has to do with Nona's admiration of
the older woman's intellect. The portraits of the novel's
two protagonists are elaborately drawn but the only significant impression of Masefield gained by the reader is
that it is a dreadfully hot place in the summer.

Susan Jean Sherman was born in New York City in 1939.
She attended the University of Vermont, Harvard, the New
School, and Sarah Lawrence. *Give Me Myself* was her first
novel.

265.   Terry, Marshall, Jr. *Old Liberty*. New York: Viking
        Press, 1961.

This brief (181-page) and sprightly novel describes
the freshman year at "Liberty College" of Redwine Walker,
a wealthy and hedonistic lad from Texas. Liberty College
is a small, non-elite institution in "Olive Hill," Pennsylvania. The story is told in the first person by Redwine, whose major accomplishment during the year is to
invite the town prostitute to the spring prom. Toward
the conclusion of the book Liberty's only dormitory is
destroyed by fire and it remains an open question as to
whether or not the school will be in existence for Redwine's possible return as a sophomore. The faculty and
administration at Liberty are accorded significant space
in Redwine's narrative. The portrait of the institution's
president is especially intriguing. Known only as "Mon-
key," he bubbles with unwarranted enthusiasm and speaks
in polysyllabic language which none of his students can
understand.

After attending Amherst and Kenyon, Marshall Terry received a B.A. from Southern Methodist University in 1953.
He received an M.A. from Southern Methodist in 1954. *Old
Liberty* was his first novel. At the time the book was
published Terry was director of public relations, instructor of English, and editor of the alumni magazine
at Southern Methodist.

266. Thorp, Roderick. *Into the Forest*. New York: Random
       House, 1961.

       Into the Forest details the involved, late-adolescent
       exertions of an institutionally diverse set of under-
       graduates. Some of the students are from Ithaca, New
       York, but attend City College in New York City. Others
       are from the greater New York City area but attend Cor-
       nell. And still others are enrolled at Cortland State
       Teacher's College and at Hunter. The plot centers on
       Charlie Cumberland, one of the CCNY students, and on
       Cal Torrenson and Elaine Spellman, two Cornellians. The
       two young men at the center of the story do battle over
       Elaine. Charlie, a Korean War veteran who is studying to
       become a high school teacher, emerges victorious in the
       romantic combat. Cal, the pampered son of a bus company
       owner, finds consolation in the beds of various co-eds.
       And Elaine, a nice Jewish girl from New York, alienates
       her parents who oppose her impending marriage to the
       gentile Charlie. Some of the action in the book takes
       place at Cornell and some takes place in New York City.
       From the standpoint of college fiction, the most note-
       worthy scene is an exceedingly graphic depiction of
       pledge-hazing at a CCNY fraternity house.
          Roderick Thorp attended CCNY in the 1950s. *Into the
       Forest* was his first novel. In later years Thorp became
       a well-respected writer of mystery and suspense stories.

267. [Bayer, William, and Nancy Harmon]. *Love with a Harvard
       Accent*. By Leonie St. John (pseud.). New York: Ace
       Books, 1962.

       The protagonists of this novel are three affluent Rad-
       cliffe roommates named Heather, Ginny, and Sara. The
       story takes place during the girls' junior year. Also
       in the cast are assorted Harvard students who help the
       girls forget the burdens of their wealth by engaging
       them in sexual diversions. While the basic plot of the
       book is relatively routine, the narrative includes a
       great amount of Radcliffe-Harvard marginalia. Moreover,
       it offers many glimpses of the academic side of Ivy League
       undergraduate life in Cambridge. We learn, for example,
       that at the termination of English 188 for the semester
       the professor thanks his students for their contributions
       to his intellectual development, accepts his applause,
       and "humbly" walks from the room.
          Leonie St. John was a pseudonym employed by William
       Bayer and Nancy Harmon, two Harvard-Radcliffe undergradu-
       ates during the late 1950s. *Love with a Harvard Accent*,

published only in paperback, was the first novel for
both of its authors.

268.   Brantley, Russell. *The Education of Jonathan Beam*.
        New York: Macmillan Co., 1962.

    When Jonathan Beam leaves his rural Southern home to
attend North Carolina's "Convention College," he is in-
structed by his local Baptist minister to report back
about "sin" on the Convention campus. A church college,
Convention has recently liberalized its policies to allow
such shocking pursuits as on-campus dancing. Jonathan's
minister wants data with which he can persuade Convention's overseers to rescind the school's new rules.
Once enrolled at Convention, Jonathan has a series of
misadventures which make him a participant in the sinful
goings-on. He gets drunk in public, consorts with girls,
and thanks to an iconoclastic faculty member he even begins to doubt his own fundamentalist beliefs. Toward
the end of the story Jonathan attends a state-level Baptist conference where he hears himself described from
the platform as a leading example of Convention College's
subversion of young minds. The novel contains some humor
but, for the most part, it is a serious attempt to explore
the dilemmas of students with strict religious backgrounds
who are confronted with "temptations" in college.
    At the time *The Education of Jonathan Beam* was published
Russell Brantley was director of communications at Wake
Forest.

269.   Glassman, Joyce. *Come and Join the Dance*. New York:
        Atheneum, 1962.

    This slim (176-page) and pithy novel takes place in the
week before a Barnard College graduation. The protagonist, Susan Levitt, is a senior. Afraid of leaving college for the world beyond, but at the same time anxious
to become a full-fledged adult, Susan loses her virginity
and, in an unrelated incident, has a bitter quarrel with
her parents. The latter is prompted by a notification
from the college that Susan has failed physical education--
for irregular attendance--and hence will not be graduating after all.
    Joyce Glassman was born in 1935 in New York City. As
a child she appeared on Broadway in the cast of *I Remember Mama*. She attended the Professional Children's School
and Barnard College. *Come and Join the Dance* was her
first novel.

270. Morrah, David Wardlaw, Jr. *me and the liberal arts*.
Garden City, New York: Doubleday and Co., 1962.

In a style which is reminiscent of Max Shulman's *Bare-foot Boy with Cheek* (165), this comic novel reviews the
collegiate career of one Wilbur Hare, a boy from a small
town in North Carolina. Wilbur attempts to enroll in
"King City College" but gets in the wrong line on regis-
tration day and is employed as a member of the school's
groundskeeping staff. Thinking he has been given a work-
study scholarship Wilbur attends classes, stars on the
football team, and even uncovers a financial scandal in
the ranks of the college administration. The physically
attractive Wilbur also is nearly raped by Miss Beasley,
his libidinous biology instructor. Attempting to lure
Wilbur to her apartment Miss Beasley offers, in seductive
tones, to show him her Ph.D. Wilbur speaks in fractured
English throughout the story. Reflecting on the value
of a college education, at the end of the book he comments: "Everybody which possibly can owes it to their-
selves to go off to college and get them a degree."
David Wardlaw Morrah, Jr., was born in Atlanta, Georgia,
in 1914. He received a B.S. from North Carolina State
College in 1935. A frequent contributor to *The Saturday
Evening Post*, and a columnist for the *Greensboro (North
Carolina) Sunday News*, Morrah was director of development
at Guilford College when this novel was published.

271. Perutz, Kathrin. *The Garden*. New York: Atheneum, 1962.

The "garden" in the title of this brief (185-page)
novel is an exclusive college for women in New England.
The protagonist-narrator is a bright Jewish undergraduate
named Kathy. Through a slowly paced series of remin-
iscences, Kathy offers the reader descriptions of the
institution's often banal student subculture and information about her own adjustments to it. One way in which
Kathy adjusts is to develop a lesbian attachment to a
classmate whom she identifies only as "The Blossom."
As the book proceeds, the relationship between Kathy and
her lover becomes the dominant theme of the story.
Kathrin Perutz received a B.A. from Barnard in 1960.
The Garden was her first novel.

272. Sullivan, Scott. *The Shortest Gladdest Years*. New York:
Simon and Schuster, 1962.

This conventional student-centered novel deals with
the exploits of four Yale undergraduates in the 1950s.

The book begins with the four students' entrance as
freshmen and ends, after 381 pages, when three of the
protagonists graduate. The odd man out, a lady killer
named Kevin, is suspended in his senior year after being
caught by campus security in flagrante delicto with a
girl from Vassar. The story is told in multiple first
persons; each of the four central characters takes a
quarter of the book to recount his impressions of the
chums' adventures. The narrative, straight from the
Yalies' mouths, is told with heavy doses of adolescent
sophistication. The book offers little information
about academic matters but it is a virtual Baedeker of
Yale social life of the period.

Scott Sullivan graduated from Yale in 1958. *The Shortest Gladdest Years* was his first novel. At the time the
book was published Sullivan was living in Paris.

273. Cuomo, George Michael. *Jack Be Nimble*. Garden City,
New York: Doubleday and Co., 1963.

Set at a large state university in the Midwest, this
mildly satirical novel has as its protagonist a frisky
undergraduate named Jack Wyant. Jack is a part-time
reporter on the local newspaper, a straight-A student,
and a paid tutor for numbskull football players. He
also is the paramour of Caroline Walters, the wife of the
school's football coach. The plot involves Jack in a
series of escapades from which he escapes by combining
his considerable natural charm with convenient white
lies. Indeed, Jack emerges as a modern version of those
Harvard and Yale undergraduate rogues who populated turn-
of-the-century student-centered novels.

George Michael Cuomo received a B.A. from Tufts in 1952
and an M.A. from the University of Indiana in 1955. *Jack
Be Nimble* was his first novel. At the time the book was
published Cuomo was an associate professor of English at
Victoria University in Victoria, British Columbia.

274. Farrell, James Thomas. *The Silence of History*. Garden
City, New York: Doubleday and Co., 1963.

This frankly autobiographical novel chronicles the
undergraduate days of Eddie Ryan at the University of
Chicago. The story is set in the 1920s. Eddie is a
poor boy who supplements his scholarship by working at
a gas station. The novel includes numerous classroom
scenes and some well-drawn portraits of professors.

James T. Farrell attended the University of Chicago

during the 1920s. An earlier Farrell novel, *My Days of Anger* (163), describes the struggles of Danny O'Neil, a poor but highly motivated commuter student at Chicago during the immediate pre-Depression years. The plots of *My Days of Anger* and *The Silence of History* are similar. In terms of writing style, however, the two books are quite different. *My Days of Anger* is an exemplar of the "realistic naturalism" which Farrell helped pioneer during his early days as a writer. *The Silence of History*, on the other hand, is less angry, more polished, and contains considerably more introspective reflection than action. Reviewing the book for *The Saturday Review* (April 6, 1963), David Dempsey noted that "so little happens in the novel, and it happens so relentlessly, that the reader would welcome an occasional seduction or a good family brawl."

275. Smith, Betty. *Joy in the Morning.* New York: Harper and Row, 1963.

The protagonist of this pleasant story is Annie Brown, the nineteen-year-old wife of Carl, an impoverished law student. The setting is a Midwestern state university and the time is the late 1920s. Annie's formal education ended at the eighth grade but she yearns to be a playwright. With the encouragement of the law school dean, and with the permission of the professors in question, she is able to audit creative writing classes. By the end of the novel one of Annie's dramas is about to be published by the university's press. The only human villain in the piece is Annie's mother who, through her letters from Brooklyn, does her best to discourage the marriage. The couple's real fight is against grinding poverty. When Carl graduates in the last chapter, and takes a position with a small-town law firm, it is clear that better financial times lie ahead.

Betty Smith was born in Brooklyn in 1904 and left school after the eighth grade. At the age of nineteen she married a law student at the University of Michigan. She attended classes at Michigan as a special student from 1927 to 1930. From 1930 until 1934 she attended the Yale Drama School. Smith began her professional career as a playwright but found greater success as a novelist. Her first novel, *A Tree Grows in Brooklyn* (New York: Harper and Row, 1943), was a best-seller. *Joy in the Morning* was her fourth novel.

276.   Larner, Jeremy. *Drive, He Said*. New York: Delacorte/
       Dial Press, 1964.

       Drive, He Said is a brief (190-page), semi-comic novel
       about a college basketball player who seeks to find a
       meaning to his life beyond studies and athletics. The
       protagonist is Hector Bloom, a student at "a small uni-
       versity upstate along the Hudson from New York City."
       Hector and his nonathletic friend Gabriel Reuben seduce
       professors' wives, take drugs, experiment with radicalism,
       and in a variety of other ways seek to get beyond the
       narrow strictures of traditional college life. Gabriel
       dies when, on a drug trip, he sets fire to a college
       building. But at the end of the book Hector is alive,
       well, and still engaged in his search.
           Jeremy Larner received a B.A. from Brandeis University
       in 1958 and did graduate work at the University of Cali-
       fornia at Berkeley. *Drive, He Said* was his first novel.
       It was published after the manuscript was selected (among
       1017 competitors) by Walter Van Tilburg Clark, Leslie
       Fiedler, and Mary McCarthy as the winner of the first
       Delta Prize, in 1964. Larner subsequently adapted the
       novel for a 1971 motion picture, with the same title,
       released by Columbia Pictures. Larner's second novel,
       The Answer (291), also is included in this bibliography.

277.   White, Robin. *All in Favor Say No*. New York: Farrar,
       Straus and Company, 1964.

       Julian "Deke" Dekker is a twenty-six-year-old perpetual
       student at "Peninsula University," a state institution
       near San Francisco. A flower child, Deke lives in a
       ramshackled cottage in a decrepit student ghetto known
       as "Bear Creek Canyon." Deke's major ambition is to
       travel to India, where he hopes to learn the secrets of
       meditation. The plot of the story has Deke falling in
       love with Alison Bojer, a Canyon neighbor who is raising
       two illegitimate children. Toward the end of the book
       Deke and Alison are married. Written as comedy, the novel
       pays minimum attention to academic matters.
           Robin White was born in 1928 in Kodaikanae, India. He
       received a B.A. from Yale in 1950, was a Bread Loaf Fellow
       at Middlebury College in 1956, and held a creative writing
       fellowship at Stanford the following year. *All in Favor
       Say No* was his fourth novel.

278. Leigh, James Leighton. *What Can You Do?* New York:
      Harper and Row, 1965.

      Philip Fuller, the protagonist-narrator of this mildly
comic novel, is a freshman at a California state college.
The year is 1960, though Philip often flashes back to
recount exploits during his high school years. Philip
specializes in sex and literature. His tastes in the
former are eclectic and his conquests include various
college co-eds, nymphets in his nearby hometown, and the
thirty-year-old wife of his high school gym teacher. At
one point in the narrative Philip describes himself as a
"genital on wheels." Philip's reading tastes, on the other
hand, are more selective. As respite from his amorous
activities he consumes Proust, Faulkner, Hemingway, and
the Marquis de Sade. The only faculty character in the
book who is accorded more than a quick, cynical slap on
the mortarboard is Mr. Mallory, Philip's English instructor. Mallory is fascinated with Philip's literary sophistication and envious of his sexual conquests. In return
for A's on his term papers, Philip arranges for Mallory
to sleep with a luscious co-ed named Antonia.
      James Leighton Leigh received a B.A. from San Jose
State College in 1957 and did graduate work at Stanford
in the late 1950s. *What Can You Do?* was his first novel.
At the time the book was published Leigh was an assistant
professor of English at San Francisco State College.
What Can You Do? was subsequently adapted for film and the
motion picture, entitled "Making It," was released by
Twentieth Century-Fox in 1970.

279. Nichols, John Treadwell. *The Sterile Cuckoo*. New York:
      David McKay Co., 1965.

      The Sterile Cuckoo is a brief (210-page) but frenzied
tale of adolescent love. The protagonists are Jerry
Payne and Pookie Adams, two undergraduates who attend
nearby Eastern colleges. The story is told in the first
person by Jerry, whose idea of engrossing literary narrative is to recount how his roommate once shattered five
empty beer bottles by bombarding them with hockey pucks.
Some of the plot takes place off campus, in such dispar-
ate locales as New York City and "Friarsburg," Oklahoma.
Most reviewers panned the book. Nonetheless, the work
was adapted for the screen. The motion picture, released
in 1969, starred Liza Minelli.
      John Treadwell Nichols graduated from Hamilton College
in 1962. *The Sterile Cuckoo* was his first novel.

280. Thom, Robert. *The Earthly Paradise*. New York: Trident
      Books, 1965.

      The protagonist of this disspiriting saga is Homer
      Glover, a self-indulgent undergraduate at Yale. Homer
      comes from Long Island where his family consists of his
      corporate-executive father, his alcoholic mother, and
      Jamie, his retarded deaf-mute brother. Homer takes time
      from his other extracurricular pursuits to impregnate
      Lisa, a New Haven waitress. Suddenly in the marrying
      mood, Homer brings Lisa home to meet the Glover clan.
      But Lisa finds brother Jamie more appealing than Homer,
      and the waitress and the deaf-mute disappear to a walkup
      in Greenwich Village. Homer searches for Lisa, finds her
      at the end of the book, and is rewarded for his trouble
      by being told to leave her life forever. Though much of
      this novel is set in New Haven, the academic routines of
      Yale life do not figure prominently in the plot.
          Robert Thom received a B.A. from Yale in 1951. *The
      Earthly Paradise* was his first novel. Thom's written
      output includes a great number of screenplays, teleplays,
      and dramas for the stage. Among his movie credits are
      "All the Fine Young Cannibals" (1960), "Wild in the
      Streets" (1960), and "Bloody Mama" (1970).

281. Buchan, Perdita. *Girl with a Zebra*. New York: Charles
      Scribner's Sons, 1966.

      This whimsical comedy is set in Cambridge in the 1960s.
      The protagonist is Emily Ames, a Radcliffe student from
      "Phillida," Indiana. Emily has a romance with an ego-
      centric Harvard undergraduate named Blaise. She also is
      entrusted by an addled professor with the care of a zebra.
      Moreover, Emily develops a friendship with an aging Cam-
      bridge eccentric--Miss Helen Figwort--who is pursuing
      her bizarre interests in animal husbandry by attempting
      to produce a live phoenix. The novel received generally
      favorable reviews. Some critics saw it as a unique if
      not entirely intelligible allegory about American life
      in the mid-period of the twentieth century.
          Born in Great Britain, and the daughter of author John
      Buchan, Perdita Buchan graduated from Radcliffe in 1962.
      Girl with a Zebra was her first novel.

282. Farina, Richard. *Been Down So Long It Looks Like Up to
      Me*. New York: Random House, 1966.

      This ultra-hip comic novel has as its protagonist one
      Gnossos Papadopoulis, an undergraduate at "Ithake

University." An aspiring revolutionary, Gnossos is seen
in Cuba during Castro's takeover of the country as well
as on the Ithake campus during quieter moments in world
history. The plot of the book has to do with Gnossos'
growing awareness that people, whether they posture on
the left or the right of the political spectrum, are not
always what they seem to be. The characters in the story
include an opportunist radical co-ed and a flagitious,
politically conservative dean who aspires to become Ithake's president. The story contains an abundance of sex,
drug tripping, student protest, and idiomatic writing.

Richard Farina was born in Brooklyn in 1936. He attended Cornell in the 1950s. After college he became a
singer and songwriter. *Been Down So Long It Looks Like
Up to Me* was his first novel. Farina was killed in a
motorcycle accident on April 30, 1966, two days after the
novel was published.

283. Hersey, John. *Too Far to Walk*. New York: Alfred A.
Knopf, 1966.

John Hersey received a B.A. from Yale in 1936. A
decade later, as one of America's outstanding writers,
he was awarded an honorary M.A. by his alma mater. From
1950 until 1965 he was a fellow of Berkeley College at
Yale and in 1965 he began a five-year stint as master of
Yale's Pierson College.

Too Far to Walk was completed just before John Hersey
assumed his Pierson responsibilities. The novel tells
the story of John Fist, an undergraduate at an institution
which Hersey calls "Sheldon College." John yearns to
avoid conformity and he sells his soul to a Mephistoph-
elean fellow student named Chum Breed. In return John
begins to experience "freedom," which in his case consists of women, drugs, and political protest. After a
diet of these delights, however, John sees that real
freedom must be sought within one's mind. He renounces
his bargain with Breed, makes up with his estranged
parents, and seems prepared to resume a more traditional
student existence.

284. Hoff, Marilyn. *Dink's Blues*. New York: Harcourt, Brace,
and World, 1966.

Narrated by Sarah Lodge, a student at an unnamed college in the North, this intense novel concentrates upon
the enigmatic exploits of Diane "Dink" St. Claire, Sarah's
roommate. Dink, who is from Tennessee, claims that she

is part Black and, on occasion, she seeks companionship
in the Black section of the nearby town. Dink also has
an affair with Andrew Jefferson, a married humanities
instructor. When Dink announces she is pregnant, Andrew
attempts suicide. Sarah, whose wide-eyed innocence at
the beginning of the story gradually is replaced by skep-
ticism, comes to doubt Dink's Black lineage as well as
her supposed pregnancy. But the book ends before either
of Dink's contentions is proven or disproven.

Marilyn Hoff was born in Iowa Falls, Iowa, in 1932.
She received a B.A. from Macalester College in 1964 and
an M.A. from Syracuse in 1968. *Dink's Blues* was her
first novel.

285. White, Milton. *A Yale Man*. Garden City, New York:
      Doubleday and Co., 1966.

The Yale man referred to in the title of this brief
(155-page) novella is Dave Miller, class of 1936. The
story covers Dave's first and only year in New Haven.
Only eighty-nine pounds, soaking wet, the diminutive Dave
engages in a variety of customary freshman pursuits. At
the end of his freshman year—and at the end of the book—
Dave's father dies and family finances dictate the end
of Dave's Yale career. Although the plot of this book
is neither exciting nor unusual, *A Yale Man* provides un-
matched detail about Yale undergraduate life in the early
1930s. Parts of the book originally appeared, though in
somewhat different form, in *The New Yorker*, *Seventeen*, and
Harper's.

Milton White attended Yale for one year, as a member of
the class of 1936. He received a B.A. and an M.A. from
Miami University of Ohio. At the time *A Yale Man* was
published White was a member of the department of English
at Miami University of Ohio.

*286. Kolb, Kenneth. *Getting Straight*. Philadelphia and New
       York: Chilton Books, 1967.

This anti-establishment satire has as its protagonist
a young man named Harry. As the story begins Harry is
studying both for an M.A. in English and a teaching cer-
tificate at a college in San Francisco. He also holds a
part-time job as an advertising assistant at a department
store and, in his spare time, he hosts a series of live-
in girlfriends. In the course of the book Harry is expelled from the teacher-training program, fails his M.A.
orals, and loses his position at the department store.

At the close of the novel he is without job or education prospects but he is about to take yet another feminine companion into his abode. Many professors appear in the text and all of them are portrayed as suffering from advanced forms of absurdity. Indeed, Harry flunks his orals when he suddenly decides to give inane answers to the inane questions put to him by a gaggle of faculty inquisitors.

Kenneth Kolb was born in 1926 in Oakland, California. He received a B.A. from the University of California at Berkeley in 1950 and an M.A. from San Francisco State College in 1953. *Getting Straight* was Kolb's first novel, although he had previously published many short stories and had sold many television scripts and screenplays. In 1970 Columbia Pictures transformed *Getting Straight* into a motion picture starring Elliott Gould.

287. Theroux, Paul. *Waldo*. Boston: Houghton Mifflin Co., 1967.

The title character of this inventive comic novel is an incorrigibly suggestible young man who attends "Rugg College" after his release from the "Booneville School for Delinquent Boys." Waldo stays at Rugg only for a month before he is spirited away by Clovis Techy, an aging movie starlet who yearns for his body. But during his brief time at Rugg--which takes up a third of the 208-page story--Waldo meets a wide array of bizarre campus characters and has a series of misadventures. Inspired by a huge colored chart on the wall of one of his lecture rooms, for example, Waldo stands in front of the hanging before class, giving it careful scrutiny. When the professor enters he castigates Waldo for his prurient interests. The chart, it turns out, is not a map of the Louisiana Purchase territories, as Waldo believes. Instead, it is a huge color plate of the female urogenital system.

Paul Theroux received a B.A. from the University of Massachusetts in 1963. For the next ten years he taught English in a series of African and Asian universities. *Waldo*, his first novel, was published when he was a lecturer at Makerera University in Uganda. Theroux's later books, most notably *Family Arsenal* (Boston: Houghton Mifflin Co., 1976), projected him into the front rank of American writers.

288. Walton, Stephen. *No Transfer*. New York: Vanguard Press,
      1967.

      No Transfer would be a routine novel of undergraduate
      life if it were not for the particular motivational pro-
      gram of "Modern University," the book's setting. In
      many respects, Modern is a progressive school. Students
      may cut classes as they wish, and when a male and female
      student desire to live together the administration assigns
      them an apartment. But, as the title of the work sug-
      gests, Modern does not allow its students to transfer to
      other institutions. A half-dozen or so times per year
      klaxons summon the Modern undergraduates to a mandatory
      assembly in a giant auditorium. One student with high
      grades and one with an "unacceptable" scholastic average
      are chosen by lot to walk down to the stage. The low-
      ranking student puts his or her head on the block of a
      guillotine, and the high-ranking student pulls a cord to
      activate the machine. John Clark, the president of
      Modern, is perhaps the only college president, in or out
      of fiction, who can tell a freshman class at orientation
      that "there are one thousand and twelve of you here today
      (and) more than one thousand of you will graduate."
      Against the backdrop of Modern's "self-discipline" plan,
      the protagonist of the story, Gary Fort, leads a sur-
      prisingly normal collegiate existence. Not until his
      live-in girlfriend is separated from the college, and
      from her head, does Gary seriously consider the impli-
      cations of Modern's unique stimulus for studying.
          Stephen Walton graduated from Michigan State University
      in the late 1960s. *No Transfer*, written while he was
      still an undergraduate, was his first novel.

289. Yount, John Alonzo. *Wolf at the Door*. New York: Random
      House, 1967.

      This seamy story deals with a mentally unbalanced under-
      graduate who is determined to do harm to himself and to
      those around him. Thomas Rapidan, an army veteran, is a
      junior at "Briston University." The plot centers upon
      the breakup of Tom's marriage and upon his subsequent
      affair with a barmaid. The wolf in the title of the
      book is a decrepit stuffed animal which Tom buys for com-
      panionship after his wife leaves him. Since Tom lives
      off-campus and seldom attends classes, very little of this
      novel is concerned with the usual undergraduate activities.
          John Alonzo Yount received an A.B. from Vanderbilt in
      1960 and then attended the Writers' Workshop at the State

University of Iowa. After a brief stint in the English
department of Clemson University he moved to the University of New Hampshire in 1965. *Wolf at the Door* was his
first novel.

290. Hawes, Evelyn Johnson [Mrs. Nat H. Hawes]. *A Madras-
        Type Jacket*. New York: Harcourt, Brace and World,
        1968.

This bubbly novel is told in the first person by Margo
Brown, an eighteen-year-old co-ed at a large state university in the Pacific Northwest. The book covers Margo's
freshman year. Although Margo has many escapades her
frolics are all of the harmless variety and the story is
full of good cheer and optimism. Margo even studies!
Some days she gets up before dawn to grind away at her
books. The madras-type jacket in the title belongs to
one Andy Peterson, a fellow student with whom Margo has
a platonic romance. Reviewing the book for *The Library
Journal* (October 15, 1967), W.L. Tefft praised the work
for its wholesomeness, but noted that it was "far out of
touch with the kids of today."
Evelyn Johnson Hawes received an undergraduate degree
from the University of Washington in 1936 and then did
graduate work at the University of Cincinnati, Purdue
University, and the State University of New York at Buffalo. At various points in her career she taught speech,
literature, and creative writing at the University of
Washington, Cincinnati, and SUNY-Buffalo. *A Madras-Type
Jacket* was her second novel. The book won the National
League of Pen Women award for the best published novel
of 1968.

291. Larner, Jeremy. *The Answer*. New York: Macmillan Co.,
        1968.

Steeped in ironies, this novel follows the exploits of
Alex Randall, a twenty-year-old university student, as
he seeks truth through drugs. Alex attends a high-status
institution in New England. Much of the story takes
place in "Heavenly House," the mansion of Dr. Magus Tyrtan, a former academic who is now a guru of the drug culture. Alex is at first one of Dr. Tyrtan's more willing
disciples. But he turns upon his mentor when his roommate dies after internalizing an overdose of good doctor's
wonder potion. The last chapter of the novel is a postscript, presumably written in the 1980s, in which Alex
tells how, after a long trip to Mexico, he finally

finished college. He tells, too, about the decline of
drugs during the 1970s and how children of the eighties
"scorn their druggie parents."

The Answer was Jeremy Larner's second novel. His first
novel, *Drive, He Said* (276), is included in this bibliography. In between these novels Larner published *The
Addict in the Street* (New York: Grove Press, 1965), an
edited book of interviews with heroin addicts.

292.   Spacks, Barry. *The Sophomore*. Englewood Cliffs, New
        Jersey: Prentice-Hall, 1968.

The protagonist of this hip, farcical novel is Harry
Zissel, a directionless twenty-two-year-old sophomore at
an unnamed university in "Fear of Reprisals," Connecticut. Harry has a live-in, pregnant girlfriend who rides
a unicycle, a dog-eared copy of *The Kama Sutra*, and an
unfulfilled desire to take up residence in a drugstore
phone booth. Searching for the meaning of his life, at
one point in the narrative Harry visits an old roommate,
now a Ph.D. and an instructor of humanities at the "Cordelia (New Jersey) College for Women." But Cordelia
College proves to be as absurd a place as the Connecticut
university which, for reasons unknown, retains Harry on
its student rolls.

Barry Spacks received a B.A. from the University of
Pennsylvania in 1952 and an M.A. from the University of
Indiana in 1956. *The Sophomore* was his first novel. At
the time the book was published Spacks was a member of
the humanities staff of the Massachusetts Institute of
Technology.

293.   Yafa, Stephen H. *Paxton Quigley's Had the Course*.
        Philadelphia and New York: J.B. Lippincott Co., 1968.

As this brief (195-page) book opens Paxton Quigley, a
Williams College student, has been held prisoner for two
weeks in the attic of a Bennington dormitory. Three
Bennington women, his captors, visit him--one every four
hours--for sex. Most of the story consists of flashbacks, through which the tiring Paxton reviews his own
pre-captivity pursuits of each of his three jailors. The
end comes when one of the girls decides to leave Bennington. She releases Paxton who, though happy to be out of
the dark and dingy dormitory attic, finds his sexual
freedom a mixed blessing.

Stephen H. Yafa received an A.B. from Dartmouth in
1963 and an M.F.A. from Carnegie-Mellon University in

1965. *Paxton Quigley's Had the Course* was his first
novel. At the time the book was published Yafa was an
elementary school teacher in Los Angeles. Yafa subsequently adapted the novel for a motion picture which was
released in 1968 under the title "Three in the Attic."

294. Garbo, Norman. *The Movement*. New York: William Morrow,
      1969.

The Movement is a violent novel about student protest
in the 1960s. The setting is "Chadwick University," a
state institution in the Midwest. Although the protagonist of the story is a Black student dissident named
Joshua Lecole, the most noteworthy character from the
standpoint of college fiction is Hadley Young, Chadwick's
president. Young is the most egregious presidential
failure in any college novel. Described as a "tall,
square shouldered, virile-looking man," Young believes
he can charm his rioting students into quiescence. Yet
while Young is charming some of his students, others
break into the ROTC building and carry off an arsenal
of weapons. With machine guns and bazookas they wipe
out contingents of state police and national guardsmen
sent to the campus to keep order. Even as Lecole and
his chums hold Young hostage in his office, the valiant
president pleads with the governor for more time in which
to negotiate. But his entreaty is to no avail. Young
and the student radicals perish when a fleet of air force
phantom jets bombs Chadwick's administration building
into oblivion.
Norman Garbo was born in New York City in 1919. He
attended City College of New York and the New York Academy
of Fine Art. During his career Garbo has combined paint-
ing, writing, newspaper work, and lecturing at various
American colleges and universities. *The Movement* was his
second novel.

295. Gold, Herbert. *The Great American Jackpot*. New York:
      Random House, 1969.

This often funny satirical novel is set at Berkeley in
the early 1960s. The protagonist is Al Dooley, a graduate student in sociology. Bored with academe, Al tries
a career in crime and unsuccessfully attempts to rob a
bank. Also in the cast is Jarod Howe, a Black sociologist who is Al's mentor. At one point in the narrative
Jarod sheds his bourgeois academic garb and joins the
Black Muslims. Despite the many campus scenes in the

book, the work is not a mainstream college novel. Most
reviewers saw it as a broad fictive statement about general American manners and morals.

A major American writer, Herbert Gold received a B.A.
from Columbia in 1946 and an M.A. from that institution
in 1948. Al Dooley and Jarod Howe appear again in a later
Gold novel, *Waiting for Cordelia* (New York: Arbor House,
1977). In this story, which takes place almost entirely
off campus, Dooley is now a member of the Berkeley sociology faculty. Accused by Howe of "coasting on his reputation as a bankrobber," he studies prostitution in San
Francisco in order to obtain data for quick and easy
publications.

296. Leggett, John Ward. *Who Took the Gold Away*. New York:
      Random House, 1969.

This well-told, often matter-of-fact novel traces the
lives of two Yale students, from their entrance into Yale
in 1938 until the death of one of the protagonists twenty-
two years later. The boys-cum-men in the story are Ben
Moseley and Pierce Jay. Ben is a scholarship student
and Pierce, who is killed in 1960 in a New York City mug-
ging, is the wealthy scion of an airline magnate. Despite
their differences in social background, Ben and Pierce
become chums and their relationship--though not always a
smooth one--continues after graduation. The first half
of the 468-page book is set in New Haven, and the Yale
scenes, rich in detail, are presented with a high degree
of verisimilitude.

John Ward Leggett received an A.B. from Yale in 1942.
From 1950 until 1960 he was an editor with Houghton
Mifflin, and from 1960 until 1967 he was a senior editor
at Harper's. *Who Took the Gold Away* was Leggett's third
novel. At the time the book was published he was a full-
time professional writer.

297. Von Hoffman, Nicholas. *Two, Three, Many More*. Chicago:
      Quadrangle Books, 1969.

This intense, kaleidoscopic novel describes the events
leading up to a violent outbreak of student protest at
an unnamed, high-status American university. A host of
characters, from both the student ranks and from the
university's power structure, appear in the book. Most
of the principals are clearly modeled after well-
publicized, real-life campus figures of the late 1960s.
Despite the mediation efforts of Myron Mirsky, a social

scientist, the students and their antagonists manage to plunge headlong toward disaster. As the book concludes police have just opened fire on a rampaging mob of student dissidents.

Two, Three, Many More was Nicholas Von Hoffman's first novel. As a reporter and columnist for *The Washington Post* Von Hoffman covered most of the major campus disturbances of the Viet Nam era. His nonfiction work *We Are the People Our Parents Warned Us Against* (Chicago: Quadrangle Books, 1968) is often regarded as the most insightful journalistic study of anti-establishment college students of the 1960s.

298. Segal, Erich. *Love Story*. New York: Harper and Row, 1970.

Interviewed in *The Saturday Review* (September 14, 1970), Erich Segal described *Love Story* as "a very short novel about a Harvard boy, old New England, and a Radcliffe girl, Italian-American, who fall in love, are married despite family opposition, enjoy early success and great happiness in New York, and then are struck by tragedy." As millions of people around the world know from reading the book and/or from seeing the motion picture of the same title, the tragedy is the girl's death from cancer. Although future students of college fiction are not likely to find that *Love Story* reveals a great deal about American higher education in the late 1960s, they certainly will be intrigued by the work's immense commercial success. In the first year after its publication the book sold 450,000 hardbound and over 9,000,000 paperbound copies. Moreover, during its initial release the motion picture, which was written by Segal, was second in box office receipts only to "Gone with the Wind," then the reigning revenue champion of filmdom.

Erich Segal received an A.B. from Harvard in 1958 and a Ph.D. from Yale in 1974. He was an assistant professor of classics at Yale when *Love Story* was published. The novel, Segal's first, was adapted from his screenplay. Prior to "Love Story," Segal had a number of other screenplays to his credit. One of them, "R.P.M.," a 1970 Columbia Pictures release starring Anthony Quinn and Ann-Margret, is the story of a sociologist who vaults into a college presidency during a student uprising.

299.   [Crichton, Michael J., and Douglas Crichton]. *Dealing:*
       or The Berkeley-to-Boston Forty-Brick Lost-Bag Blues.
       By Michael Douglas (pseud.). New York: Alfred A.
       Knopf, 1971.

       Dealing is a lively, if sensationalistic, novel which
       ferrets into the mechanics of the drug trade at Harvard
       and Berkeley. The protagonist is a fallen-away Harvard
       student named Peter Harkness. Peter renounces his con-
       ventional values and becomes a prime mover in the cross-
       country transport of marijuana. Also in the cast are
       assorted drug-involved students and a corrupt narcotics
       officer.
       "Michael Douglas" was a pseudonym employed by Michael
       and Douglas Crichton, brothers who co-authored this book.
       Michael Crichton, who received an A.B. from Harvard in
       1965 and an M.D. from Harvard Medical School in 1969,
       is best known as the author of *The Andromeda Strain* (New
       York: Alfred A. Knopf, 1969).

300.   Knowles, John. *The Paragon.* New York: Random House,
       1971.

       Set at Yale, this well-written novel of undergraduate
       awakening centers on the exploits of Lou Colfax. Lou
       enters Yale in the early 1950s after a short stint in
       the Marine Corps. An individualist, he squabbles with
       his tweedy roommate, attends classes when the spirit
       moves him, and has an affair with Charlotte Mills, a
       student at the Yale Drama School. A male child is born
       from this liaison. Annoyed by Lou's generally irresponsi-
       ble deportment, Charlotte leaves New Haven, takes the
       infant with her, and eventually marries another man.
       When she returns to New Haven a year later, Lou kidnaps
       his son. He returns the child after five days. At this
       point--which comes at the end of the story--the suddenly
       sympathetic Charlotte declines to prosecute Lou and,
       instead, offers him visiting privileges with his boy.
       The book includes many scenes on the Yale campus.
       John Knowles received a B.A. from Yale in 1949. *The*
       Paragon was his fourth novel. Knowles' first novel,
       A Separate Peace (New York: Macmillan Co., 1960), is now
       considered a classic story of prep school life.

*301. Osborn, John Jay, Jr. *The Paper Chase.* Boston: Houghton
       Mifflin Co., 1971.

       This intense novel describes the stressful first year
       of a group of students at the Harvard Law School. The

student scrutinized most closely is Hart, a bright but
often naive lad from Minnesota. Hart compounds his academic problems by falling in love with the daughter of
his contract law instructor, Professor Kingsfield. Kingsfield, one of the most brilliant but least popular teachers
in college fiction, terrorizes his pupils by subjecting
them to merciless classroom inquisitions. The book pays
a great amount of attention to the grinding and grade
grubbing of law school life.

John Jay Osborn, Jr., received a B.A. from Harvard in
1967 and a J.D. from Harvard Law School in 1970. *The
Paper Chase*, written while the author was a law student,
was Osborn's first novel. The book was adapted for a
1973 motion picture bearing the same title, and in 1978
The Paper Chase was employed as the basis for a weekly,
prime-time television series on CBS.

302. [Chitty, Sir Thomas Willes]. *Generally a Virgin*. By
      Thomas Hinde (pseud.). London: Hodder and Stoughton,
      1972.

Generally a Virgin is an intricate and intense novel
about the radical American student scene of the late
1960s. The protagonist is Jo Victor, a junior from the
Midwest who is attending "Eastern University." Jo is
politically conservative and he sometimes acts as an
undercover informant for the F.B.I. Jo's girlfriend,
Sherry Holiday, is a hippie who becomes a dedicated
devotee of violent protest. As the story progresses
Sherry flirts not only with arrest and expulsion from
the university but with a nervous breakdown as well. One
indication of Sherry's precarious mental condition is
the fact that she gets so emotionally involved in the
lectures of her leftist sociology professor that she sobs
with ecstasy in his classroom. For his part, Jo goes
through various tortures of conscience as Sherry races
toward disaster. At the end of the book he is attempting, in vain, to dissuade her from manufacturing bombs
in her apartment.

During the 1969-1970 academic year Sir Thomas Willes
Chitty served as a visiting professor at Boston University. *Generally a Virgin* was his twelfth novel. An earlier Chitty novel, *High* (375), also appears in this bibliography.

*303.   DeLillo, Don. *End Zone*. Boston: Houghton Mifflin Co.,
        1972.

        Although this book centers on intercollegiate football
        it is much more than a conventional college-sports novel.
        Sometimes allegorical, sometimes a parody of college
        fiction, and sometimes a satire on academe, it is a com-
        plex work which defies easy categorization. The pro-
        tagonist of the story is Gary Harkness who arrives at
        "Logos College," deep in the Southwest, for the express
        purpose of playing football. Gary already has played for
        Syracuse, Penn State, Miami, and Michigan State and has
        been asked to leave all of these institutions for various
        rules infractions. Logos, which aspires to the national
        championship, has as its president Mrs. Tom Wade, who is
        not only one of the few women presidents in college
        fiction but one of the few women in all of literature
        who can be described as "Lincolnesque." Mrs. Wade is
        the tough, spare widow of Logos' founder, a mute who could
        only make "disgusting sounds." Although the Logos team
        does well, losing only its final game, Gary ends up in
        the hospital with brain fever, his football career pre-
        sumably at an end. In addition to Gary and Mrs. Wade,
        the cast of the novel includes an ROTC major whose
        language consists almost totally of military jargon, a
        fat co-ed who loses weight in an attempt to capture
        Gary's attention, and Coach Emmett Creed, who employs
        religion, profanity, and down-home sayings in an effort
        to motivate his players.
        Don DeLillo attended Fordham University in the 1950s
        and then worked for five years at a New York City ad-
        vertising agency before becoming a full-time writer.
        End Zone was his second novel.

304.   Scott-Heron, Gil. *The Nigger-Factory*. New York: Dial
        Press, 1972.

        This often acrid novel takes place at "Sutton Uni-
        versity," a Black, state-supported institution in Vir-
        ginia. The plot centers upon an attempt by a violence-
        prone student group--called "the Mjumbe"--to force the
        school's administration into accepting thirteen "non-
        negotiable" demands. The protagonist of the story is
        Earl Thomas, president of the student council, who tries
        to moderate between the dissidents and Sutton's con-
        fused and bitter president, Ogden Calhoun. President
        Calhoun is by far the novel's best-developed character.
        A liberal Black psychologist, he was a leading civil

rights activist in the 1950s. Yet to the more immoderate
of his students in the early 1970s he is the "Head Nig-
ger," and his home is "The Plantation." Many of the demands in question seek to shift power from Calhoun--who
is portrayed as a moderately authoritarian administrator--
to the student government. Eventually Calhoun is forced
to call in the National Guard and one of the leading
student agitators is killed when a Guard bullet detonates
a bomb he is carrying. At the end of the novel Sutton is
closed. Calhoun plans to reopen the institution only
after invoking a "readmission" policy which will screen
out those students who took major roles in the insurgency.
    Gil Scott-Heron was born in Chicago in 1949. He at-
tended the Fieldston School of the Ethical Culture Society and Johns Hopkins University. He received an M.A.
from Johns Hopkins in 1972. *The Nigger-Factory* was his
second novel.

305. Klamkin, Lynn. *Hello, Good-Bye*. New York: Dodd, Mead
      and Co., 1973.

      The protagonist of this short (123-page) novella is
Jane Potterman, an undergraduate at "Laurencelle College."
Laurencelle is an experimental, coeducational institution
in Vermont. It is the sort of school where, in Jane's
words, "a ... teacher does not get pissed off by a lousy
student ... only concerned." The book follows Jane
through her freshman year, during which she acquires an
ability to spout great bursts of pseudo-sophisticated
dialogue and has two affairs with male students. Despite
(or perhaps because of) the trivial nature of the book's
plot, the author is able to suggest that experimental
education--Laurencelle style--is something short of
higher education at its finest.
      Lynn Klamkin was born in Waterbury, Connecticut, in
1950. She received a B.A. from Goddard College in Vermont in 1971. *Hello, Good-Bye* was her first novel.

306. Lukas, Susan. *Fat Emily*. New York: Stein and Day,
      1974.

      The title character of this novel of adolescent re-
bellion is a plump Jewish girl from California. Brimming
over with sarcastic one-line commentaries about those
with whom she comes in contact, Emily attends the University of California at Los Angeles. Her traditionalist
parents hope that she will lead a routine college life,
join a sorority, and marry a fiscally promising young

young man. Instead, Emily takes up with Tali, a young
Israeli theater major whose lack of both manners and
money offends her mother and father. Some of the story
takes place in New York City after Emily is sent to a
"citizenship camp" in the Bronx. She is packed off to
New York by her parents in the vain hope that she will
forget her boorish boyfriend. Although the book contains
many scenes at UCLA it is probably more valuable as a
study of middle-class Jewish family life than as a fictive
investigation of the college experience.

Susan Lukas received a B.A. from UCLA in 1962. *Fat
Emily* was her first novel.

307. Rooney, Frank. *Valedictory*. New York: Harcourt Brace
Jovanovich, 1974.

The protagonist of this semi-satirical novel about
student protest is Fred Harbach, a star discus thrower
and football player at "David Thoreau College." David
Thoreau, built on the site of the former "Dinwood School
for Boys," and located next door to the "Emily Dickinson
College for Women," is a private institution for the
mediocre in New England. When leftist dissidents take
over the school's science building, Fred tries to remain
aloof from the fracas. However, a group of conservative
student athletes breaks into the building, assaults its
occupiers, and Fred is unjustly accused of leading the
violent counter-protest. Dean Willie ("The Vermont
Weasel") Wilson then offers Fred as a sacrifice to the
left-wingers. He suspends Fred indefinitely and the
campus returns to normal. At the close of the book Fred
tries and fails to make the squad of the New York Football
Giants and, as we last see him, he is playing in Canada
with the Toronto Argonauts. The list of characters includes Harriet Myer Nielson, Fred's girlfriend who eventually deserts him to join "the movement," and a host of
campus radicals. Dean Wilson is portrayed as a pompous
administrator whose natural loathsomeness is raised to
new heights during moments of crisis.

Frank Rooney was born in Kansas City, Missouri, in
1913. He did not attend college. A professional writer,
his short stories and nonfiction articles have appeared
in virtually every major American magazine. *Valedictory*
was his sixth novel.

308. Rose, Louise Blecher. *The Launching of Barbara Fabri-kant*. New York: David McKay and Co., 1974.

Barbara Fabrikant, the heroine of this sometimes satirical novel, is an overweight Jewish co-ed at "Harter University." Harter is a middling-status institution in
New England which caters to students who cannot get into
better places. During her time at Harter Barbara throws
out more than her quota of cynical remarks, gains and
loses great quantities of fat depending upon her mood of
the moment, and has affairs with a weak, pasty student
and with a professor of political science. The portrait
of Dr. Appel, Barbara's professorial paramour, is offered
in considerable detail. Obsessed both with sex and his
Jewish heritage, Appel insists that Barbara wear a cruci-
fix around her neck when they have intercourse. As for
Harter University, Barbara observes that it is a school
which "is ordered around itself, which exists strictly
for the benefit of itself, and has students only because
it would look mighty foolish without them."
    According to information on the dust jacket of *The
Launching of Barbara Fabrikant*, Louise Blecher Rose was
a teacher of literature and writing at a college in New
York City when the novel was published.

*309. French, Marilyn. *The Women's Room*. New York: Summit
Books, 1977.

Mira, a thirty-eight-year-old housewife in suburbia,
is divorced by her husband. She enrolls in Harvard to
pursue a Ph.D. in English. In Cambridge she acts as
mother figure to a set of younger female graduate students. After her group is beset by a series of misfortunes, including unhappy romances (both heterosexual
and homosexual), mental breakdowns, and a rape, Mira
manages to complete her thesis and graduate. But, of
course, no high-status institution will hire a fortyish
female Ph.D. So Mira takes a job at a junior college
in Maine where, at the end of the story, she walks along
the beach talking to herself. The first half of this
book details Mira's years as an exploited suburban housewife. The second half chronicles her experiences at
Harvard.
    Marilyn French received a B.A. from Hofstra in 1951
and a Ph.D. from Harvard in 1972. From 1964 until 1968
she was an instructor of English at Hofstra. In 1967 she
was divorced from her husband of seventeen years. French
became an assistant professor of English at Holy Cross in

1972. In 1976 she became a Mellon Fellow in English at
Harvard. *The Women's Room* was her first novel. *The
Women's Room* also was the first novel to be published by
Summit Books, a division of Simon and Schuster, and its
appearance was accompanied by an aggressive advertising
and public relations campaign. Paperback rights to *The
Women's Room* were sold for $750,000 even before hardbound
copies went on sale. In 1980 the novel was adapted for
a made-for-television motion picture.

310.   Larson, Charles Raymond. *Academia Nuts: Or, The Collected
       Works of Clara Le Page.* Indianapolis and New York:
       Bobbs-Merrill Co., 1977.

       Told in the first person by a harassed professor of
       English, this amusing book is less a novel than a col-
       lection of vignettes. The book is broken into twenty-
       eight short chapters, most of them four or five pages in
       length. All of the stanzas deal with the professor's
       attempts to teach an aggressively ingenuous co-ed named
       Clara Le Page. After reading her class assignments Clara
       insists, for example, that Rip Van Winkle was impotent
       and that the "grass" in Walt Whitman's most famous poem
       was marijuana. Although the professor is never able to
       bring Ms. Le Page to accept more orthodox interpretations
       of the classics, he unintentionally inspires her to pur-
       sue her creative scholarship. At the end of the book she
       announces her intention to go on for a Ph.D. in liter-
       ature.
       Calvin Raymond Larson received a B.A. from the Uni-
       versity of Colorado in 1959 and a Ph.D. from Indiana
       University in 1970. At the time *Academia Nuts* was
       published he was a professor of literature at American
       University. Larson is best known for his professional
       writings on fiction by Third World authors.

311.   Sayles, John Thomas. *Union Dues.* Boston: Little, Brown
       and Co., 1977.

       This intense, richly textured novel explores the radi-
       cal demimonde of Cambridge in the late 1960s. The plot
       centers on the unsuccessful efforts of a working-class
       father, forty-five-year-old Hunter McNatt, to find his
       runaway son. The boy, seventeen-year-old Hobie McNatt,
       is a member of a commune dedicated to revolution. Al-
       though Hobie is not a student, much of the action in the
       book takes place in and around Harvard Square and many
       of Hobie's companions are or were students at institutions

of higher learning in the Boston area. Reviewers generally praised the novel as an insightful look at radicalism, Cambridge-style, at the height of the Viet Nam War.
   John Sayles received a B.A. from Williams in 1972.
Union Dues was his second novel.

312. Wakefield, Dan. *Home Free*. New York: Delacorte Press/
      Seymour Lawrence, 1977.

   Home Free is a gloomy story about a twenty-three-year-
old male student at Northeastern University who seduces
and then lives with his female, twenty-seven-year-old
history instructor. The student, named Gene, is heavily
into drugs, Janis Joplin music, and loafing. The instructor, named Louise, is so laconic that her character never
becomes clear. After a time Gene tires of Louise and
drifts across America to Venice, California, where he becomes an integral part of the hippie scene. One of Gene's
stops along the way is the University of Iowa. At Iowa
he lounges on the periphery of the campus and takes up
with a co-ed.
   Dan Wakefield received a B.A. from Columbia in 1955.
At one point in his student career he served as a research
assistant to sociologist C. Wright Mills. Wakefield has
been a visiting lecturer at a number of universities,
including the universities of Massachusetts, Illinois, and
Iowa. Although he has published several novels, most of
his career has been spent writing investigatory, nonfiction books about American social problems.

313. DeLynn, Jane. *Some Do*. New York: Macmillan Co., 1978.

   Some Do is a quasi-satirical but joyless novel about a
gaggle of radical students and assorted campus hangers-
on at Berkeley in the late 1960s. The book is kaleidoscopic in format. The various characters, most of them
women, enter the story, leave, and then reappear at climactic moments. The plot involves its participants in
anti-Viet Nam political action, the then-incipient women's
liberation movement, drug taking, and lesbianism. Some
of the characters are into only one of these activities
but the more energetic of them take part in two, three,
and even all four. Since academic work is only a side-
line for the book's cast, the author pays little attention to the traditional routines of college life.
   Jane DeLynn was born in New York City in 1946. She
received a B.A. from Barnard in 1968 and an M.F.A. from
the University of Iowa in 1970. *Some Do* was her first
novel.

*314.   Myrer, Anton. *The Last Convertible*. New York: G.P.
        Putnam's Sons, 1978.

        An especially well-written exercise in nostalgia,
        this novel follows four Harvard students, class of 1944,
        from their entrance into college in 1940 until their
        twenty-fifth reunion. All four have their educations
        interrupted by military service; thus there are scenes
        of post-war Harvard as well as descriptions of student
        life before Pearl Harbor. The convertible in the title
        is a luxurious 1938 Packard brought to Cambridge by a
        wealthy French refugee who enters Harvard with the four
        principal characters. When he is killed in the war the
        automobile passes into the hands of the protagonists.
        Eventually the car becomes the property of George Virdon,
        the student whom the novel follows most closely. It sits
        unused in George's garage until the reunion, when George
        refurbishes it and drives it back to the Harvard campus.
        Anton Myrer graduated from Harvard in 1947. A pro-
        fessional writer, his best-known novel before *The Last
        Convertible* was *The Violent Shore* (Boston: Little, Brown
        and Co., 1962). *The Last Convertible* received general
        critical acclaim and, in 1979, was adapted for a tele-
        vision drama.

*315.   Epstein, Jacob. *Wild Oats*. Boston: Little, Brown and
        Co., 1979.

        This funny, satirical novel is set at "Beacham Uni-
        versity," a private institution in Connecticut. Beacham
        is a school populated from top to bottom by dull normals.
        The protagonist of the story is Billy Williams, an under-
        graduate with good intentions but without excessive in-
        telligence. Billy routinely demonstrates his academic
        incompetence by grinding out term papers which are unin-
        tentional parodies of scholarship. Nonetheless, Billy's
        written work more than meets the not-very-rigorous
        standards set by his mentors. The book includes some
        devastatingly caustic portraits of Beacham faculty mem-
        bers and administrators. Philip Russo, for example, is
        an uptight teacher of English who is trying, and failing,
        to publish before he perishes. Philip and Billy compete
        for the affections of Zizi Zanzibar, a co-ed whose physi-
        cal assets far exceed her mental gifts. And the author
        offers a brief but penetrant glimpse of Beacham's unnamed
        president. This worthy invites all of the institution's
        freshmen to a reception on the lawn of his mansion. Un-
        fortunately, it rains on the day of the gathering and the

students stand drenched in a "long, long line" along the
curb in order to shake their host's hand. They receive
their reward when Beacham's chief executive, almost un-
recognizable in his rain gear, mumbles "glad you could
make it" to each of his youthful guests.

Jacob Epstein was awarded a B.A. from Yale in 1978.
Wild Oats was written while he was an undergraduate and
finished just before he received his degree.

316. Howard, Joseph. *Breaking Away*. New York: Warner Books,
1979.

This story concerns a group of "cutters," local high
school boys in Bloomington, Indiana, who invade the
Indiana University campus to sample the extracurricular
delights of undergraduate life. Resented by the Indiana
students, the cutters do not add to their popularity when
their bicycle team defeats all undergraduate comers in
a marathon race. At the very end of the book the action
is telescoped a few years into the future. Dave, the
former leader of the cutters, is glimpsed as an Indiana
freshman. Since to this point Indiana undergraduates
have been portrayed as rich, spoiled brats, while the
cutters have been depicted as fundamentally decent offspring of the underprivileged, one wonders how Dave will
fare during his college career.

As a novel, *Breaking Away* is characterized by one
sentence paragraphs, staccato dialogue, and a minimum
of lingering description. The book was adapted from the
screenplay of the popular 1979 motion picture of the
same title. The original screenplay was written by Steve
Tesich, who received a B.A. from Indiana University in
1965.

317. Jaffe, Rona. *Class Reunion*. New York: Delacorte Press,
1979.

This slick, professionally written novel follows four
Radcliffe students from their entrance into college in
1953 until their twentieth reunion. The first third of
the 338-page story takes place in Cambridge during the
protagonists' undergraduate years. As is usual in follow-
the-graduates novels, the central characters are from
varied social backgrounds and they possess significantly
different physical and mental attributes. And, also in
the best traditions of this sub-genre of the college
novel, the principals experience diverse fates after
graduating. In the case of *Class Reunion*, the post-

graduate experiences of the book's heroines have to do
largely with divorces and otherwise unsettling marital
experiences. The girls' Radcliffe years are described
with great attention to detail about the norms pertaining
to female college students of the 1950s. Thus when Emily,
a nice Jewish girl from a New York City suburb, wants to
take a pre-med program, her advisor, one Mrs. Tweedy,
suggests that she major in social relations and marry a
doctor instead. And, in fact, that is exactly what Emily
does.

Rona Jaffe received a B.A. from Radcliffe in 1951 and
went on to become one of America's most successful writers
of commercial fiction. *Class Reunion* was her tenth novel.

318. Roome, Katherine Ann Davis. *The Letter of the Law*. New
      York: Random House, 1979.

Set at a fictive version of the Cornell Law School, this
novel is written in journal format. The diarist, Ixias
Smith, is a second-year law student. An ambitious and
highly competitive young woman, Ixias does anything to
get good grades. At one point she even seduces and blackmails one of her professors. Occasionally humorous, but
predominantly bitter in tone, the book probes the frenetic
life of law students in considerable detail.

Katherine Ann Davis Roome received a B.A. from Williams
College in 1974 and a J.D. from the Cornell Law School
in 1977. With her mother--mystery writer Mildred Davis--
Roome co-authored *Lucifer Land* (New York: Random House,
1977), a gothic romance set during the Revolutionary War.
Letter of the Law was her first solo novel.

319. Stimpson, Catherine. *Class Notes*. By Kate Stimpson.
      New York: Times Books, 1979.

Class Notes covers ten years in the life of Harriet
Elizabeth Springer, a 1959 graduate of "Harwyn College."
The story begins with Harriet in high school in North-
ville, Washington. It follows her through Harwyn and
then into the world of work in New York City. Harwyn is
an exclusive Eastern college for women. Harriet's undergraduate adventures take up the middle part of the book.
Harriet is bright, brash, and liberal. Moreover, in
keeping with the traditions of college novels set at
institutions for women, Harriet is a lesbian. Much of
her time at Harwyn is spent discovering and adjusting to
her sexual preference for women.

Catherine Stimpson was born in Bellingham, Washington,

in 1936. She received an A.B. from Bryn Mawr in 1958
and a Ph.D. from Columbia in 1965. She was a member of
the English department at Barnard College when this book
was published. *Class Notes* was her first novel.

320. Weil, Dorothy. *Continuing Education*. New York: Ransom,
      Wade Publishers, 1979.

Laura Hoffman, thirty-eight years old and the mother
of three, decides to return to college after nearly twenty
years. Entering an art program at an unnamed university
in Cincinnati, she meets a variety of faculty members and
fellow students. The book is written as light comedy-
satire and most of Laura's university contacts are modern-
day stereotypes. Her sculpture instructor, for example,
is a radical feminist. Her art history teacher is an
aging male lecher. And her mentor in drawing is a stuffy
Yale graduate who wears three-piece suits and speaks in
indecipherable professional jargon. Meanwhile, back at
the Hoffman residence, Laura's psychiatrist husband and
her three children learn to adjust to mother's departure
from all-consuming domesticity. At the end of the story
Laura receives her degree and has embarked on an as-yet-
unsuccessful search for fulfilling employment.
Dorothy Weil was co-founder of the Cincinnati Women's
Press. At the time *Continuing Education* was published
she was a member of the English department of Edgecliff
College in Cincinnati.

STAFF-CENTERED NOVELS

*321. Aldridge, John Watson. *The Party at Cranton*. New York:
       David McKay Co., 1960.

       Faculty social gatherings are a favorite plotting device
    for authors of college novels. By including these affairs
    in their stories, authors are able to introduce large
    numbers of characters and, perhaps of more importance,
    they are able to have these characters engage each other
    in witty, if often banal, dialogue. Aside from some
    limited flashback material *The Party at Cranton* takes
    place, as its title implies, entirely at one faculty party
    at "Cranton University." The affair is described by
    Richard Waite, a professor of English, and through Waite's
    eyes the author of the piece offers a series of detailed
    and often unflattering character sketches. The center of
    attention at the gathering is Arthur Buchanan, the leading
    member of Cranton's English department and a man who takes
    perverse pleasure in ruining the careers of junior faculty.
    Also in the roster of guests is Dorothy Murchison, a
    visiting classicist, who supplies the book's most dramatic
    incident by stripping off her clothes after imbibing more
    than her share of liquid refreshment. College novel buffs
    will be especially appreciative of the depictions of
    Lester Fleischmann and Miriam Hornblower, two members of
    the Cranton English department who write their own college
    fiction. These academic authors, whose novels do not ap-
    pear in this bibliography, spend most of their time in the
    kitchen assassinating each other verbally and, in calmer
    moments, comparing notes on the other partygoers in prep-
    aration for their next college sagas.
       John Watson Aldridge received a B.A. from the University
    of California at Berkeley in 1947. One of America's foremost
    literary critics, he served in various faculty capacities
    at the University of Vermont, Princeton, Sarah Lawrence,
    Queens College, and New York University before becoming
    a Fulbright lecturer at the University of Munich during
    the 1958-1959 academic year. Upon his return from Germany

Aldridge was a visiting professor at Hollins College from
1960 until 1962. After another Fulbright lectureship in
Europe, this time at the University of Copenhagen, Aldridge
became professor of English at the University of Michigan
in 1963. *The Party at Cranton* was his first novel.

*322. Fisher, Vardis. *Orphans in Gethsemane*. Denver: Alan
       Swallow, 1960.

This massive (987-page) volume is made up of revised
versions of the four novels in Vardis Fisher's Vridar
Hunter tetralogy. It also contains approximately 100
pages of new concluding material. Three of the novels
in the tetralogy are "college novels" in the sense that
they deal with Vridar's experiences as a college student
and as a faculty member. These novels are *Passions Spin
the Plot* (114), *We Are Betrayed* (117), and *No Villain Need
Be* (147). The new concluding material in *Orphans in
Gethsemane* follows Hunter's career as a novelist during
the Depression and the 1940s.
       Vardis Fisher was a prolific writer. *Orphans in Geth-
semane*, itself an augmented tetralogy, was the final work
in yet a larger series of twelve novels which Fisher
called his "Testament of Man." During the 1960s Pyramid
Books divided *Orphans in Gethsemane* into two segments and
published paperback editions of both segments under new
titles. The first half of *Orphans in Gethsemane* was
issued in paperback as *For Passion, For Heaven*. The
second half was titled *The Great Confession*.

323.   Hardy, William Marion. *Year of the Rose*. New York:
       Dodd, Mead and Co., 1960.

At forty-two David Shelby has just been promoted to
the chairmanship of the English department at "Tryon
University" in North Carolina. David has an attractive
wife named Fran and an energetic teenage daughter named
Debbie. Then he meets Roberta ("Bert") Heller, an allur-
ing graduate student, and his troubles begin. An enterprising male undergraduate finds out about their affair
and threatens to reveal all unless he is awarded with
perpetual A's. Fran begins to suspect that something is
amiss and she and David engage in a series of verbal
sparring sessions. In an effort to get away from these
travails David takes Roberta to New York City for a week
of fun and games. As a pretext he claims to be consulting
with his publisher. But as the week proceeds David finds
himself longing for Fran and inadvertently calling Roberta

by his daughter's name. At the end of the book the fate-
ful New York junket is concluding and David is preparing
to tell Roberta that their romance is over. Most of the
story takes place on the Tryon campus and the academic
backdrop to the romance is drawn in considerable detail.

William Marion Hardy received a B.S. from Duke in 1943
and an M.A. from the University of North Carolina in 1954.
He was an assistant professor of English at Purdue when
Year of the Rose was published.

324. Leslie, Warren. *Love or Whatever It is*. New York:
      McGraw-Hill, 1960.

The first two-thirds of this 335-page, broken-backed
novel consists of a reasonably routine faculty-centered
romance. Hans Grimm, a bachelor professor of music at
"Caruth College" falls in love with Ann Bowen, the daughter
of a faculty colleague. Hans is fiftyish. Ann is in her
mid-twenties. Caruth College is a bastion of academic
gentility in the quaint town of "Hester," Massachusetts.
During the romantic phase of the book the story is but-
tressed with faculty dinner parties, witty conversations,
and gossipy discussions of college people and politics.
But Ann begins to have doubts about her love for Hans.
When she tells the professor that their relationship is
finished he puts a Segovia record on the phonograph and,
in a fit of rage, strangles her to death. With Ann's
demise the novel becomes a study in human degradation.
Ann's death is attributed to Ricki Pulaski, the town
half-wit who discovers her body. Ricky is soon shot flee-
ing the police and Hans, exuding guilt from all pores,
takes up with Ricki's sister "Beavertooth," the local
Hester prostitute. Beavertooth is not immediately aware
of Hans' crime, and she agrees to spend Christmas vacation with him in New York. There, in a hotel room, she
watches as Hans goes into delirium brought on by a combination of hepatitis and nervous exhaustion, and she
listens as he attempts to call the police to confess Ann's
killing. Hans passes out before he can complete the call
and, at the end of the story, Beavertooth is dialing the
number.

Warren Leslie was born in New York City in 1927. He
was educated at Phillips Exeter Academy and at Yale.
Love or Whatever It is was his second novel. At the time
the book was published Leslie was vice-president and
director of sales promotion for the Neiman-Marcus department store in Dallas, Texas.

325. Mann, Georg. *The Dollar Diploma*. New York: Macmillan
      Co., 1960.

      This satirical novel focuses upon fund raising by aca-
      demic institutions. It is set at "Fox University," a
      struggling private school located in the town of "Garden
      Prairie," a community which university brochures describe
      as "the Babylon of the Midwest." The protagonist of the
      story is Tom Mears, humanities editor for the Fox Universi-
      ty Press. Tom is assigned temporary duty as an assistant
      on a major capital fund drive. Through Tom's eyes readers
      observe the political machinations and unscheduled events
      which, eventually, cause the campaign to fail. The final
      blow comes when a visiting female professor reduces dona-
      tions to a trickle by giving a public lecture in which she
      criticizes capitalism, American foreign policy, and the
      depressed status of women. In the end, however, the uni-
      versity survives. Though the Fox administration is rock-
      ribbed conservative, President Wells Thornton eagerly ac-
      cepts a huge donation from a wealthy man whose late father
      was a Communist. In return, the university agrees to name
      its entire undergraduate school for the deceased leftist.
      The novel is populated by a variety of unsavory academic
      types and the author pays particular attention to the
      blustering, self-aggrandizing behavior of Fox's petty
      administrators.
         Georg Mann received a B.A. from the University of Chicago
      in 1934. *The Dollar Diploma* was his first novel. At the
      time of its publication Mann was director of public rela-
      tions for Case Institute of Technology in Cleveland.

326. [Cassill, Ronald Verlin]. *Night School*. By R.V. Cassill.
      New York: New American Library, 1961.

      Night School is a novel about higher education as of-
      fered in the evening program of a large New York City
      university. At the center of the action is Houston
      Parker, a professor of creative writing, but the book
      explores the lives of many of Parker's students as well.
      A notation on the cover of the Dell paperback edition
      (1961) suggests the ethos of the plot. "Parker's class
      had no homework," reads the blurb, "the students found
      their material in extracurricular activities--most of
      their work was written in bed." Not one to let his stu-
      dents toil without supervision, Parker joins them in their
      horizontal labors. At the end of the book he is spending
      the summer at the St. Louis home of his favorite co-ed.
      The girl's mother, an aspiring novelist herself, also
      finds Parker's bedroom lessons absorbing.

Born in 1919, Ronald Verlin Cassill received a B.A.
from the State University of Iowa in 1939 and an M.A.
from the same institution in 1947. At the time *Night
School* was published he was an instructor at the Iowa
Writers' Workshop. Although *Night School* is not generally regarded as one of his most meritorious works, Cassill is a highly respected American novelist. One of his
more prestigious novels, *The President* (351), appears in
this bibliography. Two more of Cassill's novels have
academic connections. One of them, *Dormitory Women* (New
York: Lion Books, 1954), is a paperback suspense story
which centers upon the mental hallucinations of a university co-ed. The other, *La Vie Passionnee of Rodney
Buckthorne* (New York: Bernard Geis, 1968), is a satirical
comedy about a former professor of classics from "Vistu-
lar University" in Wyoming. The ex-professor finds his
destiny through sexual escapades in Greenwich Village.

327. Evans, Fallon. *The Trouble with Turlow*. Garden City,
      New York: Doubleday and Co., 1961.

The protagonist of this comic satire is Henry Turlow,
a member of the English department at a small Catholic
college for women in the West. Henry fights a losing
battle against both poverty and his own professional las-
situde until he is asked to host an educational television
show produced by the college. Henry hopes to use his
television exposure as a springboard to a full-time video
career. Unfortunately, the show ends in disaster when
one of Henry's fellow faculty participants attempts to
light his pipe and succeeds in burning down the TV studio
just as Henry's television debut is commencing. The novel
contains a great deal of inside humor about lay faculty
life at Catholic colleges. However, one need not be employed by a Catholic institution to appreciate the scene
in which Henry is promoted to associate professor but
denied a salary increase because the school's pay scales
for assistant and associate professors "overlap."
      Fallon Evans received an A.B. from Notre Dame in 1951
and a Ph.D. from the University of Denver in 1953. At
the time *The Trouble with Turlow* was published Evans was
an associate professor of English at Immaculate Heart
College in California. *The Trouble with Turlow* was Evans'
first novel. His second novel, *Pistols and Pedagogues*
(New York: Sheed and Ward, 1963), is a comic-mystery which
describes the struggles of an instructor of English to
combat a drug ring at a small Catholic college in the
Midwest.

328. Kelly, Robert Glynn. *A Lament for Barney Stone*. New
      York: Holt, Rinehart and Winston, 1961.

        Barney Stone is an unworldly bachelor professor of
      English at "Castleton University." Castleton is a pri-
      vate institution in the West. Written as satire, this
      novel reviews Barney's eighteen years at the school.
      Much of the plot involves Barney's continuing rivalry
      with Donald Creel, a loutish faculty colleague. Creel's
      "unconventional" behavior only seems to propel him up
      the academic status hierarchy at a pace which exceeds
      that of Barney. However, after nearly two decades of
      loyal if unspectacular service Barney is about to be
      named dean. Creel, unhappy about Barney's sudden good
      fortune, pays an actress to register for one of Barney's
      classes. Then, under Creel's direction, the woman seduces
      Barney and makes the affair known on the campus. In the
      book's last scene Barney unleashes his frustrations by
      knocking Creel down in a fistfight. But by this time
      Castleton's president has already decided to let the
      matter of the deanship "slide for awhile." The book is
      full of sardonic passages about academic politics, teach-
      ing, and research. And a great number of well-drawn facul-
      ty members and administrative characters grace its pages.
        Robert Glynn Kelly received a B.A. from San Diego State
      College in 1946 and a Ph.D. from Stanford in 1952. *A
      Lament for Barney Stone* was his first novel. At the time
      the book was published Kelly was a member of the English
      department at Indiana University.

*329. Malamud, Bernard. *A New Life*. New York: Farrar, Straus
      and Cudahy, 1961.

        A New Life is the classic satirical novel about faculty
      life in the academic bush leagues. The protagonist is
      S. Levin, a Jewish non-Ph.D. from New York who comes to
      "Cascadia College" to teach English. Cascadia is a state
      institution in the Pacific Northwest. Levin finds the
      school populated by a set of aggressively mediocre faculty
      members and administrators. He also finds and has an
      affair with Pauline Gilley, the wife of a departmental
      colleague. As Levin discovers the awful truths about
      Cascadia, and as he discovers truths about himself in the
      process, the story touches upon academic freedom, faculty
      politics, and the place of research in a teaching-oriented
      state college. Rich in insight and often very funny, the
      book defies reasonable summarization.
        Bernard Malamud is one of America's outstanding writers.

He received a B.A. from City College of New York in 1936 and an M.A. from Columbia University in 1942. *A New Life* was his third novel. Malamud was a member of the English department at Oregon State University from 1949 to 1961. In 1961 he became a member of the division of language and literature at Bennington College.

330. Manchester, William Raymond. *The Long Gainer*. Boston: Little, Brown and Co., 1961.

The Long Gainer is a long (494-page) and intriguing novel about a state university president who unsuccessfully runs for governor. The president is Adam "Doc" River and the state is in southern New England. A former football hero at the university he now heads, Doc obtains the Democratic nomination but loses the general election when the campus "Gridiron Queen" besmirches his administration by posing nude for a girlie magazine. Doc, a crusty, no-nonsense type, is portrayed as a wise university administrator but naive about politics. So many campus characters trot across the pages of the book that the author prefaces the book with a roster of thirty-nine of the primary players. The state university is located near an exclusive private institution--"Peabody College"-- and there are innumerable passages in which the open, democratic nature of "State" is compared to Peabody's snobbishness.

William Raymond Manchester received an A.B. from the University of Massachusetts in 1946 and an A.M. from the University of Missouri in 1947. *The Long Gainer* was his third novel. After writing *The Long Gainer* Manchester turned to nonfiction. Publication of Manchester's *Death of a President* (New York: Harper and Row, 1967), a book about the assassination of John F. Kennedy, was a major American literary event.

331. Sarton, May. *The Small Room*. New York: W.W. Norton and Co., 1961.

This commanding novel is set at "Appleton College," an exclusive New England institution for women. The protagonist is Lucy Winter, a neophyte instructor of English. Lucy discovers plagiarism on the part of Jane Seamon, the reigning intellectual queen of Appleton's student body. Lucy's finding sets off a series of chain reactions involving various Appleton faculty and staff. Most shaken by the events is Carryl Cope, an internationally famous anthropologist who refuses to believe that

Jane, her protégée, could commit a misdeed. The book
includes a lesbian relationship between Carryl and a female trustee of the college, and it offers many well-
constructed portraits of Appleton personages. Because
it depicts women in the serious pursuit of academic ex-
cellence, *The Small Room* became popular reading in the
1970s among feminists in higher education.
   Another of May Sarton's novels, *Faithful are the Wounds*
(240), appears in this bibliography.

332.   Shaw, Russell B. *The Dark Disciple*. Garden City, New
       York: Doubleday and Co., 1961.

   The protagonist of this extremely intense novel is
Christopher Gavin, a young instructor of English at
"Webster University." Webster is a second-rate, secular
institution in the midst of a large city. Christopher
is a convert to Catholicism and the plot of the story
concerns his efforts to spread his faith among Webster's
generally agnostic faculty and students. One of his
prospective converts, a male student, commits suicide
after Christopher's ministrations. And when Christopher
begins to proselytize Julie Brodie, the wife of a faculty
colleague, he nearly drives the Brodies to a divorce.
Toward the end of the novel the discouraged Christopher
resigns his faculty appointment. Then, meditating in a
deserted Catholic church, he realizes that his zealousness
has been prompted by a desire for self-aggrandizement,
not by a sincere love of God.
   Russell B. Shaw received a B.A. from Georgetown University in 1956 and subsequently received an M.A. in
English from the same institution. *The Dark Disciple*
was his first novel. At the time the book was published
Shaw was a staff writer for the National Catholic Welfare
Conference News Service in Washington, D.C.

*333.   Lafore, Laurence Davis. *Learner's Permit*. Garden City,
       New York: Doubleday and Co., 1962.

   Learner's Permit is a farce about an academic imposter.
Nicholas Torrente, whose highest educational attainment
is a high school degree, comes to "Parthenon College" to
teach English. Parthenon is a small, Protestant-affili-
ated college in "Acropolis," New York. Torrente is im-
personating a real Ph.D., hired by Parthenon in absentia,
who is detained in Europe providing sex education to
Torrente's wealthy female employer. Torrente learns a
few catch phrases--he finds "water imagery" especially

useful--and he conducts classes by allowing his students
to discuss their own questions about the assigned read-
ings. He is voted the best teacher on campus. But, alas,
his deception is discovered and he is called to the office
of President Helmsford Scantleberry Overton. In the course
of the interview President Overton discovers that Torrente
was once a military policeman and, for four years, acted
as his employer's paramour. An expert in police work,
and familiar with "the psychology of sex," Torrente is
just the person Overton needs for his administration.
Overton dismisses Torrente from the school's teaching
staff and immediately hires him as dean of students.

Laurence Davis Lafore received a B.A. from Swarthmore
in 1938 and a Ph.D. from the Fletcher School of Law and
Diplomacy in 1950. *Learner's Permit* was his first novel.
At the time the book was published Lafore was a professor
of history at Swarthmore. *Learner's Permit* was published
in Great Britain under the title *The Pride of Parthenon,
New York* (London: Gollancz, 1963).

334. Lurie, Alison [Mrs. Jonathan Peale Bishop, Jr.]. *Love
and Friendship*. New York: Macmillan Co., 1962.

Love and Friendship is set at "Converse College," a
small, coeducational institution in New England. The
protagonist of the story is Emily Stockwell Turner, the
twenty-eight-year-old wife of Holman Turner, a rather
insipid instructor in the "languages and literature
division." Although Holman's salary is so low as to be
almost nonexistent, Emily has an independent income of
$8000 per year. The plot centers on Emily's affair with
Will Thomas, a free-loving member of Converse's music
department. At the conclusion of the book Emily returns
to Holman, but the reader has the distinct impression that
she may not remain with him forever. Written with considerable wit and polish, the novel is alternatively
serious and satirical. Some of the plot is carried forward by gossipy letters from Allen Ingram, a Converse
professor of English, to various out-of-town correspon-
dents.

Alison Lurie was born in Chicago in 1926. She received
an A.B. from Radcliffe in 1947. *Love and Friendship* was
her first novel. Three other Lurie novels feature academics in leading roles. *The Nowhere City* (New York:
Coward-McCann, 1965) has as its protagonist a Harvard
historian who spends a year in Los Angeles writing the
official history of a California corporation. *Imaginary
Friends* (New York: Coward-McCann, 1967) deals with two

sociologists who study a millenarian religious sect in
upstate New York. In both of these books the protagonists
spend the bulk of their time off·campus, thus neither work
is accorded a separate entry in this bibliography. Lurie's
The War Between the Tates (397), on the other hand, is
hard-core college fiction at its zenith, and that novel
is included in this bibliography.

335. Morrison, Theodore. *The Whole Creation*. New York:
      Viking Press, 1962.

      The Whole Creation is the third and final Theodore
      Morrison novel to be set at "Rowley University," a private
      institution in New England. The first two novels in the
      Rowley series are *The Stones of the House* (233) and *To
      Make a World* (247). *The Whole Creation* has three pro-
      tagonists: Kent Warner, an industrial engineer with a
      local business firm; Arthur Schur, a professor of biology
      at Rowley; and Malcolm Isley, a writer-in-residence at
      the university. The plot of the story, which is too
      intricate for meaningful summarization, articulates the
      world of industry with university politics. Most re-
      viewers saw the book as a series of character sketches,
      and as an exposition of the different viewpoints of cor-
      poration men and academics. Rowley's president, Andrew
      Aiken, who is the sagacious protagonist of *The Stones of
      the House*, continues his wise reign over the university
      in this novel.

336. Nabokov, Vladimir. *Pale Fire*. New York: G.P. Putnam's
      Sons, 1962.

      Pale Fire is an exceedingly intricate satire which,
      since its publication, has provided literary scholars with
      considerable food for intellectual mastication. The basic
      plot of the book deals with the efforts of John Shade, a
      poet-in-residence at "Wordsmith College," to finish an
      epic 1000-line autobiographical poem. Just as Shade com-
      pletes line 999, however, he is shot to death by a luna-
      tic murderer who mistakes him for his neighbor, a judge.
      The novel contains the full text of the nearly completed
      poem and a line-by-line commentary upon it. The com-
      mentary is the work of Charles Kinbote, a homosexual
      emigre professor who has persuaded Shade's widow to allow
      him to prepare the manuscript for publication. At yet
      another, emergent level of plot Kinbote turns out to be
      the deposed "King of Zembla" and Shade, so it seems, is
      shot by mistake by a Zemblanian secret agent sent to kill

the king. Nabokov experts continue to debate the various
meanings of this novel. But most agree that it can be
read as a telling burlesque of academic manners.

An earlier Nabokov novel, *Pnin* (248), also is included
in this bibliography.

337. Roth, Philip Milton. *Letting Go*. New York: Random House,
1962.

The protagonists of this long (630-page) but highly
polished novel are Gabe Wallach and Paul and Libby Herz.
The three meet in 1953 when Gabe and Paul are graduate
students in English at the University of Iowa. Shortly
thereafter Gabe obtains a teaching post at the University
of Chicago and, when another staff vacancy occurs at
Chicago, Gabe engineers an appointment for Paul. Although
academe serves as a background device for the story, most
of the plot centers upon the Herz' fiscal and domestic
difficulties and upon Gabe's attempts to break free from
habitual stodginess and indecisiveness. Gabe and Paul
are Jewish (Libby is the daughter of Catholic parents)
and, as in most of Roth's fiction, considerable attention
is paid to modern American Jewish culture.

Philip Roth received an A.B. from Bucknell University
in 1954 and an M.A. from the University of Chicago in 1955.
Early in his career he served in junior faculty positions
at Chicago and at the University of Iowa. At the time
Letting Go was published Roth was writer-in-residence at
Princeton. *Letting Go* was Roth's first novel. The work
was preceded, however, by *Goodbye, Columbus* (Boston:
Houghton Mifflin Co., 1959), a book of stories which won
the 1960 National Book Award. Two later Roth works have
as their protagonist one David Kepesh, a professor of
English at SUNY-Stony Brook. These books are *The Breast*
(New York: Holt, Rinehart and Winston, 1972) and *The Professor of Desire* (New York: Farrar, Straus and Giroux,
1977). In neither of these works does Professor Kepesh
spend an appreciable amount of time on the SUNY-Stony
Brook campus. Hence neither book is accorded a separate
entry in this bibliography.

338. Sewell, Elizabeth Margaret. *Now Bless Thyself*. New
York: Doubleday and Co., 1962.

This novel is told in the first person by a female poet-
in-residence at "Auber University." Auber is a state
institution in the Midwest. The narrator has come to
Auber from her native Great Britain after her husband's

suicide. Seeking to lose herself in teaching and writing,
she finds herself embroiled instead in a variety of extracurricular activities. In particular, she joins forces
with a group of liberal faculty and students in an attempt
to save the job of an ex-Communist professor. Auber University is next door to a small Catholic college. Of all
the academics with whom the narrator comes in contact,
Father Clavery, the president of the Catholic college,
emerges as the most understanding and humane. Much of
this novel is reflexive; the narrator submerges the events
of the plot in a torrent of introspective monologue. As
Irma Brandeis noted while reviewing the novel for *The
Saturday Review* (August 11, 1962): "When one puts the
book down one recalls, not its life, but its themes."
These themes include adjustment to domestic tragedy, the
emerging role of a foreign female visitor on an American
campus, and the virulence of right-wing political thought
in America.

Elizabeth Margaret Sewell received a B.A. from Cambridge
in 1942 and a Ph.D. from the same institution in 1949. A
well-known British poet and novelist, she taught at Ford-
ham University during the 1954-1955 and 1958-1959 academic
years.

339.   Deal, Babs Hodges. *The Grail*. New York: David McKay
       Co., 1963.

The protagonist of this slickly written novel is Arthur
Hill, the forty-five-year-old head football coach at
"Castle University." Castle is located "in the heart of
the Southeastern Football Conference." Arthur's ambition--
his "grail"--is a perfect season. But when his young wife
has an affair with his star quarterback, Arthur becomes
so unnerved that he loses the last game of the year through
poor coaching. The novel contains some non-football scenes
on the Castle campus, as well as some romantic interludes,
but readers are left with no doubt that the dominant interest of the Castle community is football.

Babs Hodges Deal received a B.A. from the University of
Alabama in 1952. *The Grail* was her fourth novel. In an
acknowledgment at the beginning of the book Deal thanks
Paul Bryant, head football coach at Alabama, for "reading
the manuscript for technical detail." Interestingly
enough, the team which defeats Castle in the last game,
thereby ending Coach Hill's dream of a perfect season, is
Bryant's Alabama "Crimson Tide."

340. Duncan, Bob. *The General and the Co-Ed*. Garden City,
     New York: Doubleday and Co., 1963.

     The general in the title of this semi-satirical novel
     is Frederick C. ("Frederick the Great") Garner, a retired
     U.S. Army officer who is chosen to become president of
     "McDermott College." McDermott is a private institution
     in California. Garner finds the school lacking in disci-
     pline and he begins to turn it into something resembling
     a military post. Instead of routine administrative
     memoranda he issues "orders of the day," and he forms a
     collection of his most macho male undergraduates into a
     military police force which patrols the campus. As might
     be expected, McDermott's faculty and administrative staff
     find Garner's reign unbearable. But before they can mount
     an effective offensive against him he is named president
     of a higher-status college in Pennsylvania. The co-ed
     who is associated with Garner in the book's title is
     Stacy Dove. The neurotic daughter of a wealthy college
     benefactor, Stacy's favorite pastime is to pretend to
     be a rape victim. Though she never accuses Garner of
     any impropriety, she levels rape charges against a
     number of students and faculty members and the problems
     which arise from these accusations hasten Garner's exit.

341. Fuller, Edmund. *The Corridor*. New York: Random House,
     1963.

     The Corridor is a sobering story about a professor of
     history whose hospitalized wife is fighting for her life
     after an operation. For three days, before his wife is
     pronounced out of danger, the professor paces the hospital
     halls reflecting upon his marriage. Somewhat incidentally,
     he also reflects upon the nature of his occupation. Mal-
     colm Adamson, the professor, is a member of the faculty
     at "Camden College," a prestigious women's college in
     upper New England. At its core this novel is a study of
     a husband-wife relationship and it deals only in passing
     with issues relating to academe. Nonetheless, there is a
     modest amount of material about academic job changing and
     about the frustrations of college teaching.
     The Corridor was Edmund Fuller's third novel. His
     reputation in literary circles is built less upon his
     novels, however, than upon his essays, editing, and criti-
     cism. During the early stages of his career Fuller taught
     at the New School and at Columbia.

342.   Johnson, Pamela Hansford [Mrs. Charles Percy Snow].
       Night and Silence: Who is Here? New York: Charles
       Scribner's Sons, 1963.

       Matthew Pryor, a middle-aged bachelor Englishman, is
       invited to spend a year at the Center for Advanced Studies
       of "Cobb University." Cobb is located in the most rural
       portion of New Hampshire. Pryor is an unaccomplished
       writer whose claim to academic fame is that he is a friend
       of Dorothy Merlin, a noted British poet. Throughout this
       often very funny satire Pryor attempts to write Merlin's
       biography, but various obstacles--including his own mental
       vacuity--make the task impossible. Much of the plot deals
       with Pryor's sometimes strained relationships with the
       six other fellows of the Center. One of these scholars
       is attempting to prove that Emily Dickinson was an alco-
       holic, and Tiepolo, a boorish sociologist, is writing a
       book on "rape and its role in the community." Also in
       the cast is Dr. Dominick Maudlin Parke, the director of
       the center, who tries and fails to keep order among his
       resident collection of zanies.
       Born in 1912, Pamela Hansford Johnson is one of Great
       Britain's most respected writers. She is the widow of
       the late Sir Charles Percy Snow.

343.   Kubly, Herbert. *The Whistling Zone*. New York: Simon
       and Schuster, 1963.

       Christian Mawther, an associate professor of humanities
       at an institution in New England, is sent by a foundation
       to teach an experimental course at "Alakoma University."
       Alakoma is a state university in the southern Midwest.
       And, as Mawther quickly discovers, Alakoma is populated
       largely by lethargic students, pompous administrators,
       and intellectually deceased faculty. Moreover, the state
       itself is dominated by right-wing politicians who object
       to Mawther's liberal philosophies of education. Eventu-
       ally, the state fathers make it clear that Mawther and
       his Yankee ideas are not welcome at Alakoma. But he has
       begun to stimulate the minds of the youngsters in his
       course. Though his person is at some risk, at the end
       of the story he decides to stay at Alakoma in the interests
       of his newly enlightened students. The book contains a
       number of sub-plots, one of which deals with Mawther's
       desertion by his wife, and it includes a large number of
       portraits of Alakoma campus characters. Though the over-
       all tone of the novel is serious, some portions are writ-
       ten as satire.

Herbert Kubly received a B.A. in 1937 from the University of Wisconsin. During most of the 1940s he worked in the publishing business in New York City. From 1944 until 1947 he was music critic for *Time Magazine*. In 1949 Kubly became an associate professor of speech at the University of Illinois. He left this post in 1954 to write plays, nonfiction books, and short stories. From 1962 until 1964 he was a lecturer at Columbia University and at the New School. In 1964 he became a professor of English at San Francisco State College. *The Whistling Zone* was his first novel.

344. Lockwood, Mary [Mrs. James B. Spelman]. *Child of Light*. New York: William Morrow, 1963.

Melinda White is the wife of Peter, a young instructor of history at an unnamed college in Seattle. A faculty child—the daughter of a sociologist—Melinda is blase about rules and regulations, especially about those pertaining to academe. When Frank Munger, one of her husband's students, tells her that he is afraid of exams, Melinda goes to Peter's desk and provides Frank with a draft of an upcoming examination. Peter finds out. He fails Frank and castigates Melinda. Then Frank commits suicide and Melinda leaves home. The last third of the novel describes Melinda's life in a California beach commune to which she flees after her tiff with Peter. At the end of the novel she and Peter are reconciled. The book contains many atmospheric passages about the social milieux of faculty wives in the late 1950s.

Mary Lockwood received a B.A. from Smith College in 1955. *Child of Light* was her first novel.

345. Ludwig, Jack. *Confusions*. New York: Graphic Society Publishers, 1963.

Confusions is a breezy and irreverent first novel about a new Ph.D. from Harvard who journeys to "Royce College" in California for his first teaching position. The protagonist (and narrator) of the story is Joseph Gillis who has labored long and hard in Cambridge to become an expert in the later novels of Dickens and George Eliot. Royce, he discovers to his dismay, is the kind of institution where professional competence is less important than "fitting in." The highlight of each academic week at Royce is the dean's Friday evening square dance seminar for faculty families, and no one except Joseph is overly concerned about the fact that many of the school's

attractive, pleasant students are functionally illiterate.
Joseph is Jewish. His wife Nancy, who comes with him from
Harvard, is a gentile. Thus Joseph's problems of professional adjustment are sometimes compounded by frenzied
domestic squabbles brought on by cultural misunderstandings.

Jack Ludwig was born in Winnipeg, Canada, in 1922. He
received a B.A. from the University of Manitoba and a
Ph.D. from UCLA. He taught at Williams and at Bard College before going to SUNY-Stony Brook in 1961. In 1963
he was a professor of English at Stony Brook.

346. O'Hara, John Henry. *Elizabeth Appleton*. New York: Random
      House, 1963.

The title character of this late-in-career John O'Hara
novel is the wife of a professor of history and sometime
dean of students at "Spring Valley College." Located in
western Pennsylvania, Spring Valley is an institution
attended by students who cannot gain admission to Ivy
League schools. Elizabeth Appleton is youngish, attractive, and from a wealthy family. Husband John is well
into middle age and, as the son of a former Spring Valley
professor, his only income comes from his modest salary.
Elizabeth prods John into aspiring to Spring Valley's
presidency. But thanks to the underhanded tactics of the
college's retiring chief executive--who recommends someone else for the post--John is passed over in the selection
process. Meantime, the energetic Elizabeth has an affair
with a local socialite and John, who is something less
than a human dynamo, trudges through his domestic and academic duties. The book contains several detailed portraits of John's faculty and administrative colleagues.
The most vivid of these depictions is of President Bruce
McAndrew, a man whose outstanding characteristics are
pomposity, opportunism, and cowardice.

John O'Hara was born in Pottstown, Pennsylvania, in
1905. He did not attend college. He worked as a journalist before becoming one of mid-twentieth-century
America's most popular and prolific fictionalists. *Elizabeth Appleton* was O'Hara's fourteenth novel. Reviewers
generally found it well written but not one of the outstanding examples of his literary art. O'Hara died in
1970.

347. Wagner, Geoffrey Atheling. *The Asphalt Campus*. New
York: Macmillan Co., 1963.

This synoptic satire is set at "Lincoln College," a
division of the City College of New York. The book follows assorted members of Lincoln's English department
through a variety of situations. The centerpiece of the
plot is the suspension of Professor Orrin Bunch for allegedly fondling a co-ed. But the book explores a great
number of other issues, including the difficulty of cop-
ing with lowbred students, the problems associated with
creeping academic bureaucracy, and the frustrations of
research in the field of English literature. Academic
readers may find the portrait of Mesrob Mins, the department chairman, of particular appeal. Mesrob wants to
be president of Lincoln and he attempts to display his
administrative talents by requiring his faculty to punch
time clocks. As the reviewer for *The New Yorker* (March
16, 1963) noted: "The book seems to be a catalog of the
author's personal complaints."
Geoffrey Atheling Wagner was born in 1927 in Malaya.
He received a B.A. from Christ Church College, Oxford,
in 1948 and a Ph.D. from Columbia in 1954. At the time
The Asphalt Campus was published Wagner was a member of
the English department at CCNY. *The Asphalt Campus* was
his eleventh novel.

348. Walter, Robert Henry Keamer. *Stacy Tower*. New York:
Macmillan Co., 1963.

Stacy Tower is an immense (536-page) synoptic novel
set at a large state university. The intricate plot
follows a galaxy of university students, faculty members,
and administrators through a series of interlocking adventures. Among the book's more noteworthy characters
are Whitney Robbins, Chester Nordstrom, and Johnny Gold.
Robbins, a former professor of political science, is the
institution's acting president. In an unsuccessful effort
to become the school's permanent president Robbins slavishly follows the dictates of the university's conservative trustees. Chester Nordstrom is an assistant
professor of political science. A liberal, Chet is
turned down for tenure when his department chairman
responds to Robbins' wishes that the department purge
itself of radical malcontents. And Johnny Gold, a Jewish
undergraduate, finds himself the victim of anti-Semitism
both on the university campus and in the nearby town.
The plot includes student riots, campus muggings, and

various sexual pairings. Slickly written, the book is a "good read." But academic readers will have to judge for themselves whether or not the author overstates the attendant evils of American state universities.

Robert Henry Keamer Walter received an A.B. from Pomona College in 1942 and an L.L.B. from the University of California at Berkeley in 1952. After receiving his law degree Walter embarked on a varied career which, during the next decade, included work as a Richmond, California, probation officer, as a writer's agent, and as senior editor for Bantam Books in New York. *Stacy Tower* was his first novel.

349.   Wilson, Sloan. *Georgie Winthrop*. New York: Harper and Row, 1963.

The title character of this slick, professionally written story is the vice-president of "Wellington College." Wellington is a high-status institution in New England. Georgie--known to most of his associates as George--is forty-five, married, and has two teenage children. He also is a promising president-in-training with a bright administrative future. It all threatens to unravel, however, when George falls in love with the seventeen-year-old daughter of a drunken visiting writer. George and the girl have a secret affair, but she jilts him just as he is about to ask his wife for a divorce. Thus, at the end of the book, George's marital status has gone back to quo and only his psyche has been damaged. Much of the novel takes place in New York, where George finds it convenient to meet his nymphet. Hence even though the book pays relatively little attention to George's official functions as a vice-president, it has the distinction of revealing what at least one fictive administrator does during his many off-campus trips.

Sloan Wilson received a B.A. from Harvard in 1942. Although he served as an assistant professor of English at the University of Buffalo from 1952 until 1955, most of his career has been devoted to the writing of novels and screenplays. *Georgie Winthrop* was Wilson's fifth novel. His best-known work is *The Man in the Grey Flannel Suit* (New York: Simon and Schuster, 1955).

350.   Bellow, Saul. *Herzog*. New York: Viking Press, 1964.

Moses Herzog is a Canadian-born Jew. Once a barely distinguished professor of history at Columbia and the University of Chicago, he leaves academe in his waning

years for an introspective existence in the Berkshire
Hills. Twice divorced, and ridden with uncertainty over
the meaning of his life, Herzog ruminates, writes mental
letters to the dead and to the living, and recalls his
past mistakes. Although there are flashback scenes of
college life in the novel, the book is essentially a study
of Herzog's character. Bellow takes the reader deep inside Herzog's sometimes rational, sometimes paranoic
mind. *Herzog* is a classic psychological novel and a
classic novel of ideas as well. The book won the 1964
National Book Award for fiction.
     Saul Bellow was born in Lachine, Quebec, in 1915. He
received a B.S. from Northwestern University in 1937 and
did graduate work in anthropology at the University of
Wisconsin. At the time *Herzog* was published Bellow was
a professor of English at the University of Chicago.
Herzog was his sixth novel. In 1976 Bellow received the
Nobel Prize for literature.

351. [Cassill, Ronald Verlin]. *The President*. By R.V.
      Cassill. New York: Simon and Schuster, 1964.

     When Royce Morgan returns to "Wellford College" after
World War II he expects to become the school's president.
After all, his father was Wellford's president for thirty-
five years. But the college trustees appoint Winfred
Mooney, a huckster from the business world, and Royce
grudgingly accepts a top job in Mooney's administration.
As Mooney transforms the small Midwestern college into a
bustling, though low-quality university, Royce bides his
time by having an affair with the president's wife and by
allowing his own home to turn into a domestic disaster
area. Finally Mooney is removed from office after it is
discovered that he is a closet homosexual, and Royce is
named president. Although Royce is confident that he
will have a successful reign, readers are led to suspect
that he may not turn out to be ideal presidential timber.
Reviewers universally praised *The President* as well
written. They were not in agreement, however, about the
author's intent. Some saw the novel as satire. Some
read it as serious melodrama. In any event, *The President*
contains a great deal of material about presidential politics and about Winfred Mooney's conduct of presidential
business.
     An earlier Cassill novel, *Night School* (326), is in-
cluded in this bibliography.

352. Curley, Daniel. *A Stone Man, Yes*. New York: Viking
      Press, 1964.

      This sometimes comic novel is set at a rural state
   college. The protagonist is George Scott, chairman of
   the English department. George's wife, Alice, is frigid
   toward George but not at all reluctant to share her bed
   with a young instructor in George's department. For his
   part, George tries to seduce various women but circumstances always stop him short of success. At one point
   in the plot George vainly attempts to breathe some zest
   into his life by taking an assembly line job in a tin can
   factory. Amidst all of these goings-on Steven Pratt,
   Alice's paramour, is writing a college novel about happenings at the school. Unfortunately, Steven commits suicide
   at the end of the story and leaves his novel unfinished.
   Thus Pratt's book does not appear in this bibliography.
      Daniel Curley was born in 1918 in East Bridgewater,
   Massachusetts. *A Stone Man, Yes* was his second novel.
   Curley taught at Plattsburg State College in New York
   from 1952 to 1955. At the time *A Stone Man, Yes* was
   published, he was a professor of English at the University
   of Illinois.

353. Donohue, H.E.F. *The Higher Animals*. New York: Viking
      Press, 1964.

      The protagonist of this complex novel is Daniel Conn
   ("the Connman"), a clerk in a bookstore on the edge of
   the University of Chicago campus. A mentally scarred
   veteran of the Korean War, and a law school drop-out,
   Daniel interacts with a variety of bookstore customers
   and barroom drinking companions during the course of the
   story. All of his associations bring Daniel to a better
   understanding of himself and of life. Many of Daniel's
   unwitting mentors are academic types--University of
   Chicago faculty and students--but also in the sizeable
   cast of characters are three villainous thugs from the
   hills of Kentucky, a teenage nymphomaniac, and several
   members of the Chicago police force. The book is steeped
   in symbolism and, as Guy Davenport noted when reviewing
   the work for *The National Review* (February 23, 1965):
   "Clarity is not this novel's foremost virtue."
      A graduate of the University of Chicago, H.E.F. Donohue
   was fiction editor of *Ladies Home Journal* during the late
   1950s and early 1960s. *The Higher Animals* was his first
   novel.

354.   Isherwood, Christopher. *A Single Man*. New York: Simon
       and Schuster, 1964.

       This brief (186-page) but eloquent novel recounts the
final day in the lonely life of an aging, homosexual professor. The protagonist is a British emigree named George,
a member of the English department of "San Tomas State
College" in California. George has recently lost his
lover, Jim, in an automobile accident. He would like to
take up with Kenny, a friendly student in one of his
classes. But Kenny is heterosexual. George and Kenny
have an evening swim in the Pacific and George nearly
drowns. Home alone after his enervating experience,
George ruminates on his miserable existence and dies.
Some of the novel consists of flashbacks. There are a
few classroom scenes, and George occasionally muses about
American higher education, but the book is much less a
conventional college novel than it is an intense character
study of George.
       Born in Great Britain in 1904, Christopher Isherwood
became a naturalized American citizen in 1946. With the
publication of his first novel, *All the Conspirators*
(London: Jonathan Cape, 1926), Isherwood launched what
was to become a brilliant literary career. *A Single Man*
was his tenth novel. During the early 1960s Isherwood
served as a visiting writer at Los Angeles State College
and at the University of California at Santa Barbara.

355.   Litwak, Leo. *To the Hanging Gardens*. Cleveland and New
       York: The World Publishing Co., 1964.

       To the Hanging Gardens is an involved and sometimes
murky first novel about a problem-ridden group of adults
in a university town. Among the central characters are
a stuffy thirty-five-year-old professor of philosophy,
his unhappy wife, a fifty-four-year-old itinerant instructor of philosophy, and the instructor's Black paramour. Also in the cast is a young, mentally unbalanced
male novelist with pronounced sadistic tendencies. These
characters, and others, form various sexual alliances and
engage each other in verbal and physical abuse. Part of
the plot involves the university's refusal to offer the
instructor a new contract. The Hanging Gardens of the
novel's title is a local nightspot to which the book's
characters repair at various junctures in the story.
       Leo Litwak was born in Detroit in 1924. He received
a B.A. from Wayne State University in 1948 and did graduate work at Columbia from 1948 until 1951. At the time

To the Hanging Gardens was published Litwak was an assistant professor of English at San Francisco State College.

356.   Astrachan, Samuel. *The Game of Dostoevsky*. New York:
       Farrar, Straus, and Giroux, 1965.

   "The Wolgamuts," a group of faculty and students at
"the University of Y," meet regularly in the apartment of
one of its members to play monopoly. The idea is that
monopoly will help the participants displace their frustrations. When regular monopoly begins to lose its impact, the group invents a derivative in which players try
to win spiritual grace by confessing to one or more of
the seven deadly sins. A "grand inquisitor" substitutes
for a banker, and since the players are all associated
with the university's English department, sins are con-
fessed in the name of a literary character. As the novel
proceeds the author intermixes reality with phenomeno-
logical passages and it is up to the reader to sort out
the various levels of the narrative. Since many of the
players are high on marijuana it is doubtful that even
they know what is happening at all times. Some reviewers
found the book a brilliant literary achievement, replete
with overtones not only of Dostoevsky but of Henry James,
T.S. Eliot, and even Jane Austen. Other reviewers found
it confusing and pretentious.
   Samuel Astrachan received a B.A. from Columbia in 1955.
The Game of Dostoevsky was his second novel.

357.   DeVries, Peter. *Let Me Count the Ways*. Boston: Little,
       Brown and Co., 1965.

   This broken-backed, comic novel has two protagonists,
both of whom narrate their own halves of the book. The
first narrator is Stan Waltz, an aging piano mover who,
among other misfortunes, develops a hernia after carrying
a prospective mistress into his bedroom. The second
narrator is Stan's son, Tom, a puckish instructor of
English at "Polycarp University." Tom embarrasses the
Polycarp English department by winning two twenty-five-
words-or-less writing contests, one of which brings him
a highly publicized date with Angela Ravage, a beautiful
movie star. Then, in short order, Tom rises from instructor to acting chairman of English (after the old
department chairman has a heart attack and the other senior
staff leave the university to take jobs elsewhere) and
then on to the acting presidency of Polycarp (when the
incumbent has a heart attack brought on, in part, by Tom's
behavior).

A virtuoso of the comic novel, Peter DeVries was born in Chicago in 1910. He received an A.B. from Calvin College in 1931. *Let Me Count the Ways* was his ninth novel. A later DeVries work, *The Cat's Pajamas and Witch's Milk* (372), also appears in this bibliography.

358. Fiedler, Leslie Aaron. *Back to China*. New York: Stein and Day, 1965.

Back to China is a semi-comic novel set at a university in Montana. The protagonist is a middle-aged Jewish professor of philosophy named Baro Finkelstone. Married to a gentile with alcoholic tendencies, Baro has an affair with a Japanese girl who is the wife of an American Indian graduate student. When the Indian kills himself after a drug overdose, Baro is left to sort out his complicated domestic and quasi-domestic relationships. Much of the novel is told via flashbacks. These deal with Baro's experiences as a Marine officer in China and Japan just after the end of World War II. In one flashback scene Baro submits to a vasectomy by a Japanese doctor. Thus when both his mistress and his wife claim to be pregnant by him near the end of the book Baro is understandably confused.

Leslie Aaron Fiedler is one of America's leading literary scholars, critics, and creative writers. He received a B.A. from New York University in 1938 and a Ph.D. from Harvard in 1941. From 1941 until 1964 he was a member of the English department at Montana State University. In 1964, one year before *Back to China* was published, Fiedler moved to the State University of New York at Buffalo.

359. Ford, Daniel Francis. *Now Comes Theodora*. Garden City, New York: Doubleday and Co., 1965.

One of the three protagonists of this unusual novel is Boris, a thirty-nine-year-old photographer employed by a university in upper New England. Boris lives alone in a quonset hut at the periphery of the campus. His overriding interest is taking nude photographs of co-eds. The second protagonist is Colin Merchant, a married undergraduate, who feels the need to see the world. The third central character is Theodora ("Teddy"), Colin's wife. When Theodora becomes pregnant Colin decides to take a trip to Europe. Theodora seeks refuge in Boris' hut, where the photographer treats her with kindness before, during, and after the birth of her child. Theodora files for divorce from Colin and plans to marry Boris. But at

the end of the novel Colin returns to the university,
seduces Theodora, and demands that she and the infant
return to him. Murmuring "only you--no one but you,"
Theodora willingly agrees to leave Boris and to resume
her wifely duties. In addition to the peripatetic Colin,
a number of other university students cross the pages of
this sometimes satirical, sometimes serious book. One
of them, Marvin Peabody, is an organizer of peace marches.
Another, Hal Pappajohn, is an enterprising lad who has an
affair with a dean's daughter. Boris, one of very few
university photographers in college fiction, and certainly
the only photographer-protagonist in a college novel, is
portrayed as a warmhearted slob.

Daniel Francis Ford received a B.A. from the University
of New Hampshire in 1954. At the time *Now Comes Theodora*,
his first novel, was published, Ford was an editor in the
University of New Hampshire office of publications.

360. Harrison, George Bagshawe. *The Fires of Arcadia*. By
      G.B. Harrison. New York: Harcourt, Brace and World,
      1965.

George Bagshawe Harrison was born in 1894 in Great
Britain and was educated at Cambridge and the University
of London. He began his academic career at the University
of London in 1924, moved to Queen's University in Canada
in 1943, and became a professor of English at the University of Michigan in 1949. Internationally known as a
Shakespearean scholar, he became a professor emeritus at
Michigan in 1964. This brief (153-page) book, published
a year after his retirement, was his first novel.

The Fires of Arcadia is set at "Arcadia College" in New
England. It tells of a series of bizarre events which
follow the successful attempt of a professor of biology
to breed satyrs on the college farm. The climax comes
when the hedonistic daughter of Arcadia's president stages
an orgy with the satyrs and her brother, outraged by the
affair, kills the creatures and burns down the college's
main building. Although *The Fires of Arcadia* is less a
conventional novel than it is a satirical academic fable,
it includes a series of academic sub-plots and a sizeable
roster of campus characters. Moreover, Harrison takes
good-humored delight in tweaking "progressive" education-
alists, pompous college presidents, and those who conduct
scientific research in academe.

361. Williams, John Edward. *Stoner*. New York: Viking Press,
      1965.

      This novel is not recommended for those considering
      college teaching as a profession. The book traces the
      dismal life of William Stoner, from his undergraduate
      days at the University of Missouri through forty-plus
      years in the university's English department. Stoner be-
      gins his teaching career as a promising young man but his
      enthusiasms are soon sapped by his neurotic wife and by
      an evil department chairman. The latter assigns him end-
      less freshman composition classes. The chairman also
      dismisses from the faculty a young female instructor with
      whom Stoner has a brief and poignant romance. The epitome
      of the competent but unspectacular teacher, Stoner is
      never promoted and he retires as an assistant professor.
      Shortly thereafter he dies of cancer.
          John Edward Williams received a B.A. from the University
      of Denver in 1949 and a Ph.D. from the University of Mis-
      souri in 1954. In 1954 he joined the English department
      at Denver and was a professor of English there when *Stoner*
      was published. *Stoner* was his third novel.

362. Barth, John. *Giles Goat-Boy: Or, The Revised New Syl-
      labus*. Garden City, New York: Doubleday and Co., 1966.

      This massive (710-page) novel is set at an institution
      of higher learning and includes a large roster of aca-
      demic characters. However, it is hardly a traditional
      college novel. *Giles Goat-Boy* is a complex allegory.
      Its locale, "the University," is by implication the world
      of the early 1960s. The university has a West Campus and
      an East Campus (both subdivided into self-contained col-
      leges), and a Kennedy-like leader (Chancellor Rexford)
      and a Khrushchev figure (Comrade X). Campus Riot I and
      Campus Riot II have ended and the university is now in-
      volved in the Quiet Riot (the Cold War). The protagonist
      of the story is Billy Bocksfuss, a boy raised as a goat
      on a university experimental farm. Billy is a heroic
      archetype. As the novel progresses Billy becomes "George
      the Undergraduate" and, as the book proceeds into its
      final stages, he takes on the role of "Giles the Grand
      Tutor," a god figure. No precis of *Giles Goat-Boy* can
      possibly do justice to the depth and intricacy of the
      novel. Indeed, since its publication the book has become
      a favorite subject for dissection by literary scholars
      and critics.
          Another, somewhat less reticular John Barth novel, *The
      End of the Road* (254), is included in this bibliography.

363.   Birstein, Ann [Mrs. Alfred Kazin]. *The Sweet Birds of Gorham*. New York: David McKay Co., 1966.

The protagonist of this often funny, satirical novel is Daisy Lerner, an attractive young Jewish girl who arrives at Gorham College to teach English. Daisy has no graduate degrees but she has just published a modestly well-received novel. Gorham is an exclusive Eastern women's college and its faculty (as well as its faculty spouses) treat their newest recruit with disdain. Most of the plot focuses upon Daisy's efforts to gain acceptance on the campus and upon her affair with George Auerbach, the school's self-centered, forty-year-old poet-in-residence. Fans of college novels will be happy to learn that Daisy takes advantage of her situation to begin a fictive expose of Gorham.

Ann Birstein received a B.A. from Queens College in 1948. During the 1950s and 1960s she taught at Queens, the New School, City College of New York, and the University of Iowa. *The Sweet Birds of Gorham* was her third novel. With her husband, author Alfred Kazin, she was co-editor in 1959 of *The Works of Anne Frank* (Garden City, New York: Doubleday and Co.).

*364.   Bradbury, Malcolm. *Stepping Westward*. Boston: Houghton Mifflin Co., 1966.

James Walker, a visiting novelist-in-residence from Great Britain, tries to adjust to the breezy but not very intellectual atmosphere of "Benedict Arnold University." Benedict Arnold is a part private and part state-supported institution in America's far Midwest. Walker leaves before the expiration of his one-year appointment, after refusing to sign a loyalty oath. But before his departure he encounters one of the funniest and most mercilessly satirized set of academics in college fiction. Representative of Benedict Arnold's inhabitants is Ralph Zugsmith Coolidge, the institution's energetic president. Each year the school's new visiting writer composes a scurrilous novel about Benedict Arnold, and each of these tomes includes a lampoon of Coolidge. Instead of taking offense, however, Coolidge collects the novels in his office and has his public relations department give them maximum publicity. "Kids like coming here after reading those books," he tells his associates. "My guess is that (the novels have) boosted enrollment by around twenty percent."

Malcolm Bradbury received a B.A. from the University

College of Leicester in 1953, an M.A. from Queen Mary College, University of London, in 1955, and a Ph.D. from the
University of Manchester in 1963. He studied at Indiana
University during the 1955-1956 academic year. In 1965
he became a member of the English faculty at the University of Easy Anglia and in 1970 he became a professor of
American studies at that institution. *Stepping Westward*
was Bradbury's second novel. His first and third novels
also are set in academic locales, both of them British
provincial universities. These novels are *Eating People
is Wrong* (New York: Alfred A. Knopf, 1959) and *The History
Man* (Boston: Houghton Mifflin Co., 1976). Like *Stepping
Westward*, these novels are satires, but in all three works
Bradbury underlies his satire with a serious theme—the
decline of liberal humanism in the modern academic world.

*365.   Hudson, Helen (pseud.). *Tell the Time to None*. New York:
        E.P. Dutton and Co., 1966.

    Set at a high-status university in the East, this epi-
sodic novel tunnels into the generally selfish and mean-
ingless lives of a series of academics and their spouses.
Part of the plot centers on the inevitable jockeying for
political position which accompanies the lingering death,
from cancer, of Philip Boswell Darling III, the institution's beloved president. Another segment of the story
involves the suicide of Kevin Tweed, a mentally disturbed
graduate student whose sufferings at the hands of unfeel-
ing faculty members lead to his self-destruction. Social
scientists may be especially interested in the portrait
of Werner Woulff, a sociologist. Werner imprisons his
wife in a world of domestic servitude, dominates his
faculty colleagues, and is convinced that he is "a giant
in a world of pygmies." In one chilling scene Werner
bursts into President Darling's office as the critically
ill president is attempting to spend one last, reflective
day at his desk. Recognizing the president's weakened
state, Werner attempts to bully him into signing an application for a cost-inefficient research project.
    Considering the almost totally negative tone of *Tell
the Time to None*, it is little wonder that the author of
this first novel employed a pseudonym. Her identity remains a publishing secret although many past and present
Yale faculty are convinced that she was the wife of one
of Yale's leading social science professors. A second
novel by "Helen Hudson," *Meyer Meyer* (367), is included
in this bibliography.

366.   Ballard, Phoebe, and Willis Todhunter Ballard. *The Man
       Who Stole a University*. Garden City, New York: Double-
       day and Co., 1967.

       Out at "Wellington University" in Ohio the natives are
       getting restless. The school has mounting debts and a
       declining number of admissions applications. The only
       person who can save the institution is Emory Monck, a
       twenty-nine-year-old alumnus who is now a big wheeler-
       dealer in the oil business. The trustees appoint Emory
       as Wellington's chancellor. But the trustees prove to
       be a recalcitrant lot. They fight Emory's new policies
       and eventually fire him. So Emory, the very epitome
       of presidential aggressiveness, sets up a rival university
       in temporary quarters a few miles away and steals all of
       Wellington's faculty and students. When Wellington then
       goes bankrupt, Monck and his oil tycoon backers simply
       buy Wellington's physical assets and move everyone back
       to the Wellington campus. Although this book is written
       as serious fiction, many academic readers may well inter-
       pret much of it as satire. For example, at one point
       Emory is followed to an out-of-town speaking engagement
       by an infatuated co-ed. She gains entrance to his hotel
       room and slips nude into his bed. When the startled Emory
       discovers the girl he first lectures her on the necessity
       for pristine presidential-student relations and only then,
       when his remonstration is finished, does he order her to
       put on her clothes.
           Phoebe and Todhunter Ballard were married in 1936.
       Their collaborative efforts have produced over 150 books
       (including mysteries and westerns) as well as more than
       fifty motion picture and television scripts. Much of their
       work has been published under pseudonyms. As pen names
       they have employed Brian Agar, P.D. Ballard, Parker Bonner,
       Sam Bowie, Nick Carter, Hunter D'Allard, Brian Fox, Har-
       rison Hunt, John Hunter, Neil MacNeil, Clint Reno, John
       Sheperd, Jack Slade, and Clay Turner.

367.   Hudson, Helen (pseud.). *Meyer Meyer*. New York: E.P.
       Dutton and Co., 1967.

       The title character of this study in dramatic ironies
       is Meyer Benjamin Meyer, a forty-seven-year-old professor
       of history at a New York City university in Greenwich
       Village. Unmarried, Meyer's only close companion is
       Mendel Berg, a middle-aged bachelor professor of history
       at an uptown university in New York. Meyer has an affair
       with Lena Hoffman, a wealthy Connecticut widow. Berg
       has an affair with Josie Molumphy, a nurse. Meyer tries
       to impede Berg's romance. When Lena dies, Meyer is left

once again to his celibate existence. But despite
Meyer's interference, Berg marries Josie and then leaves
New York to accept an offer to join the Harvard faculty.
Meyer is portrayed as weak, egocentric, and meddlesome.
Berg is described as a man with latent strengths. There
are a few effective campus scenes in the novel and
Meyer, on occasion, is given to reflecting upon his
lonely life as an academic.

    Meyer Meyer was the second novel by the woman who em-
ployed "Helen Hudson" as a pseudonym. Her first novel,
Tell the Time to None (365), also appears in this bibliography.

*368. McInerny, Ralph Matthew. *Jolly Rogerson*. Garden City,
      New York: Doubleday and Co., 1967.

    Jolly Rogerson is a rich, satirical novel about a pro-
fessor of humanities who is deep in the throes of mid-
career disillusionment. The protagonist, Matthew "Matt"
Rogerson, is employed by "Fort Elbow College," a low-
status private institution in Ohio. Lacking the publications to move to a better school, Matt reacts to his
plight by sardonic gamesmanship. In incident after incident he takes himself to the brink of disaster, not in any
serious effort to improve his fundamental condition, but
simply to add interest to his otherwise drab life. At
one point, for example, Matt decides that there is no
particular distinction to being a mediocre professor in
a mediocre college. He realizes that he cannot be good,
so he determines to be the worst teacher on campus. One
of his tactics is to avoid prepared lectures. Instead,
he delivers disjointed spur-of-the-moment commentaries to
his classes. This backfires, however, when he is voted
Fort Elbow's outstanding instructor. A great many Fort
Elbow faculty and administrators act as Matt's foils during
the story. Most of these individuals already have come
to terms with their own mediocrity and Matt, who still
nurses discontent, emerges as a paragon of academic cre-
ativity by comparison.

    Ralph Matthew McInerny received a B.A. from St. Paul
Seminary in 1951 and a Ph.D. from Laval University in 1954.
At the time *Jolly Rogerson* was published he was a professor
of philosophy at Notre Dame. *Jolly Rogerson* was his first
novel. Three other novels by McInerny--*Gate of Heaven*
(403), *Spinnaker* (409), and *Rogerson at Bay* (406)--also
appear in this bibliography. *Rogerson at Bay* chronicles
the further adventures of Matthew Rogerson.

369. Pease, Robert. *The Associate Professor.* New York: Simon
      and Schuster, 1967.

      The Associate Professor is a black comedy which covers
      a week in the life of James Knudsen, an associate professor
      of physics at "Borough College." Borough is a public
      institution in New York City. Knudsen's tenure decision
      is in the immediate offing and the story follows him as
      he moves in near panic through his daily routines. Bor-
      ough College, headed by a president whose chief concern
      is efficiency, is depicted as heartless and impersonal.
      Indeed, Knudsen's tenure is denied, in part, because twice
      in a single year he has been five minutes late for his
      8 A.M. class. The book includes frosty portraits of
      Borough's registrar and of Knudsen's department chairman.
      Registrar Harry Mulcahy invents ingenious computer pro-
      grams through which the administration can measure faculty
      teaching productivity. And Chairman Blumberger, a dedi-
      cated toady to the school's president, spends much of his
      time making certain that his faculty do not dismiss their
      students before their full allotment of classroom time has
      expired.

370. Adams, Hazard. *The Horses of Instruction.* New York:
      Harcourt, Brace and World, 1968.

      Set in the halcyon days of the late 1950s and early
      1960s, when expanding American colleges and universities
      were beginning feverish recruitment of faculty, this
      novel deals with three young men hired as assistant pro-
      fessors of English at "Walton University" in Ohio. At-
      tracted to Walton by promises of elaborate research fa-
      cilities, an honors program, and a yet-to-be-founded
      literary magazine, the three neophytes discover that, in
      fact, Walton has more detriments than assets. After run-
      ning afoul of the English department's moss-laden old
      guard, and after realizing that the university will never
      make good on most of its pledges, all three leave Walton
      for greener academic pastures. Although the book is
      serious in tone it is lightened by judicious injections
      of humor. Academic nostalgia buffs will appreciate the
      scenes in which Jack, Will, and Jason, the three pro-
      tagonists, weigh the relative merits of various job offers,
      many of them unsolicited, which they receive throughout
      the story.
          Hazard Adams was awarded an A.B. from Princeton in 1948
      and a Ph.D. from the University of Washington in 1953.
      He taught in the English departments of Cornell, the

University of Texas, and Michigan State before moving to
the University of California at Irvine as professor of
English and chairman of the department in 1964. He became dean of the School of Humanities at Cal-Irvine in
1970 and vice chancellor for academic affairs in 1972.
The Horses of Instruction was Adams' first novel.

*371. Brace, Gerald Warner. *The Department*. New York: W.W.
       Norton, 1968.

Less a novel than a series of ruminations, this book
has as its narrator Robert Sanderling, an about-to-retire
professor of English at a university in Boston. In prep-
aration for his farewell speech Sanderling mentally reviews his career and muses about many of his past and
present faculty colleagues. As he gives thought to his
forty years in academe, Sanderling emerges as a man of
reasonable modesty and humanity. However, some of those
about whom he cogitates do not fare as well. As Sanderling reflects on his life he offers in-depth character
studies which speak to the weaknesses, as well as to the
strengths, of a range of academic types. These faculty
portraits are among the most penetrating in American
college fiction, and no serious student of the American
college novel can afford to ignore *The Department*.
     An earlier work by Gerald Warner Brace, *The Spire* (229),
is included in this bibliography.

372.   DeVries, Peter. *The Cat's Pajamas and Witch's Milk*.
       Boston: Little, Brown and Co., 1968.

This book consists of two comic novellas which are
linked together by the presence in both of Tillie Shilep-
sky Seltzer, a social worker. Only the first of the
novellas, *The Cat's Pajamas*, deals with life in academe.
The protagonist of *The Cat's Pajamas* is Hank Tattersall,
an unenthusiastic teacher of creative writing at "Chichester College." Although Hank is a member of the institution's faculty disciplinary committee, he joins the
picket line at a student demonstration over dormitory
curfews. The college administration, unhappy over this
seeming conflict of interest, suggests that Hank might
be happier elsewhere, and he leaves Chichester to join an
advertising agency. Unfortunately, the advertising business does not prove to be any more satisfying than did
college teaching. Unemployed, Hank descends to life in
a squalid flophouse, where he comes to the attention of
the intrepid Tillie. Shortly thereafter, he freezes to

death one bitter winter night when he catches his head in
a dog-door at the bottom of the entrance to his residence.
Although the portrait of Hank is not intended to be taken
seriously, it is perhaps as insightful as are many of the
other depictions of self-destructive academics in fiction.
    Another work by Peter DeVries, *Let Me Count the Ways*
(357), is included in this bibliography.

373. Morressy, John. *The Addison Tradition*. Garden City, New
      York: Doubleday and Co., 1968.

        The Addison Tradition is a sometimes angry, sometimes
humorous novel which probes many of the moral and professional problems of college faculty members. Among the
issues explored in the book are teaching versus publishing, academic freedom, and the often strained relations
between faculty and administration. The protagonist of
the story is Matthew Grennan, an untenured instructor of
English at "Addison College." Addison is a small liberal
arts college in the East. Grennan resolves to put publication at the head of his personal agenda but he is in-
eluctably drawn into campus politics. Eventually he is
caught up in an imbroglio which arises from a student
sit-in in the dean's office. The sit-in is prompted by
the administration's instant dismissal of a student who
writes a satirical story on "the Addison Tradition" for
the campus humor magazine. Grennan manages to survive
the immediate backwash of the sit-in, but at the end of
the novel he knows that his days at Addison are numbered.
    John Morressy received a B.A. from St. Johns University
in 1953 and an M.A. from the same institution in 1961.
He taught English at St. Johns from 1963 until 1966, when
he left after becoming involved in a strike against the
administration. At the time *The Addison Tradition* was
published Morressy was an associate professor and chairman
of the English department at Franklin Pierce College in
New Hampshire. *The Addison Tradition* was Morressy's
second novel.

374. Turnbull, Agnes Sligh. *Many a Green Isle*. Boston:
      Houghton Mifflin Co., 1968.

        Many a Green Isle is a simply written story about a
professor with complex problems. Gavin McAllister is head
of the English department at "Marsden College," a second-
rate private institution in western Pennsylvania. Among
those who contribute to McAllister's woes are his unwed
pregnant daughter, a local attorney who covets his wife's

affections, and the college president who has a habit of
assenting to any and all demands made by prospective benefactors. When the president and McAllister disagree over
the former's policies, McAllister is fired. Since he
lacks a Ph.D. he is reduced to teaching English in the
local high school. Yet, by the end of the story, things
are looking up. McAllister's daughter gets married. His
wife remains faithful. And, best of all, he inherits
$25,000 which will allow him to return to graduate school
for his doctorate. With a Ph.D., so we are led to pre-
sume, McAllister will find ready employment in the academic big leagues.

Agnes Sligh Turnbull was born in New Alexandria, Pennsylvania, in 1888. She graduated from Indiana State College
in Pennsylvania. After a brief career as a high school
English teacher she devoted her full professional attention to writing, specializing in romances, volumes of
short stories, and books for juveniles.

375. [Chitty, Sir Thomas Willes]. *High.* By Thomas Hinde
     (pseud.). New York: Walker and Co., 1969.

Maurice Peterson is a British professor of English who
is serving as a visiting lecturer at "Flatville University," a huge state institution in the Midwest. Maurice
has an affair with Jill, a co-ed whose encumbrances include both a husband--who is away in Australia--and a
jealous boyfriend. Maurice is writing a novel about his
stay in Flatville. The characters in his novel are fictive
versions of himself, Jill, and a number of other Flatville
inhabitants. Passages of Maurice's novel are interspersed
with the main narrative, and the story is carried forward
through both presentations. *High* includes classroom
scenes, sex, and an abundance of drug taking. Portions
of Maurice's manuscript are clearly hallucinatory. Some
reviewers found the novel to be a tour de force of modern
writing. Others thought it a case of literary self-
indulgence.

Sir Thomas Willes Chitty, son of a Baronet, was born in
Great Britain in 1926. Educated at Oxford, he worked
during the 1950s for the British Inland Revenue Service
in London and, toward the end of the decade, for the Shell
Oil Company in Nairobi, Kenya. In 1960 he left the world
of business to concentrate on writing. *High* was his tenth
novel. From 1965 until 1967 Chitty was a visiting lecturer at the University of Illinois. During the 1969-1970
academic year he served as a visiting professor at Boston
University. Another of Chitty's novels, *Generally a Virgin* (302), is included in this bibliography.

376. Rader, Paul. *Professor Wilmess Must Die*. New York:
      Dial Press, 1969.

      Professor Wilmess Must Die is a satire on student pro-
      tests of the 1960s. The setting is "Los Angeles Western
      College," known locally as "LAW." The protagonist is
      Earnest Wilmess, a liberal professor of English who takes
      upon himself the role of intermediary between LAW's dissi-
      dents and its establishment. Earnest also takes Susan
      Rapture, a rebellious co-ed, as his bed partner. At the
      end of the novel Susan stabs Earnest to death after inter-
      course in order to make a political statement. The prob-
      lems at LAW stem from the administration's diversion of
      student activity funds into construction of "The Uni-
      torium," a massive administration office building and
      auditorium. At the height of the uproar LAW's president,
      Marshall Stride, suddenly resigns to conduct a study of
      "Wesleyan doctrine as it relates to young people of
      today."
          During most of the 1960s Paul Rader served as a public
      relations officer at New York University. *Professor
      Wilmess Must Die* was his second novel. According to the
      book's dust jacket Rader was a vice-president for develop-
      ment at a university in the Southwest when *Professor
      Wilmess Must Die* was published. Before entering academe
      Rader was a writer and producer in motion pictures and in
      television.

377. Wiebe, Dallas. *Skyblue the Badass*. Garden City, New
      York: Doubleday and Co., 1969.

          The protagonist of this satire, a young man named Sky-
      blue, is followed from his boyhood in Kansas into a career
      as a college teacher of English. Most of the book's aca-
      demically relevant passages are set at the University of
      Wisconsin-Madison, where Skyblue holds his initial faculty
      appointment. Skyblue is portrayed as a dreamer, in search
      of his true destiny. One notable Madison scene is en-
      riched by the appearance, at a dinner party, of all of
      the university's neophyte instructors of English. Each
      of these individuals feels that he can escape academe at
      any time by writing a best-selling college novel. The
      book contains very little dialogue and, in fact, the plot
      itself is of only minor importance. Of more significance,
      at least from the author's standpoint, is the constant
      employment of literary fireworks. Long and often meta-
      phorical passages reminiscent of the work of John Barth,
      Thomas Pynchon, and even Thomas Wolfe are regularly

injected into the narrative. Reviewing the novel for *The Atlantic* (February, 1969), Phoebe Adams noted: "The novel Mr. Wiebe intended to write is presumably buried somewhere under a pile of paraphrased quotations." Dallas Wiebe received an A.B. from Bethel College in Kansas, and a Ph.D. from the University of Michigan. His first teaching post was at the University of Wisconsin-Madison. At the time *Skyblue the Badass* was published Wiebe was a member of the department of English at the University of Cincinnati.

378. Brookhouse, Christopher. *Running Out*. Boston: Little, Brown and Co., 1970.

Running Out is an intense, existential novel which follows the misfortunes of three Harvard graduates in their young adult years. One of the protagonists, Bingham Fairchild, is an employee of a Boston publishing house. Bingham is shot to death by a thug who takes revenge after Bingham thwarts his attempt to stage a street robbery. The second protagonist is Bingham's sometimes mistress, Rachel, who is stalked by Bingham's killer after the murder. The third central character, named George, teaches English at "Cape Fear State College" in North Carolina. After Bingham is shot, George flies to Cambridge and persuades Rachel to move with him to North Carolina. There are a number of flashbacks about Harvard, but from the standpoint of the college novel the most significant scenes take place at Cape Fear. George finds the institution to be an intellectual graveyard. In desperation, he holds long conversations with the operator of a local pizza parlor--the only individual in town with even a smattering of erudition--and he eases his frustrations by taking up backyard vegetable growing as a hobby.
Christopher Brookhouse received an A.B. from Stanford in 1959 and a Ph.D. from Harvard in 1964. He was a member of the department of English at the University of North Carolina when this book was published. *Running Out* was his first novel.

379. Slavitt, David Rytman. *Anagrams*. Garden City, New York: Doubleday and Co., 1970.

Anagrams is an acerbic satire about the academic literary circuit. Jerome Carpenter, a poet of minor reputation and a professional ghostwriter of doctoral dissertations, takes part in a literary festival at "Rockville College." Rockville is a small Midwestern institution with large

pretentions. The novel explores the intellectual tricks,
the bad manners, and the loose morals of the festival's
participants. The Rockville faculty sponsors of the
event are portrayed as negatively as are Carpenter's
fellow visiting writers. Indeed, the only serious student
of literature in the story is a retired chemical engineer
who sits next to Carpenter on the first leg of the flight
to Rockville. The engineer passes the time by reading
Thomas Wolfe's *The Web and the Rock* (129).

David Rytman Slavitt received an A.B. from Yale in 1956
and an M.A. from Columbia in 1957. He taught English at
Georgia Tech for one year after his graduation from Columbia. An accomplished poet, an author of fiction for
juveniles, and a sometimes serious novelist, Slavitt also
has written a number of best-selling commercial novels
under the pseudonym Henry Sutton.

380. McConkey, James Rodney. *A Journey to Sahalin*. New York:
     Coward, McCann and Geoghegan, 1971.

Set in the traumatic sit-in and revolution days of the
late 1960s, this serious novel follows the attempts of
George Chambers, a dean of students, to calm the troubled
waters at "Brangwen University." Brangwen is a private
multiversity in the East. George's efforts at campus
conciliation are impeded by his own none-too-placid domestic life. He has two budding-revolutionary teenage children, a liberated but not loving wife, and a weepy mistress. Despite his personal harassments, George has a
certain amount of success in negotiating with dissident
student organizations. But just as he seems about to
restore the campus to its normal state of somnambulance,
George is killed by a shot fired by an unknown sniper.
A variety of campus characters appear in the novel. These
include a dogmatically liberal president, who resigns
after George is assassinated, and a dogmatically conservative faculty member whose proposed solution to the
university's problems is literal application of the student rule book.

James Rodney McConkey received a B.A. from Western
Reserve University in 1943 and a Ph.D. from the State
University of Iowa in 1953. *A Journey to Sahalin* was his
second novel. At the time the book was published McConkey
was a professor of English at Cornell.

381. Read, Piers Paul. *The Professor's Daughter.* Philadelphia
and New York: J.B. Lippincott Co., 1971.

    The Professor's Daughter is an old-style melodrama
furnished with modern academic trappings. Henry Rutledge
is a professor of political theory at Harvard. He is
wealthy, liberal, the husband of an unfaithful wife, and
the father of two physically attractive but badly disturbed daughters. The older of his two offspring,
twenty-year-old Louisa, is the book's title character.
Already divorced, a failed suicide, and a nymphomaniac,
she is under a psychiatrist's care. Louisa arises from
her various couches long enough to role play at radicalism,
and she joins forces with some of her father's most promising students in a plan to kill a United States senator.
Learning of the plot to assassinate the politico (who also
happens to be his wife's paramour), Henry tries to intervene. But he is accidentally shot and killed by one of
the would-be gunmen. Some of the book consists of flashback passages in which Henry's academic career is reviewed.
And there are several intriguing scenes in which Henry's
students meet to hatch their revolutionary plots.
    The son of British cultural historian Sir Herbert Read,
Piers Paul Read was educated at Cambridge University.
The Professor's Daughter was his fourth novel. Subsequent
Read books, most notably *Alive: The Story of the Andes
Survivors* (Philadelphia and New York: J.B. Lippincott Co.,
1974), have gained him stature as a major British writer.

382. Shapiro, Karl. *Edsel.* New York: Bernard Geis, 1971.

    A first novel, published at the age of fifty-eight by
one of America's foremost poets, *Edsel* probes the professional and sexual miseries of Edsel Laserow, a seasoned
professor of English at "Milo University." Milo is a
large, state-run emporium of academic mediocrity in the
Midwest. In the course of the first-person narrative
Edsel samples the various sexual wares of several women,
attends a wild party at the home of a husband and wife
team of sociologists, and becomes involved in revolutionary
dissent on the Milo campus. He also lectures with studied
pomposity to his poetry classes. Though some reviewers
found the frequent scatological passages in *Edsel* dis-
tasteful, the book includes a great deal of crackling
dialogue, more than a little wit, and a collection of
deft characterizations of Milo students, faculty members,
and administrators.

Karl Shapiro was born in Baltimore, Maryland, in 1913.
He attended the University of Virginia and Johns Hopkins
University. After teaching at Johns Hopkins and Loyola
University of Chicago, Shapiro joined the department of
English at the University of Nebraska in 1956. He was a
professor of English at Nebraska when *Edsel* was published.

383. Caute, David. *The Occupation*. New York: McGraw-Hill,
     1972.

The Occupation is an intense probe into the tortured
mind of Stephen Bright, a visiting British professor at
an unnamed university in New York City. Stephen's academic discipline is not identified but clues in the text
suggest that it is one of the social sciences. The novel
mixes flashbacks and dream sequences--some of which have
British settings--with narrative about Stephen in New York.
A middle-aged masochist and a would-be revolutionary,
Stephen interacts with pornography purveyors in Times
Square, with voluptuous co-eds, and with angry student
militants. All the while fantasy is juxtaposed with
reality to convey the fact that Stephen is experiencing
a breakdown.
     Educated at Oxford and Harvard, David Caute was a fellow
at All Souls (Oxford), a visiting professor at New York
University and at Columbia, and a reader in social and
political theory at Brunel University in London at various
times during the 1960s. *The Occupation* was first published
in Great Britain (London: Andre Deutsch, 1971). It was
the final component of a three-part, interconnected, mixed-
media series of works which Caute termed "The Confronta-
tion." The first portion of the series was a dramatic
play entitled *The Demonstration* (London: Andre Deutsch,
1970). The second portion was an extended essay, *The
Illusion* (New York: Harper and Row, 1972).

*384. Frankel, Charles. *A Stubborn Case*. New York: W.W.
      Norton, 1972.

John Burgess, a professor of English at a major Eastern
university, returns to the campus after a harrowing sojourn in Venezuela only to find that his institution is
embroiled in student protest. In Venezuela, where he went
to instruct teachers of English, Burgess was kidnapped
and nearly killed by terrorists. Back home he finds that
the rebellious American students suspect him of CIA involvement. His office is trashed and he receives threaten-
ing phone calls. Toward the end of the novel Burgess

becomes a hostage once again when students occupy the building in which he has his office. And, again, he is nearly killed, this time when a brick is thrown through his window. The book is written in spare, crisp prose. Burgess is portrayed as intellectually detached from the disturbances, and as the campus unrest escalates he is increasingly bewildered about its meaning.

Charles Frankel received an A.B. from Columbia in 1937 and a Ph.D. from the same institution in 1946. He joined the Columbia department of philosophy as an instructor in 1939 and, over the next four decades at Columbia, he became one of America's most distinguished academics. He served as Assistant Secretary of State in the administration of Lyndon B. Johnson and later held the post of director of the National Center for the Humanities. *A Stubborn Case* was his only novel. Frankel and his wife were killed in their home by burglars on May 10, 1979.

385. Lynn, Jack. *The Professor*. New York: Dell Publishing Co., 1972.

Joe Pastore, a brilliant professor of psychology at New York University, is passed over for the department chairmanship. Angry over this slight, Joe resigns and accepts a far more lucrative position tutoring teenage children of the Mafia. He has problems with his charges—some of them threaten to kill him when he assigns them too much work—but Joe perseveres. Eventually he becomes the Mafia's beloved Mr. Chips, with a life-style beyond the fondest dreams of most academics. Problems arise, however, when a congressional committee begins to investigate the activities of his bosses. Joe is called to testify. His professorial ethics suggest that he should tell all he knows. But by sending a goon to give him a sample beating the Mafia chieftains strongly suggest the wisdom of silence. Indeed, Joe takes the fifth amendment and lives to teach another day. The book was first printed—in a hardbound edition—by the London publishing firm of Allison and Bushy in 1971. It was issued in America only in paperback.

Jack Lynn was born in 1927. *The Professor* was his first novel. At the time the saga was published Lynn was a television and motion picture producer.

386. Spivak, Talbot. *The Bride Wore the Traditional Gold*. New York: Alfred A. Knopf, 1972.

This brief (196-page) but rambling novel is told in the first person by Jason Chambert, an instructor of Latin at

"Lutzen College." Lutzen is a Mennonite institution in
a rural section of the Midwest. Jason's wife, Devi, is
from India, and the title of the book refers to the gold
sari which she wears at the couple's wedding. Much of
the novel consists of flashbacks through which Jason--a
keeper of voluminous diaries--describes his initial meeting with Devi at Cornell, tells about their year in
England at Cambridge, and discusses their love/hate relationships with cats. The book includes many satirical
passages about graduate student and junior faculty life
in the 1960s. At Lutzen, Jason's Latin courses become
the most popular classes on campus because he shuns the
usual methods of teaching the language and, instead,
instructs his students in the Latin drug formulae used
in his grandfather's apothecary in Luxembourg. And during one flashback Jason recounts Adolf Hitler's visit to
his grandfather's shop during World War II. Thus *The
Bride Wore the Traditional Gold* is the only American
college novel which includes Hitler in a speaking part.

Talbot Spivak was born in Philadelphia in 1937. He
received a B.A. from Trinity College in Hartford, Connecticut, in 1959, an M.A. from Cornell in 1962, and a
Ph.D. in French Literature from the university of Iowa
in 1976. *The Bride Wore the Traditional Gold* was his
first novel. At the time the book was published Spivak
was a graduate student at Iowa and an instructor of French
at Augustana College.

387. Lelchuk, Alan. *American Mischief*. New York: Farrar,
     Straus, and Giroux, 1973.

American Mischief is a long (501-page) satirical novel
set principally at "Cardozo College," "that prestigious
school twelve miles from Cambridge, Massachusetts." The
book has two protagonists who take turns narrating the
story in the first person. One of the protagonist-
narrators is Bernard Kovell, a middle-aged professor of
literature and dean of humanities at Cardozo. Kovell's
major problem is women. He collects them and, singly and
in combination, they provide him with both satisfaction
and harassment. Kovell's sexual activities are described
in explicit anatomical detail. The other protagonist-
narrator is Lenny Pincus, a young radical and a former
student of the dean. Inclined more to action than to
thought, Pincus produces a number of outrages. His
masterpiece is a kidnapping of ten major academic intellectuals gathered at Hofstra for a conference on socialist thought. Some reviewers found *American Mischief*

to be an epic commentary on the 1960s. Others thought
it an exemplar of avant-garde scatology.
   Alan Lelchuk received a B.A. from Brooklyn College in
1960, an M.A. from Stanford in 1963, and a Ph.D. from
Stanford in 1965. In 1966 he joined the department of
English at Brandeis as an assistant professor. *American
Mischief* was Lelchuck's first novel. His next two novels,
Miriam at Thirty-Four (396) and *Shrinking* (416), also ap-
pear in this bibliography.

388. Maloff, Saul. *Heartland*. New York: Charles Scribner's
     Sons, 1973.

   Isaiah Greene is a forty-year-old itinerant professor
of English in New York City. Quietly observing a long-
running, save-the-Jews-of-Russia rally in Manhattan, he
is mistaken by the press as a participant and is interviewed on television. Thanks to the publicity he receives, Greene is invited to give visiting lectures at a
number of colleges and universities in the West. The last
stop on his tour is "Donner Pass College," an institution
which at his first glance seems to be populated by attractive young Protestant women. The girls of Donner Pass
turn out to be Furies, however, and in one of their more
energetic rituals they castrate one of Greene's fellow
visiting speakers. Greene returns to the safety of New
York, revisits the rally, and is this time arrested for
disturbing the peace. The New York City scenes in *Heartland* are written in a satirical-realistic style while the
episode at Donner Pass College emerges as neo-fantasy.
Greene, a fallen-away Jew, is portrayed both as self-
mocking and self-destructive. Some reviewers saw the book
as an allegory about modern urban Jews in America.
   Saul Maloff received a B.A. in 1943 from City College
of New York and a Ph.D. in 1952 from the University of
Iowa. A former book editor for *Newsweek*, Maloff taught
at a number of colleges and universities--most of them in
the New York City area--before leaving academe in the
1960s to write on a full-time basis.

389. Schaeffer, Susan Fromberg. *Falling*. New York: Macmillan
     Co., 1973.

   This well-received first novel is an intensive study of
a young woman's near breakdown and her subsequent restora-
tion to mental health. The protagonist, Elizabeth Kamen,
is pictured in a number of academic settings. As an undergraduate she attends "Simon College" in Massachusetts

before transferring to the University of Chicago. Eventually, after placing herself under the care of a psychiatrist, Elizabeth obtains a Ph.D. from Chicago. While finishing her graduate work, she teaches English at a dreary junior college in Chicago and then at a much more intellectually stimulating "Institute for Technical Studies" in the same city. Finally, she takes a job at a university in New York City. Despite the many college and university scenes in the book, academic matters are only of secondary importance in the heavily flashbacked plot. More crucial are Elizabeth's childhood relationships with her parents and her traumatic domestic life with an egotistical young medical doctor whom she marries while still an undergraduate.

Susan Schaffer Fromberg received a B.A. from the University of Chicago in 1961 and a Ph.D. from that institution in 1966. She taught English at Wright Junior College in Chicago and at the Illinois Institute of Technology before joining the faculty of Brooklyn College in 1966. *Falling* was her first novel.

390.   Stern, Richard Gustave. *Other Men's Daughters*. New
       York: E.P. Dutton and Co., 1973.

Robert Merriweather is a middle-aged M.D. who holds a post as professor of physiology at Harvard. Caught in a loveless marriage with Sarah, a lady with an immense capacity for coldness, Robert is a man ready for an affair. His eye falls on Cynthia Ryder, a Harvard summer student. Cynthia, whose natural habitat is Swarthmore, is no stranger to in-bed relationships. She has a male traveling companion--a fellow Swarthmore student--and her life is "a sexual pageant." Robert and Cynthia meet and mate, and their liaison proves so fulfilling for both that Cynthia shucks her boyfriend and Robert leaves his wife. At the end of the book the happy couple is together in an isolated cabin deep in the Colorado mountains, and neither Robert nor Cynthia is anxious to return to the world of academe.

Richard Gustave Stern received a B.A. from the University of North Carolina in 1947, an M.A. from Harvard in 1949, and a Ph.D. from the University of Iowa in 1954. *Other Men's Daughters* was Stern's sixth novel. He was a professor of English at the University of Chicago when the book was published.

391. Wallace, John. *Honk If You Love Boise Hafter.* Indianapolis and New York: Bobbs-Merrill Co., 1973.

P.R. Riffling, a young psychologist at a university in southern California, is a dedicated eccentric. One of his favorite pastimes is to haunt the university library to analyze the stains left in books by their previous readers. P.R.'s constant use of the library leads him to a sexual relationship with Miss Dunnette, a librarian. Moreover, deep in the stacks, he finds materials pertaining to a mysterious former professor, one Boise Hafter. Hafter, it appears, had learned how to turn conformists into "out-of-sync" creative deviants by manipulating their brain waves. Hoping that Hafter will be their guru, P.R. and Miss Dunnette embark for "Gallitzin College" in Pennsylvania, Hafter's last known address. They do not find the great man--he is long since deceased-- but the pilgrims have many adventures in the course of their quest. Most serious students of college fiction probably will be safe if they skip this comic-fantasy. But "out-of-syncs" (who occur in nature in only one out of every 500,000 births) may find it rewarding.

John Wallace was a member of the psychology faculty at the University of California at Irvine when this book was published. *Honk If You Love Boise Hafter* was his first novel.

392. Baird, Thomas. *Losing People.* New York: Harcourt Brace Jovanovich, 1974.

Losing People is a brief (183-page) novel about a domineering professor who, during the course of a family gathering at Christmas, loses much of his hold on the people in his life. The professorial tyrant in the story is Hugo Kerenyi, a professor of history at Princeton. Hugo's downfall begins when his long-suffering wife, unwilling to take any more of his verbal abuse, simply refuses to come downstairs to open presents on Christmas morning. Then, one by one, the other members of his clan decline to do his bidding. The last straw comes when an attractive female graduate student whom Hugo covets refuses to kiss him, claiming that he is "too old." There are no campus scenes in the novel, but the characterization of Hugo as an egotistical, aging academic is drawn in great detail.

Thomas Baird received a B.A. from Princeton in 1945 and an M.F.A. from the same institution in 1950. He served as an instructor of art history at Princeton from

1949 until 1951 and again during the 1952-1953 academic
year. At the time *Losing People* was published Baird was
a member of the art faculty at Trinity College in Hartford, Connecticut. *Losing People* was his eighth novel.

393. Caputi, Anthony Francis. *Loving Evie*. New York: Harper
      and Row, 1974.

      The protagonist of this exercise in dolorousness is
      Merrick Baines, an assistant professor of English at a
      State University of New York campus in Buffalo. Merrick
      impregnates Evie Holman, a scatterbrained but ravishingly
      beautiful co-ed. Merrick and Evie marry, a daughter is
      born, and their marriage stays alive through sex. Eventu-
      ally Merrick decides to restart his life and he leaves
      his little family. Evie, hardly the epitome of mental
      stability in the best of times, reacts to Merrick's de-
      sertion by attempting suicide. Overwhelmed by guilt,
      Merrick returns to Evie and the couple presumably lives
      happily ever after. Several of Merrick's faculty col-
      leagues appear in the story, most of them suffering do-
      mestic and/or psychological dislocations of their own,
      and there are some in-depth scenes of academic life in
      the cold snows of Buffalo.
          Anthony Francis Caputi received an A.B. from the Uni-
      versity of Buffalo (now a part of the State University
      of New York system) in 1949 and a Ph.D. from Cornell in
      1956. *Loving Evie* was his first novel. At the time the
      book was published Caputi was a member of the English
      department at Cornell.

394. Fisher, David Elimelech. *A Fearful Symmetry*. Garden
      City, New York: Doubleday and Co., 1974.

      Henry Keller is a forty-seven-year-old professor of
      geology who has gone stale. One day, in his office at
      an unnamed university, the listless Henry is going
      through his pedagogic motions when he is visited by a
      pretty co-ed named Becky Aaronson. Becky asks for an A
      in Geology 103. Henry looks up Becky's record in his
      gradebook, finds that she has not even bothered to hand
      in most of her assignments, and refuses her request.
      With that, Becky stands, strips to the buff, and announces
      that she is prepared to do anything to get the grade she
      wants. This magnanimous offer jolts Henry out of his
      lethargy and into a world made up, in equal parts, of
      ecstasy and danger. It all ends some 200 pages later
      with Becky's death in an accidental fall from a hotel

balcony and with Henry's near demise at the hands of
Becky's demented boyfriend. *A Fearful Symmetry* straddles
the line between "straight" and "suspense" fiction and
only barely qualifies for inclusion in this bibliography.
Nevertheless, the book offers a detailed portrait of
Henry as an impulsive and bumbling academic.

David Elimelech Fisher received a B.S. from Trinity
College in Hartford, Connecticut, in 1952 and a Ph.D.
from the University of Florida in 1958. A geophysicist,
he has done research at the Oak Ridge and Brookhaven
Laboratories and has taught at Cornell and the University
of Miami. He was a professor of geophysics and cosmo-
chemistry at Miami when *A Fearful Symmetry*, his third
novel, was published.

395. Irving, John Winslow. *The 158-Pound Marriage*. New York:
      Random House, 1974.

This often opaque, darkly satirical novel is set at a
prestigious university in the East. The unnamed narrator
is a member of the university's history department. With
his spouse, Utch, he participates in a wife swapping arrangement with Severin Winter, the school's wrestling
coach, and with Severin's wife, Edith. Since the narrator's professional interests lie more in the historical
novels he writes than in his classroom duties, the book
deals only peripherally with the doings of the institution's history department. On the other hand, Severin
Winter cares deeply about his wrestling team, and *The
158-Pound Marriage* offers the most detailed look at intercollegiate wrestling in American adult college fiction.

John Winslow Irving was born in Exeter, New Hampshire,
in 1942. He received a B.A. from the University of New
Hampshire in 1965 and an M.F.A. from the University of
Iowa in 1967. At the time *The 158-Pound Marriage* was
published Irving was an assistant professor of English
at Mount Holyoke College. *The 158-Pound Marriage* was
Irving's second novel. Two later novels by Irving are
set, in part, upon academic turf. In *The Water Method
Man* (New York: Random House, 1972), the protagonist is
Fred "Bogus" Trumper, a peripatetic graduate student in
comparative literature at the University of Iowa. And
in Irving's best-selling *The World According to Garp*
(New York: E.P. Dutton and Co., 1978), Garp's wife, Helen,
is a member of the English department at an unnamed state
university during part of the story.

396. Lelchuk, Alan. *Miriam at Thirty-Four*. New York: Farrar,
     Straus and Giroux, 1974.

     Miriam at Thirty-Four is a novel about a divorcee, a
     former faculty wife, who experiences devastating problems
     with her new freedom and with her sexuality. Miriam
     Scheinman, until recently the wife of Stan Brown, a Har-
     vard professor of psychology, studies photography at Rad-
     cliffe by day and bed-hops in Cambridge at night. Stan
     hopes to gain custody of their two children and he has
     Miriam followed to many of her rendezvous. At the end of
     the book Miriam is raped in a park and, in the final scene,
     she is admitted to a hospital in a state of shock. The
     Harvard-Radcliffe atmosphere pervades the story but,
     fundamentally, the novel is a psychological study of
     Miriam's mental disconnections.
        Miriam at Thirty-Four was Alan Lelchuk's second novel.
     Lelchuk's first and third novels, *American Mischief* (387)
     and *Shrinking* (416), also appear in this bibliography.

*397. Lurie, Alison [Mrs. Jonathan Peale Bishop, Jr.). *The War
      Between the Tates*. New York: Random House, 1974.

      The War Between the Tates is one of the most biting
      (and most entertaining) faculty-centered satires in all
      of college fiction. The protagonist is Erica Tate, wife
      of a professor of political science at "Corinth Univer-
      sity." Corinth is a high-prestige institution in upstate
      New York. The mother of two repulsive teenage children,
      Erica is tired of full-time housewifery. For his part,
      husband Brian is professionally stagnant and frustrated
      because he has not become the great academic of his
      dreams. The plot centers on Erica's attempts to take a
      part-time job (which Brian opposes), Brian's affair with
      an adoring but mentally muddled graduate student named
      Wendy Gahaghan, and the breakup and subsequent rejoining
      of the Tate marriage. A great many Corinth faculty and
      their spouses appear in the book and there is one espe-
      cially memorable scene in which Brian is verbally and
      physically abused on campus by co-ed feminist demonstra-
      tors. Reviewers gave the work near unanimous praise and
      the story was adapted, in 1978, as a made-for-television
      motion picture.
         The War Between the Tates was Alison Lurie's fifth
      novel. Her first novel, *Love and Friendship* (334), is
      included in this bibliography. At the time *The War Be-
      tween the Tates* was published Lurie and her husband were
      both members of the Department of English at Cornell.

398. Shreve, Susan Richards. *A Fortunate Madness*. Boston: Houghton Mifflin Co., 1974.

The protagonist of this novel, Susanna McPherson, has a mild breakdown when her husband, an instructor of English at the University of Pennsylvania, resigns his post. Hubby Peter, a man of strong principles but weak ambition, resigns in support of a homosexual colleague who is unjustly accused of soliciting a student. In order to keep food on the family table Susanna takes a job teaching creative writing to freshmen at the University of Virginia. Peter and the couple's infant son follow along. Now it is Peter's turn to undergo psychological trauma. One night he takes the family car and, though it is not made clear whether or not his death is suicidal, he is killed in a road accident. At this point Susanna must call upon all of her inner reserve to survive. By the end of the book it is clear that she will do so, with the help of a handsome colleague in the Virginia English department. Although the plot of this novel exudes soapsuds, the book offers some strong descriptions of life at Penn and Virginia.

Susan Richards Shreve received a B.A. from the University of Pennsylvania in 1961 and an M.A. from the University of Virginia in 1969. A secondary school English teacher, she was co-founder in 1972 of the Community Learning Center—an alternative school—in Philadelphia. *A Fortunate Madness* was her first novel.

399. Williams, Thomas Alonzo. *The Hair of Harold Roux*. New York: Random House, 1974.

The protagonist of this intricate satire is Aaron Benham, a professor of creative writing at a university in New England. Aaron is writing a novel, and much of the book focuses upon his efforts to clear away various harassments so that he may concentrate on his work. The protagonist of Aaron's novel is Allard Benson, a fictive version of the fictive author, and at many junctures the story within a story is interjected into the main narrative. Allard's novel takes place just after World War II and it deals with Allard's experiences as an undergraduate. One of Allard's student associates is Harold Roux, who wears an outlandish red wig to hide his premature baldness. Harold, by the way, is writing his own novel. The book offers many sardonic insights into faculty life in the 1970s and, through its subsidiary text, offers considerable insight into student life in the 1940s as well.

The novel won the 1975 National Book Award for fiction.

Thomas Alonzo Williams received a B.A. from the University of New Hampshire in 1950 and an M.A. from the same institution in 1958. He was a professor of English at New Hampshire when *The Hair of Harold Roux* was published.

400. Cherniak, Judith. *Double Fault*. New York: G.P. Putnam's Sons, 1975.

The protagonist-narrator of this study in academic frustration is Leah Middlebrook, a thirty-five-year-old newly minted Ph.D. Leah is the wife of Charles, an untenured associate professor of history at a college in the Boston area. Leah, whose doctorate is in English, is desperately seeking a teaching post. Charles, who is suffering from mid-career crisis, is having grave doubts about the meaningfulness of his own teaching career. Leah and Charles both have extramarital affairs and all that keeps them together is their bright teenage daughter, Kate, who shows signs of becoming yet another family intellectual. At the end of the book Leah proposes that Charles give up his job. Her idea is that the Middlebrook family should move to another part of America where, presumably, both adults can find employment. Since Charles has just been fired Leah's suggestion proves redundant. The two quarrel because Charles did not inform Leah immediately upon his dismissal. Telling his wife uncategorically that "I loathe you from the bottom of my heart" Charles storms out of the Middlebrook home. But because he has no money and "no place to go," Leah awaits his return.

Judith Cherniak received a B.A. from Cornell in 1955 and a Ph.D. from Yale in 1964. During the 1960s she taught English at Columbia and at Tufts. At the time *Double Fault* was published Cherniak was a lecturer at the University of London. *Double Fault* was her first novel.

401. Goulet, John. *Oh's Profit*. New York: William Morrow, 1975.

The protagonist of this bizarre fantasy-satire is a 368-pound blackback gorilla named Oh. Captured in the wilds of Uganda, Oh is brought to "Cambridge College" in deepest Indiana in order to be the subject of a language-learning experiment. Professor Norman Liedlich, a Cambridge psycholinguist, teaches Oh "American sign

sign language" ("ASL") and the gorilla proves to be at
least as intelligent as most of the college's administrators and faculty members. Oh's capacity for reasoning
certainly rivals that of President "Waspo" Hacket, a
paragon of academic daffiness who has continuous doubts
about the propriety of Professor Liedlich's research.
Toward the end of the book Oh is accused of harboring
impure thoughts about Liedlich's wife, Nancy. Then he
refuses to have dinner with the President of the United
States, who travels to the Cambridge campus to inspect
the ASL project. Out of favor, Oh is drugged and crated
for shipment to an unidentified destination, and Cambridge
College loses one of its more enlightened inhabitants.

John Goulet was born in Boston in 1942. He received
a B.A. from St. Johns College in Collegeville, Minnesota,
in 1964 and a Ph.D. from the University of Iowa in 1972.
At Iowa he attended the Iowa Writers' Workshop. After
serving as an assistant professor at Hanover College in
Hanover, Indiana, for two years, he became an associate
professor of English at the University of Wisconsin-
Milwaukee in 1974. *Oh's Profit* was his first novel.

402.   Lodge, David. *Changing Places: A Tale of Two Campuses.*
       London: Secker and Warburg, 1975.

The protagonists of this very inventive academic comedy-
satire are Philip Swallow and Morris J. Zapp. Philip is
a lecturer in English at the "University of Rummidge,"
deep in provincial Great Britain. Morris is a professor
of English at the "State University of Euphoria" ("Eu-
phoric State") in southern California. Philip is a
mousy non-publisher. Morris is an aggressive scholar
with an international reputation. The two men swap jobs
and salaries for a year. Philip's motivation is financial. He wants to save most of his American income in
order to buy a central heating unit for his Rummidge
home. Morris wants a year away from Desiree, his nagging
second wife. Both men leave their wives and children behind as they undertake the exchange. Some 200 pages
later neither of the protagonists wants to return to his
native habitat and, indeed, Philip and Morris now want
permanent swaps of wives as well as jobs. During these
200 pages the author offers innumerable satirical passages about British and American institutions of higher
learning and, through a series of uncharitable character
sketches, he pokes mischievous fun at academics on both
sides of the Atlantic.

David Lodge was born in London in 1935. He holds a

B.A. and an M.A. from University College, London, and a
Ph.D. from the University of Birmingham. He was a member
of the department of English at Birmingham when *Changing
Places* was published. A well-respected literary critic
and scholar, Lodge was a visiting associate professor of
English at the University of California at Berkeley during
the 1969-1970 academic year. *Changing Places* was his
fifth novel.

403. McInerny, Ralph Matthew. *Gate of Heaven*. New York:
      Harper and Row, 1975.

      This well-written and sensitive novel explores the ad-
ministrative politics of "St. Brendan's College" in Ohio.
Though the school has a lay board of directors it is in
fact controlled by the order of Catholic priests--The
Society of St. Brendan--which founded it. The institution's ambitious president, Father Hoyt, is determined to
modernize the campus and most of the plot revolves around
his attempt to have "Little Sem" demolished to make way
for an up-to-date dormitory. Little Sem is St. Brendan's
oldest building and many of the Society's senior members
have emotional ties to the structure. Father Hoyt eventually succeeds in having Little Sem torn down but his
aggressiveness prompts the Society's Father Superior to
remove him from St. Brendan's presidency. Little Sem's
most ardent defenders live in "Porta Coeli," a retirement
home for aged Society priests which overlooks the college
grounds, and in the course of the story the political
affairs of Porta Coeli become entwined with those of the
college.
      Three other novels by Ralph Matthew McInerny appear in
this bibliography. These novels are *Jolly Rogerson* (368),
Rogerson at Bay (406), and *Spinnaker* (409). In contrast
to the serious tone of *Gate of Heaven*, the three other
McInerny novels in this bibliography are satires, and all
three focus upon life at secular institutions.

404. Wheatcroft, John. *Edie Tells: A Portrait of the Artist
      as a Middle-Aged Cleaning Woman*. South Brunswick, New
      Jersey, and New York: A.S. Barnes, 1975.

      Edie Tells is the ultimate put-down of academics,
especially academic poets. The protagonist of the satirical story is Edith ("Edie") Duggan, a forty-five-year-
old, semi-literate cleaning woman at "Harkness College."
Harkness is a small private institution in Pennsylvania.
Edie is assigned to clean the offices of the English

department and after reading some of the discarded attempts at poetry written by the professors she is inspired to try her own hand at the craft. Eventually Edie becomes a poet of note and, even though she continues to work as a charwoman, she acts as the school's unofficial hostess at literary soirees. The book contains one mocking passage after another about academic life. For example, at one point in the narrative the English department at Harkness receives a new dictionary and puts its old one up for bids. Edie bids $10. But the department chairman sells it to her for $2 since the highest faculty bid was only $1.50.

John Wheatcroft received a B.A. from Bucknell in 1949 and a Ph.D. from Rutgers in 1960. Known primarily as a poet, Wheatcroft was a professor of English at Bucknell when *Edie Tells* was published.

405. Bourjaily, Vance. *Now Playing at Canterbury*. New York: Dial Press, 1976.

Set at "State University" in "State City," a community in the very heart of the American Midwest, this complex novel centers on the staging of an opera written by two faculty members. Some of the characters in the book are local students and faculty. Some are singers, technicians, and members of the directorial staff imported to the campus for the production. In large part the novel consists of flashbacks, through which several of the characters, like the pilgrims in Chaucer's *Canterbury Tales*, reveal portions of their life histories. Since many of the characters are theatrical people, much of the flashback material involves nonacademic matters. Perhaps the most intriguing academic scene comes when one of the opera's authors—a professor of English—describes his favorite fantasy, a seminar on F. Scott Fitzgerald attended by Fitzgerald's ghost. Some reviewers saw *Now Playing at Canterbury* as relatively straightforward satire. Others read it as an allegory in which the book's characters represent various types of citizens of the mid-twentieth-century world.

Vance Bourjaily received a B.A. from Bowdoin in 1947. A major American novelist, Bourjaily has spent much of his adult life as a professor of creative writing at the University of Iowa.

406. McInerny, Ralph Matthew. *Rogerson at Bay*. New York:
      Harper and Row, 1976.

      Matthew "Matt" Rogerson, the protagonist of this sa-
      tirical novel, was first seen as the central character
      of *Jolly Rogerson* (368). In *Rogerson at Bay* Matt con-
      tinues his self-defeating exploits at "Fort Elbow College."
      A sour professor of humanities, caught in the agonies of
      mid-life crisis, Matt attempts to add spice to his dis-
      mal life by deliberately courting disaster. In contrast
      to *Jolly Rogerson*, which focuses primarily on Matt's
      academic adventures, *Rogerson at Bay* deals at some length
      with his domestic affairs. *Rogerson at Bay* describes
      Matt's strained relations with his newly liberated wife,
      his attempts to come to grips with his Catholicism, and
      his sufferings after a circumcision operation which he
      undergoes at the age of forty-seven. Meanwhile, on the
      Fort Elbow campus Matt continues to teach badly, has a
      squabble with the institution's officious dean, and under-
      takes a clumsy affair with a female faculty colleague.
      Although *Jolly Rogerson* and *Rogerson at Bay* are both
      pessimistic in tone--the reader knows that Matt's situ-
      ation will never improve--those two books are among the
      funniest and most insightful faculty-centered satires in
      college fiction.
           In addition to the Rogerson chronicles two other
      McInerny novels--*Gate of Heaven* (403) and *Spinnaker*
      (409)--appear in this bibliography. Beyond these works,
      McInerny's publication record includes many books on
      philosophy, other novels, and the "Father Dowling" mystery
      series.

407. Morton, Frederic. *An Unknown Woman*. Boston: Atlantic
      Press/Little, Brown and Co., 1976.

      An Unknown Woman is a panoplied satire about university
      life, liberalism, sociology, and the international jet
      set. The protagonist is Trudy Ellner, whom we meet first
      as a quasi-radical sociology graduate student at "Moloch
      University." Moloch is a private institution in uptown
      New York City. Trudy has a meteoric rise to academic
      prominence. Still without her Ph.D., she marries the
      president of "Interfaith University," a new institution
      in New York bankrolled by an oil millionaire. Her hus-
      band immediately makes Trudy dean of students. Yet,
      despite her sudden good fortune, Trudy does not lose her
      zest for the underdog. Part of Interfaith's curriculum
      is a floating seminar for underprivileged corporation

presidents--those who lack college educations. The
seminar is conducted aboard a luxurious cruise ship
sailing the Caribbean. Ever the woman of action, Trudy
flies between the ship and New York, where she directs
street demonstrations in Harlem. As the book progresses
Trudy becomes a media celebrity. Dressed in outrageous
hats she gives interviews, and lobbies for her causes,
over sumptuous lunches in fashionable New York restaurants.
Liberal academics, especially sociologists, may find the
book of special interest.

Frederic Morton was born in Vienna, Austria, in 1924.
He received a B.A. from City College of New York in 1947
and an M.A. from the New School in 1949. Between 1951
and 1959 Morton taught English and creative writing at
the University of Utah, New York University, the University of Southern California, Johns Hopkins, and the
New School. Since leaving academe he has become one of
America's foremost popular novelists.

408. Gurney, Albert Ramsdell, Jr. *Entertaining Strangers*.
By A.R. Gurney, Jr. Garden City, New York: Doubleday
and Co., 1977.

This sometimes bitter satire is narrated in the first
person by Porter Platt, an associate professor of English
at a prestigious engineering "Institute" in Cambridge,
Massachusetts. The plot centers upon Platt's growing
distaste for Christopher Simpson, a mysterious academic
Adonis with a British accent. Simpson appears one day
at the institute looking for work, is hired to teach
English, and in the space of a few months is named dean
of the humanities. The fact that no one at the institute
can determine Simpson's precise personal or academic background, or whether or not he possesses any formal degrees,
seems to be troublesome only to Platt. Everyone else at
the school is mesmerized by Simpson's charm. At the end
of the novel Platt's burden is lifted when his antagonist
leaves the institute. Simpson moves "up the river," to
become director of career counseling at Harvard.

Albert Ramsdell Gurney, Jr., received a B.A. from
Williams College in 1952 and an M.F.A. from Yale in 1958.
A dramatist as well as a novelist, Gurney was a member
of the humanities faculty at the Massachusetts Institute
of Technology when *Entertaining Strangers* was published.

409. McInerny, Ralph Matthew. *Spinnaker*. South Bend, Indiana:
      Gateway Editions, Ltd., 1977.

      This brief (160-page) satire is set at "Spinnaker Col-
      lege," a low-prestige institution in the Midwest. The
      time is 1969 and though college campuses all over America
      are boiling with student unrest the climate at Spinnaker
      is one of studious dedication to scholastic inferiority.
      Displeased because Spinnaker is a grommet of calm amidst
      national academic disorder, one Professor Plosive, a so-
      ciologist, organizes a protest. A century ago the ground
      on which Spinnaker now stands was the property of the
      Ephchoke Indians, and Plosive and his newly aroused dissi-
      dents claim that the Ephchokes were swindled out of their
      land. No real Ephchokes can be found, so the protectors
      make themselves "honorary" members of the tribe and demand
      that Spinnaker be returned to them. The disturbance dies,
      however, when historical documents prove that the land in
      question was legally sold by the Ephchokes. Moreover,
      the records indicate that the Ephchokes still owe the
      palefaces fifty quandi pelts because, on the day of the
      long-ago transaction, the Indians failed to make correct
      change. Despite the small size of this book the story
      weaves its way around a sizeable number of Spinnaker
      faculty members and administrators. The president of the
      school, Howard Pringle, comes in for special attention.
      Described as "anything but a national figure," Pringle
      tries to appease all parties to the conflict and, at one
      point, he is kidnapped by the mock Indians. Also in the
      cast of characters is Andrew Abelard, a famous newspaper-
      man who has tried for years to hide the fact that Spin-
      naker is his alma mater.
          Three other novels by Ralph Matthew McInerny appear in
      this bibliography. These novels are *Jolly Rogerson* (368),
      Gate of Heaven (403), and *Rogerson at Bay* (406).

410. Penner, Jonathan. *Going Blind*. New York: Simon and
      Schuster, 1977.

      Going Blind is a singularly melancholic story about
      Paul Held, an assistant professor of English, who is
      slowly losing his sight after his eyes are damaged in
      an automobile accident. Insult is literally heaped upon
      injury when the unnamed New York City university at which
      he is employed refuses to grant him tenure. The presi-
      dent of the institution doubts the classroom effective-
      ness of a sightless person. The novel is replete with
      medical as well as academic details. Indeed, early in

the story one of Paul's faculty colleagues dies of cancer
of the intestines and the facts of his illness, like
those of Paul's impending blindness, are offered in relentless profusion.
  Jonathan Penner was born in Bridgeport, Connecticut,
in 1940. He received an undergraduate degree from the
University of Bridgeport and did graduate work at the
University of Iowa. At the time *Going Blind* was published
Penner was a member of the creative writing faculty at
Southern Illinois University in Carbondale. *Going Blind*
was his first novel.

411. Stegner, Page. *Sports Car Menopause*. Boston: Atlantic
     Press/Little, Brown and Co., 1977.

   Sports Car Menopause is a satirical entertainment which
centers on the middle-aged wanderings of Eliot Warren, a
professor of English at an unnamed college in California.
Eliot breaks with his wife and takes up with Nina Allen-
craig, a co-ed devotee of physical culture whose favorite
sport—outside of sex—is nude jogging on the campus.
The author injects many epigrammatic digs at contemporary
academe and he pays special attention to the new roles for
women in higher education. In one scene a co-ed is trying
to decide how to cope with her courses. "I got it figured
out for my religious studies course," announces the young
woman. "Like I'm going to do women in the church. And
like for my sociology course I'm going to do women in
South America. But I can't figure out what I'm going to
do for calculus."
  Page Stegner was born in Salt Lake City in 1937. He
has a B.A., an M.A., and a Ph.D. from Stanford. At the
time *Sports Car Menopause* was published Stegner was a
member of the department of English at the University
of California at Santa Cruz. He is the son of novelist
Wallace Stegner, whose *Fire and Ice* (159) appears in this
bibliography.

412. Tauber, Peter. *The Last Best Hope*. New York: Harcourt
     Brace Jovanovich, 1977.

   The Last Best Hope is an epic, panoramic novel which
takes place during the late 1960s. The protagonist is
Tyler Bowen, a peripatetic young biochemist. Tyler does
research in chemical warfare for the United States government but he increasingly finds himself in disagreement
with America's actions in Viet Nam. In the course of
this long (628-page) story Tyler is seen as a graduate

student and as an instructor at Cornell, as a post-
graduate fellow at a research center in Arizona, and as
an onlooker at Kent State on the day of the now famous
killings by the National Guard. Tyler's brother Willie,
a prominent secondary character in the book, is presented
as a combat soldier in Viet Nam and as a witness to an-
other--entirely fictive--massacre of students, this one
at Berkeley. Richard Nixon makes a cameo appearance when
he awards Willie the Medal of Honor, and the whole of the
plot transpires against a constant barrage of political
news of the period. Although much of the characters'
time is taken up with sexual escapades and political
activities, the college scenes, especially those at
Cornell, are written with considerable attention to
detail.

Peter Tauber received a B.A. from Hobart College in
1968. *The Last Best Hope* was his second novel. In addition to writing novels Tauber has been, at various points
in his career, a reporter for *The New York Times*, a
nightclub comedian, and (in 1968) an administrative
assistant in the presidential campaign of Senator Eugene
McCarthy.

413. [Tillinghast, Burette Stinson, Jr.]. *The Honeyman*. By
     B.S. Tillinghast, Jr. New York: E.P. Dutton and Co.,
     1977.

Burt Hardin, a middle-aged professor of psychology at
"Redneck University" in Florida, covets a vacant deanship
at his institution. Burt also covets Mrs. J.B. Jones, a
twenty-four-year-old graduate student who happens to be
the daughter-in-law of Redneck's most powerful trustee.
Burt and J.B. meet and mate on numerous occasions, all
of which are monitored by a detective hired by Ellen,
Burt's unloving wife. Ellen is having her own affair,
with her sex therapist, and she wants evidence through
which to win a maximum-alimony divorce. Then J.B. proves
to be an unfaithful mistress and poor Burt, mentally and
physically exhausted by his sexual entanglements, rejects
the deanship when it is offered. The novel is written
as dark satire. Burt is depicted as an energetic though
oftentimes addled academic schemer and the rest of the
cast, which includes a sizeable number of professorial
and administrative characters, is portrayed in various
stages of terminal grotesqueness.

Burette Stinson Tillinghast, Jr., was educated at Wofford
College, George Peabody, and Florida State University,
where he received an Ed.D. in 1961. From 1962 until 1967

he was a member of the education faculty at the University
of Virginia. He moved to the University of South Alabama
in 1967 and was a professor of education and counseling
at that school when *The Honeyman* was published. *The
Honeyman*, his first novel, was accepted by E.P. Dutton
after Tillinghast spent twenty-four years unsuccessfully
submitting fiction manuscripts to various publishers.

*414. Wright, Austin. *The Morley Mythology*. New York: Harper
and Row, 1977.

The Morley Mythology is an exceedingly complex novel
which explores the inner world of its protagonist-narrator,
Michael Morley. Michael is a professor of geology and
dean at an unnamed university. He receives persistent
and mysterious telephone calls from a man who somehow has
an encyclopedic knowledge of both his childhood obsessions
and his adult secrets. Michael fears that the caller intends to blackmail him but, instead, his tormentor turns
out to be a bland real estate salesman who, toward the
end of the book, commits suicide. As all of this is un-
folding, Michael's reflexive self divides into a set of
components--"the Professor," "the Dean," "the Name," etc.--
and these components discuss matters among themselves.
When Morley loses his deanship at the conclusion of the
story, "the Name" and "the ex-Dean" plan the strategy
through which Michael can reconstitute his research career.
The Morley Mythology is not a light entertainment for the
casual browser. Nor, considering the intricacy of its
plotting, is it a traditional college novel. Nonetheless,
it is one of the most intense examinations in fiction of
an academic mind.
Austin Wright received an A.B. from Harvard in 1943 and
a Ph.D. from the University of Chicago in 1959. *The Morley Mythology* was his third novel. At the time the book
was published Wright was professor of English at the
University of Cincinnati.

415. Kalpakian, Laura. *Beggars and Choosers*. Boston: Little,
Brown and Co., 1978.

The plot of this well-written first novel centers on
Alden Lundy, a professor of English at "Sheridan University." Sheridan is a small, private institution in
California. Lundy, now a stodgy pedant, was once an
aspiring poet. In the early 1950s he was a member of
the BarRoom Brawl and Bookshop poetry clique in San Francisco. During his BarRoom days Lundy behaved badly toward

a number of his associates and their wives, hence he has
no wish to see his past history brought to light. Most
of *Beggars and Choosers* concerns Lundy's efforts to prevent publication of incriminating papers left to the
university by another, recently deceased BarRoomer. The
book includes a number of well-drawn portraits of academics and, through flashback sequences, it offers glimpses of the San Francisco poetry milieu of the 1950s.
  Laura Kalpakian received degrees from the University
of California at Riverside and from the University of
Delaware. Prior to the publication of *Beggars and Choosers* she taught creative writing at the University of
California at San Diego.

416. Lelchuk, Alan. *Shrinking*. Boston: Atlantic Press/Little,
      Brown and Co., 1978.

  Lionel Solomon, a professor of English at Harvard, suffers one of the more frenetic middle-age identity crises
in college fiction. Thirty-eight years old, divorced,
and the author of two poorly received novels, Lionel
tries to recapture his youth with "Tippy" Matthews, a
ravishingly beautiful young woman who has a massive appe-
tite for sex. But when Tippy's special sexual tastes
prove too bizarre for Lionel he dismisses her and plunges
rapidly toward an emotional breakdown. Toward the end
of the novel he signs himself into "Swerdlow's Sanitarium"
and places himself under the care of Dr. Benjamin Liric.
Indeed, Dr. Liric was kind enough to write both a fore-
word and an afterword to the story. From the literary
standpoint *Shrinking* is an inventive, complex novel which
employs flashbacks, letters, explicit sex, and more to
evoke a curious blend of fantasy and reality. In terms
of the American college novel, *Shrinking* is by all odds
the most graphic account of professorial burn-out in the
genre.
  Shrinking was Alan Lelchuk's third novel. His first
two novels, *American Mischief* (387) and *Miriam at Thirty-
Four* (396), also appear in this bibliography.

417. Bonanno, Margaret Wander. *A Certain Slant of Light*.
      New York: Seaview Books, 1979.

  This impressive first novel has two protagonists. The
first is Joan Dalton Tierney, an about-to-be-divorced
young woman with a devastated ego and a three-year-old
son. The second is Sara Morrow, an aging, widowed Chau-
cerian scholar at a small Catholic college in Brooklyn.

When Sara has a paralyzing stroke she employs Joan, one
of her former students, as a companion. Gradually, Joan
assumes a role as Sara's confidant, and when Sara is
threatened with the loss of her job Joan assists her in
proving to the college administration that she is, indeed,
sufficiently recovered to resume her teaching duties.
At the end of the book the two women have helped one another to resume productive lives. Though offered rein-
statement by the college, Sara has resigned to hit the
collegiate lecture circuit. Joan has entered law school.
In addition to the interplay between the two focal characters, the book offers many glimpses, some of them unflattering, of the faculty and administrators at the
Catholic institution which forms the backdrop for the
story.
  Margaret Wander Bonanno received a B.A. from St. Joseph's College of Brooklyn in 1971.

418. Cantor, Eli. *Love Letters*. New York: Crown Publishers,
      1979.

  Love Letters is an epistolary novel told entirely
through the correspondence between Margaret Webb, a
fiftyish New York City housewife, and Brian Curtiss, a
thirtyish associate professor of sociology at the University of California at Los Angeles. Margaret initi-
ates the exchange of letters when she writes to offer
Brian an unsolicited compliment on an article he has
written about the harmful effects of fringe religions
on their adolescent disciples. They converse by mail
for over two years, discuss their domestic problems and
their philosophies of life, and develop a romantic attachment. Unknown to Brian, however, Margaret has
terminal cancer. The book ends when a mutual friend
sends Brian a totally unexpected report of Margaret's
death. Brian includes some ruminations about academe
in his dispatches but, from the standpoint of American
college fiction, *Love Letters* is most noteworthy for its
sympathetic portrait of a sociologist. Sociologists in
college novels are generally depicted as boorish simpletons. Through his letters to Margaret, Brian emerges
by contrast as kind, understanding, and intelligent.
  Eli Cantor was born in New York City in 1913. He received a B.S. from New York University in 1934 and a law
degree from Harvard in 1938. During a varied professional
career he has served as an attorney for the Columbia
Broadcasting System, an editor for *Esquire*, and as an
executive in the printing industry. A prolific writer,

Cantor has authored dramas, television scripts, and
novels. Some of the latter have been gothic romances
published under the pseudonym Agnes Wheatley.

419. Florey, Kitty Burns. *Family Matters*. New York: Seaview
      Books, 1979.

Betsy Ruscoe, a thirty-four-year-old associate professor of English at a university in Syracuse, New York,
has problems. She is single but pregnant by Judd Vandoss,
a sexually satisfying commercial photographer who is in
no mood for marriage. Judd wants Betsy to have an abortion but Betsy wants to bear the child. Meantime, Betsy's
mother, Violet, is slowly dying of cancer. Violet rou-
tinely calls her daughter in the wee hours of the morning
with bizarre requests. One of these entreaties sends
Betsy on a long search for her real grandmother, a woman
who abandoned Violet more than a half-century ago. Then,
up at the university, Betsy's pregnancy is prompting a
nasty exchange of letters to the student newspaper about
the morality of a proposed abortion-referral service for
co-eds. Betsy, you see, once signed a petition in favor
of the service, and its opponents now use her decision
not to abort her illegitimate fetus as an excuse for
accusing the pro-abortion petitioners of hypocrisy. And,
to make matters worse, Betsy's department chairman, a
chubby buffoon named Crawford Divine, offers to make
Betsy an honest woman by marrying her. With all these
difficulties, and more, it is little wonder that Betsy's
research on Alexander Pope is lagging. But Betsy is
strong. By the end of the book she still has not pro-
gressed far with her research, but most of the other important issues in her life have been resolved or are well
on their way to resolution. Her mother is dead. Her
grandmother has been found. The egocentric Judd has been
dismissed from her life. Crawford Divine is about to
marry a waitress at the Holiday Inn. The campus abortion
issue has faded into a state of quiescence. And Betsy's
baby is due any day.

420. Freely, Maureen. *Mother's Helper*. New York: Delacorte
      Press/Seymour Laurence, 1979.

This novel is a bittersweet satire on academic family
life in the early 1970s. Laura, a student at Radcliffe,
becomes a "mother's helper" to Kay Pyle, the wife of a
political scientist and herself a Ph.D. in sociology.
Kay wants more time from her three children so that she

may be free to realize her human potential. Included in
Kay's expanding, extra-familial activities is an affair
with her husband's most promising graduate student. The
Pyle household is best described as "permissive" and,
as a result, it is lacking both in organization and real
interpersonal affection. Toward the end of the book the
Pyles' youngest child commits suicide. There are some
scenes of Radcliffe dormitory life in the novel, but
most of the plot unfolds at the Pyles' home.

Maureen Freely graduated from Radcliffe in 1974.

421. LeComte, Edward Semple. *The Professor and the Coed*.
Port Washington, New York: Ashley Books, 1979.

The professor referred to in the title of this brief
(144-page) novel is Andrew Ames, a member of the English
department at "Wyandotte College." Wyandotte is a former
women's college which has only recently begun to admit
men. Andrew is forty-five, distinguished looking, and
trapped in a loveless marriage. The co-ed is Alice
Buiosco, a student in one of Andrew's classes. She has
a lummox-like boyfriend who speaks in monosyllabic language. Andrew attempts to engineer a sexual liaison
with Alice but is unsuccessful until he agrees to give
the boyfriend a passing grade in return for her favors.
Then, shortly after the affair begins, Andrew's relationship with Alice comes to a sudden halt when the boyfriend
forcibly intervenes during an Andrew-Alice coupling in
Alice's apartment. Written as satire, the book is primarily a character study of Andrew, who is portrayed as
a bumbling, would-be lecher. The book includes a few
interesting classroom scenes and, on occasion, Andrew
offers sardonic commentaries about his fellow faculty
members and about the bureaucratic routines of faculty
life.

Edward Semple LeComte was born in New York City in
1916. He received an A.B. from Columbia in 1939 and a
Ph.D. from the same institution in 1943. LeComte was a
professor of English at the State University of New York
at Albany when *The Professor and the Coed* was published.

*422. Oates, Joyce Carol. *Unholy Loves*. New York: Vanguard
Press, 1979.

Unholy Loves is a finely wrought novel which reaches
deep into the psychology of academic faculty. Albert
St. Denis, a British poet of massive reputation, arrives
at "Woodslee University" for a year in residence. Woodslee is a middling-status private university in upstate

New York. The school's English department eagerly awaits
St. Denis' coming because each of its members hopes to
use the poet's visit to further his or her career. Unfortunately, St. Denis proves to be old, feeble, can-
tankerous, and overly fond of alcohol. Eventually he
dies when his apartment is consumed by fire. Although
the plot of the book revolves around St. Denis' visit,
much of the story actually focuses upon various Woodslee
faculty and administrators, each of whom is in some
stage of personal or professional dissolution.

One of America's most prolific fictionalists, Joyce
Carol Oates was born in Lockport, New York, in 1938.
She received a B.A. from Syracuse University in 1960 and
an M.A. from the University of Wisconsin in 1961. In
1967 she became a member of the department of English
at the University of Windsor, Ontario. While *Unholy
Loves* was Oates' first college novel, it was not her
initial excursion into college fiction. In *The Hungry
Ghosts* (Los Angeles: Black Sparrow Press, 1975) she
offered seven faculty-centered stories, most of them set
at "Hilberry University" in southern Ontario.

423. Philipson, Morris. *A Man in Charge*. New York: Simon
      and Schuster, 1979.

Conrad Taylor, the head of the undergraduate division
of an unnamed but world-renowned university in New
Haven, Connecticut, suffers more than his fair share of
personal and professional crises. A homosexual faculty
member requests immediate leave to spend a semester
with his boyfriend in Paris. Conrad's trusted assistant
turns out to be a kleptomaniac. A prospective student,
refused admission to the university, enters Conrad's
office with a gun and unsuccessfully tries to kill him.
Conrad's young wife is unfaithful and his daughter by
a previous marriage runs off to an Indian reservation
to bear an illegitimate child. Meanwhile, the university provost dies, and even though Conrad is clearly
the best man for the job the president chooses someone
else. Through all of these travails, and more, Conrad
retains his composure, a measure of good humor, and his
sense of direction.

Morris Philipson was born in New Haven in 1926. He
received a B.A. from the University of Chicago in 1949
and a Ph.D. from Columbia in 1959. Early in his career
he taught at Juilliard, Hunter College, and the University
of Chicago. In 1967 he became director of the University
of Chicago Press, a post he held when *A Man in Charge*,
his third novel, was published.

424. Reed, Lillian Craig [Mrs. John Wayne Reed]. *The Ballad of T. Rantula*. By Kit Reed. Boston: Little, Brown and Co., 1979.

The Ballad of T. Rantula deals with the breakup of a faculty marriage and the impact of the dissolution on the couple's teenage son. This theme is reasonably commonplace in college fiction, but *The Ballad of T. Rantula* is unusual in the sense that the story is told through the eyes of "Futch," the fourteen-year-old boy who stands at the center of the turmoil. "Pop" is a historian at a college in the Boston area. "Mom," who has recently come upon women's liberation, leaves the family to live in a Cambridge commune. The narrator is portrayed as a hip adolescent who understands what is happening but who nurses vague hopes that Mom will return to the domestic fold. One of Futch's peers, "Tig" Tighlman, also encounters family difficulties. Tig's father, another member of the college faculty, is a sometimes homosexual who ignores his children. Tig eventually starves himself to death. Although the narrative is told in modern, teenage idiom, it contains at least one classic academic line. After Mom leaves for Cambridge, Pop begins to consort with Helen Chandler, a faculty colleague. When Futch inquires about Helen's recurrent presence in the family home Pop tries to mask his sexual interests in the woman. Explaining that he and Helen are team-teaching a course, Pop tells Futch that in a team-teaching situation "you grab all the meetings you can get." T. Rantula of the book's title is a rock music star who is idolized by Futch and his friends.

Lillian Craig Reed was born in San Diego in 1932. She received a B.A. from the College of Notre Dame of Maryland in 1954. *The Ballad of T. Rantula* was her eighth novel. Married to John Wayne Reed, a professor of English at Wesleyan University in Middleton, Connecticut, Lillian Reed was a visiting member of the Wesleyan English department when this novel was published.

425. Webber, Gordon. *The Great Buffalo Hotel*. Boston: Little, Brown and Co., 1979.

The protagonist of this exercise in ironies is Nicholas Cleveland Horne, a nonconformist, middle-aged professor of English at "Powder River College." Powder River is a small, church-affiliated institution in the far Midwest. Powder River is the ninth institution at which

Nicholas has taught. During his career the professor
has drifted westward, moving each time to a lower status
school. And now, even at Powder River, he is threatened
with the loss of his job. Therefore, in a futile bid
for retention, he volunteers to construct a huge statue
of a buffalo on the outskirts of town. The statue, so
the town fathers reason, will attract tourists. In the
course of the story Nicholas is pelted by white roses
thrown from an airplane piloted by one of his three ex-
wives, is discovered curled up in a sleeping bag with
a co-ed, and is caught in a stampede of actual buffaloes.
At the end of the book he is, once again, on his way
west. The hotel in the title of the novel is the town's
major watering hole and Nicholas' residence. On the
dust jacket of the book the publishers claim that the
theme of the story is "Horne's struggle to preserve some
measure of integrity in a cockeyed world of compromise."
From the standpoint of the college novel, the book offers
a rich portrait of a cynical, iconoclastic, and down-at-
the-heels academic.

Gordon Webber received an A.B. from Jamestown College
in 1933 and an M.A. from the University of Michigan in
1936. *The Great Buffalo Hotel* was his fourth novel.
Just before the book's publication Webber retired after
twenty-seven years with Benton and Bowles, Inc., a leading New York City advertising agency.

APPENDIX
Major American College Novels

Student-Centered Novels

Fanshawe (1828), 1
Fair Harvard (1869), 6
College Days (1894), 16
The Adventures of a Freshman (1899), 22
The Diary of a Freshman (1901), 29
Philosophy 4 (1903), 34
At Good Old Siwash (1911), 37
Stover at Yale (1912), 38
This Side of Paradise (1920), 64
The Plastic Age (1924), 75
Look Homeward, Angel (1929), 96
Bachelor--of Arts (1933), 108
Cotton Cavalier (1933), 109
Not to Eat, Not for Love (1933), 112
Doctor's Oral (1939), 128
Barefoot Boy with Cheek (1943), 165
The Cauliflower Heart (1944), 166
The Folded Leaf (1945), 169
The Primitive (1949), 180
Hangsaman (1951), 183
Getting Straight (1967), 286
The Paper Chase (1971), 301
End Zone (1972), 303
The Women's Room (1977), 309
The Last Convertible (1978), 314
Wild Oats (1979) 315

Staff-Centered Novels

The Torch (1903), 50
The Law of Life (1903), 52
The Professor's House (1925), 132
Professor (1925), 133
Chimes (1926), 134
Lone Voyagers (1929), 138
The Forbidden Tree (1933), 144
Winds Over the Campus (1936), 148
The Tree Has Roots (1937), 151
These Bars of Flesh (1938), 155
Beer for the Kitten (1939), 156
Geese in the Forum (1940), 204
The Hunted (1944), 212
We Happy Few (1946), 214
Mr. Whittle and the Morning Star (1947), 221
The Spire (1952), 229
The Groves of Academe (1952), 231
The Stones of the House (1953), 233
Pictures from an Institution (1954), 235
Pnin (1957), 248
A Friend in Power (1958), 252
Purely Academic (1958), 253
The Party at Cranton (1960), 321
Orphans in Gethsemane (1960), 322
A New Life (1961), 329
Learner's Permit (1962), 333
Stepping Westward (1966), 364
Tell the Time to None (1966), 365
Jolly Rogerson (1967), 368
The Department (1968), 371
A Stubborn Case (1972), 384
The War Between the Tates (1974), 397
The Morley Mythology (1977) 414
Unholy Loves (1979), 422

AUTHOR INDEX

TITLE INDEX